DAILY LIFE OF

WOMEN IN MEDIEVAL EUROPE

Recent Titles in
The Greenwood Press Daily Life Through History Series

Colonial New England, Second Edition
Claudia Durst Johnson

Life in 1950s America
Nancy Hendricks

Jazz Age America
Steven L. Piott

Women in the Progressive Era
Kirstin Olsen

The Industrial United States, 1870–1900, Second Edition
Julie Husband and Jim O'Loughlin

The 1960s Counterculture
Jim Willis

Renaissance Italy, Second Edition
Elizabeth S. Cohen and Thomas V. Cohen

Nazi-Occupied Europe
Harold J. Goldberg

African American Slaves in the Antebellum
Paul E. Teed and Melissa Ladd Teed

Women in Postwar America
Nancy Hendricks

Women in Ancient Egypt
Lisa K. Sabbahy

Women in Ancient Rome
Sara Phang

Women in Chaucer's England
Jennifer C. Edwards

Anglo-Saxon England
Sally Crawford

The American West
Jason E. Pierce

DAILY LIFE OF

WOMEN IN MEDIEVAL EUROPE

BELLE S. TUTEN

The Greenwood Press Daily Life Through History Series

BLOOMSBURY ACADEMIC
NEW YORK • LONDON • OXFORD • NEW DELHI • SYDNEY

BLOOMSBURY ACADEMIC
Bloomsbury Publishing Inc, 1359 Broadway, New York, NY 10018, USA
Bloomsbury Publishing Plc, 50 Bedford Square, London, WC1B 3DP, UK
Bloomsbury Publishing Ireland, 29 Earlsfort Terrace, Dublin 2, D02 AY28, Ireland

BLOOMSBURY, BLOOMSBURY ACADEMIC and the Diana logo
are trademarks of Bloomsbury Publishing Plc

First published in the United States of America by ABC-CLIO 2022
Paperback edition published by Bloomsbury Academic 2026

COVER PHOTO: Portrait of a Woman with a Man at a Casement, ca. 1440.
(Marquand Collection, Gift of Henry G. Marquand, 1889)

Library of Congress Cataloging-in-Publication Data
Names: Tuten, Belle S., author.
Title: Daily life of women in Medieval Europe / Belle S. Tuten.
Description: Santa Barbara, California : Greenwood, [2022] |
Series: The Greenwood Press daily life through history series |
Includes bibliographical references and index.
Identifiers: LCCN 2022026259 | ISBN 9781440872341 (hardcover) |
ISBN 9781440872358 (ebook)
Subjects: LCSH: Women—Europe—History—Middle Ages, 500–1500. |
Women—Europe—Social conditions. | Women—Europe—Social life and customs. | Women—Political activity—Europe—History—To 1500.
Classification: LCC HQ1147.E85 T87 2022 | DDC
305.420940902—dc23/eng/20220622
LC record available at https://lccn.loc.gov/2022026259

ISBN: HB: 978-1-4408-7234-1
PB: 979-8-2164-6157-9
ePDF: 978-1-4408-7235-8
eBook: 979-8-2160-7155-6

Series: The Greenwood Press Daily Life Through History Series

For product safety related questions contact productsafety@bloomsbury.com

To find out more about our authors and books visit www.bloomsbury.com
and sign up for our newsletters.

CONTENTS

PREFACE

Women make up approximately half the population in every human society, but sources to explore their experiences in the distant past are not abundant when compared to sources by and about men. When we think about women in the Middle Ages from our vantage point in the twenty-first century, we fill in what we don't know with our imaginations. Our imaginations provide us with both horrors and fantasies; it's sometimes hard to separate our fictional views of knights and ladies from our ideas about the real dangers, filth, and hardships of everyday medieval life. This book attempts to clarify what we know and what we do not know about women's daily lives in the Western European Middle Ages, between approximately 500 and 1500 CE.

It is important to realize that people of the time never called themselves *medieval* or called their era the *Middle Ages*. Scholars in the fourteenth and fifteenth centuries invented the term, which comes from the Latin words *medium aevum*, "the middle age." They wanted to distinguish themselves from what they saw as the backward and violent "dark ages" in between the Roman Empire and their own time. This viewpoint has persisted into our own era. Calling something *medieval* today—a technology, a person, or a point of view—is not a compliment. We imagine medieval women as oppressed and miserable, locked into drudgery, constant pregnancy, and domestic abuse. However, this book will show that women in the Middle Ages, although significantly different from us, had experiences that are familiar to us today: living good lives, working within economic systems, bearing and raising families, and contributing to the larger culture of the period. This book is arranged topically, but the topics are mainly organized chronologically. There is also a timeline of major moments in medieval women's history and a bibliography of secondary sources. Boldface terms in the text are included in the Glossary at the end of the book.

The introduction provides some basics about the Middle Ages—a quick review of the history, trends, and events of the period. This chapter also discusses some long-standing stereotypes about the Middle Ages, particularly with regard to life span, hygiene, and cultural values. We pick up with two of the issues most pertinent to medieval society's understanding of women in chapter one, "Marriage and Sexuality." In chapter two, we explore the medieval understanding of human biology and the difficulties women experienced with conception, pregnancy, and childbirth. Medieval women's relationships with reproduction dictated or shaped many of the social expectations that they experienced. Chapter three is a discussion of work, both inside and outside the home. Medieval women's functions inside the economy were much more complex and varied than many people today realize. This chapter also discusses how some daily activities, such as food preparation and housekeeping, shaped how women went through their days. Chapter four explores noble and elite women. We know somewhat more about these women because they are more visible in the sources than women of lower classes. Elite status, however, also came with some difficult challenges and opportunities that allowed some individual women to be prominent in European political life. In chapter five, we discuss women in the Roman Catholic Church, an institution that deployed many kinds of power over medieval people. At the same time, however, women who embraced a religious life had opportunities not extended to other European women, including opportunities to exert power through their reputations as holy people. Chapter six introduces women who violated society's prescriptions for proper female behavior, including sex workers, heretics, and "witches." The last chapter, chapter seven, introduces brief biographies of some European women who wrote texts that still survive. This chapter ends with five primary document excerpts of these women's works.

I would like to acknowledge debts of gratitude to my colleagues in the Department of Art and Art History at Juniata College and my readers, Jim Tuten, Tom Stoddard, Madison Caso, and Mara Revitsky. I dedicate this book to my mother.

INTRODUCTION

This book explores women's daily experiences in the European Middle Ages, a period that lasted about a thousand years. Scholars generally divide the Middle Ages into three periods: the early Middle Ages, lasting from the year 500 CE to the year 1000; the High Middle Ages, from 1000 to 1300; and the late Middle Ages, 1300 to 1500. These dates are approximate, and we use them chiefly to help us understand a long and complex period. The Middle Ages took shape when the western Roman Empire declined in power and organization, during the period of roughly 200–500 CE. In 476 CE, a Germanic king deposed the Roman emperor in the west, while the Byzantine empire, centered in Constantinople, endured. The map of western Europe was broken up into kingdoms based on various Germanic groups. For convenience's sake, scholars sometimes use 476 CE as the beginning point for the Middle Ages in the west, but the process was gradual and took several centuries.

The conflicts of the fourth and fifth centuries CE—some of purely Roman origin and some involving migrating Germanic tribes—had left the populations of western Europe diminished and Roman control greatly lessened. The three major successors of the Roman Empire in the west were the kingdoms of Gaul, Italy, and Spain, each ruled by a different Germanic ethnic group: Gaul (France) by the Franks, Italy by the Ostrogoths, and Spain by the Visigoths.

Over time, each Germanic group succeeded in making political and social connections with the Roman populations of the lands they occupied and gradually converted to Roman Catholic Christianity. The societies they created, just like the Roman societies before them, were centered on agriculture. Royal power was weak. Latin survived as the language of the highly educated, particularly those in the church, and it eventually became the language of Christian religious ritual. Everyday spoken Latin also contributed to the development of what we call Romance languages, such as French, Spanish, and Italian (Tierney 1999, 71–72).

The Franks, under King Clovis (ca. 466–511), were traditionally the first Germanic people to convert to Roman Catholic Christianity and the first to succeed in a major expansion. Frankish expansion allowed for a kingdom with imperial ambitions. Under the Frankish king Charles the Great, or Charlemagne (ca. 742–814), the Franks entered an important relationship with the popes in Rome that enabled their kings to claim the title of Roman emperor. The time of Charlemagne has sometimes been called the Carolingian **Renaissance** because of the art and literature that were produced in the period. After Charlemagne's death, his three grandsons divided the empire into thirds in 843 CE.

From the eighth to tenth centuries, incursions into western Europe by Norsemen from Scandinavia, Magyars from the East, and Muslims from North Africa destabilized many of the kingdoms that had grown up around the descendants of Charlemagne. Although medieval Europe was dominated by Roman Catholic Christianity, Christians were far from alone, especially in southern Europe. Jews were present in Europe from the time of the Roman Empire, and Muslims entered Europe not only through the conquest of Spain in 711 CE but also through the various countries and ports of the Mediterranean Sea. Magyars and Norsemen eventually settled into Hungary and Normandy and converted to Christianity; in Spain and the Mediterranean, Muslim settlements lasted until 1492. The individual kingdoms that made up western Europe continued to develop their own legal and social systems throughout the ninth and tenth centuries, influenced by the ethnic groups that settled in them.

Historians have identified the eleventh century as a period of change, and it marks the transition from the early Middle Ages to the High Middle Ages. Some historians have argued that this transition was traumatic: in the wake of the invasions, they believe that the society of western Europe entered a period of violence and disorganization that only gradually began to lift in the twelfth century. Others have seen more continuity than change and argue that despite the political fragmentation, the period was of a comparable level of violence and organization to the previous period. All acknowledge a gradual increase of state and papal power beginning in the mid-eleventh century and continuing in the twelfth and thirteenth centuries. King and popes claimed greater control over their territories and tried to exert power over wealthy, independent nobles. In the late thirteenth century, both royal and papal influence were at an all-time high, but the two spheres of power clashed with each other. Both kings and clergy wanted the right to tax their territories and to use their warrior classes to preserve them.

The period between 1050 and 1250 CE has sometimes been described as the Twelfth-Century **Renaissance**. Translators of the period, most of whom were clergy of one type or another, translated works from Greek and Arabic into Latin so that European scholars would have access both to the works of Greco-Roman antiquity and the newer philosophical and scientific works produced in the Islamic world. During this time, music, art, and literature developed in ways that reflected these outside influences. In agriculture, new crops and methods allowed for better production of food and, therefore, a rise in crop yield and in population. The twelfth and thirteenth centuries also featured a number of sociological changes, chief among which was the rise of a merchant class. Accompanying the rise of this class were works of literature in vernacular (non-Latin) languages and a rise in literacy, though the literacy rate was still well below 20 percent for the entire period.

The fourteenth century, beginning the late Middle Ages, proved to be another turning point as tension between church and state grew and caused political friction in many different countries. The early fourteenth century also began a period known as the **Little Ice Age**, when average temperatures in Europe dropped approximately 0.6 degrees Celsius (equivalent to 1.08 degrees Fahrenheit). This climate change in the early part of the century contributed to years of famine in which many people died. The chief event of the fourteenth century, however, was the arrival of the **bubonic plague**, or **Black Death**, in 1347. The plague is estimated to have killed between one-third and one-half of the population of western Europe between 1347 and 1351. The drop in population led to social changes. Workers, whose services were now in greater demand, agitated for better wages. Around western Europe, **serf** rebellions and city uprisings brought the beginning of the end of serfdom, while in eastern Europe, serfdom lasted much longer.

Culturally, the mid-fourteenth century was the period in which authors began to write vernacular literature for the moneyed and literate classes and visual artists began working with new media. This change, which occurred first in Italy and then spread to other European countries, has been called the Italian **Renaissance**. Scholars during the period looked back to Greek and Roman antiquity as great civilizations whose intellectual, political, and artistic innovations had been lost during the Middle Ages—that *medium aevum* that had stagnated, they believed, for about nine hundred years. The great intellectual writer Francesco Petrarch (1304–1374) was the first to refer to the medieval period as the Dark Ages. Writers like Petrarch advocated for humanism, a movement that emphasized the view that human beings could improve their spiritual and intellectual well-being through education and study of the Greco-Roman past. Although it is still common in modern popular culture to see the fourteenth-century Renaissance as a separate, very different period from the Middle Ages, scholars generally perceive there to have been greater continuity than change between the two time periods. That is certainly true for women, whose roles and responsibilities to home and child-rearing were consistent through both periods.

In the fifteenth century, Europeans adjusted to the new world in which plague reoccurred at intervals in different countries and cities. City and royal governments took advantage of the Catholic Church's internal problems to increase their power and exert that power over their citizens' daily lives. By the beginning of the sixteenth century, nation-states were grappling with movements that would produce the Protestant Reformation and the political and economic challenges that came with it. The Protestant Reformation and the European colonization of the New World ushered in the era that scholars call the early modern period.

As the Middle Ages progressed, women experienced both consistent and changing experiences, attitudes, and opportunities. Although women's ability to exert power or authority might have changed in the short term, women's duties and expectations stayed coupled with their biological functions throughout the period. Performing life's daily tasks, caring for the family, and bearing and raising children were women's chores; the few women who did not experience them were either religious women, nuns, and **Beguines** who were forbidden to marry or women who were rich enough to hire others to perform them. As we will see in this book, however, even the most everyday experiences had some change over time, and women's roles and responsibilities varied by time period as well as by class, race, and status.

POPULATION, URBAN GROWTH, AND DAILY LIFE

To understand what daily life was like for medieval women, it is helpful to think about what the experiences of larger groups may have been via population statistics. Throughout the High Middle Ages, the populations of most places in Europe, especially towns and cities, rose significantly from their late-antique and early medieval populations. Between the years 1000 and 1400, it is estimated that the population of western Europe, including Scandinavia and Hungary, rose from approximately 25 million to 56 million. The different regions increased at different rates. For example, France increased from 6 million inhabitants in the year 1000 to 19 million in 1430; Italy increased from 5 million to 9.3 million in the same period (Bardet and Dupâquier 1997, 172–73). Scholars have suggested reasons for this long increase, ranging from changes in agricultural techniques to fewer and less-widespread wars, but there is limited evidence to support any single reason. Rather, complex interlocking factors such as warmer temperatures, better nutrition, lower mortality, agricultural success, and political stability seem to have contributed both to the rise in population and increase of trade.

As the western European population rose, it also became more mobile. Towns and cities grew significantly in the twelfth and thirteenth centuries, and trade grew with them. Italy was the most important center of urban growth. It had the highest urban populations overall, including Venice (one hundred and ten thousand), Genoa (one hundred thousand), and Milan (one hundred thousand), although Paris was the largest city in Europe for much of this period. However large the cities and towns grew, the rural areas of Europe still remained: in 1300, only 9.5 percent of the population of western Europe lived in towns or cities (Bardet and Dupâquier 1997, 176).

Larger populations meant greater political weight for middle- and lower-class people. Beginning in the eleventh century, groups of craftspeople and merchants began to claim increasing rights from their noble overlords by leveraging their increased profits in return for concessions. These were recorded in town charters, documents that listed the rights of urban citizens to control their trades and commerce by themselves. Many of these charters stipulated that a **serf** who came to the city and lived there for a year and a day was freed from servitude. This may have contributed to the rise in urban population, as serfs escaped from servitude to come to towns and cities. Town charters also limited lords' right to tax and to demand other forms of service from their citizens (Tierney 1999, 278).

Inhabitants of the growing towns and cities organized to make the most of the rights they were granted in the charters. Craftspeople and merchants gathered into **guilds**, which functioned both as social safety nets and quality control for the products they sold and produced. Townspeople became richer and demanded concessions from their overlords. This, in turn, provoked an age of expansion and growth in trade and technology that lasted throughout the early modern period. We will talk about the roles of women in these developments in chapter three.

Hard Lives for Everyone

Despite the positive changes related to the growth in population, **paleopathology** (the study of ancient disease) has shown that life for medieval Europeans, male and female, was hard, especially in the early medieval period. For example, among the skeletons buried in the tenth- and eleventh-century cemetery of Raunds Furnells in England, 71 percent of women and 46 percent of men were found to have died before the age of thirty-five. Child mortality was also very high: at the same cemetery, roughly one-quarter of all the skeletons were under age three (Fleming 2006, 38–39). We should not fall into the error of believing that *all* medieval people died young. Men and women who passed their youth successfully could reach their sixties or seventies. Food supply, disease, and other factors shaped life expectancy across Europe throughout the period. Overall though, death rates were higher than our own and at younger ages.

One way we can understand the hardships that everyday medieval people experienced is by examining their skeletons for signs of disease and malnutrition. Archaeologists analyze bone characteristics that indicate these problems. Horizontal lines in the teeth, known as **dental enamel hypoplasia**, indicate that the person who owned the teeth had incidents of malnutrition or disease while developing the teeth; on baby (deciduous) teeth, the malnutrition occurred while the child was still in its mother's womb. Lines on the growth plate of the long bones, which are called **Harris lines**, also mark interruptions in growth caused by disease or malnutrition. For the study of women, an important indicator is an abnormal growth of bone on the skull (**porotic hyperostosis**) or in the eye sockets (**cribra orbitalia**) that are thought to be signs of anemia, or iron deficiency, in childhood. Since women must have adequate iron in their diets to carry children to term, severe anemia in skeletons suggests malnutrition could have had an impact on women's health and fertility. Some scholars have argued that the increased use of iron cooking pots in the thirteenth century might have improved iron levels and, therefore, affected the population. Another condition sometimes observable in medieval bones is rickets, which is caused by a deficiency in vitamin D and causes the bones to soften, giving the long bones of the legs a curved or bowed appearance. Archaeological digs have shown that bone markers of disease and disability occurred frequently in the medieval population. Although the amount and effects of malnutrition varied by time and place, all these problems affected medieval people's daily lives (Fleming 2006, 31–33; Steckel et al. 2019, 222–223).

Archaeological excavations have also shown that many medieval people suffered from parasite infestations, including fleas and body lice. Some medieval household books include advice on how to remove fleas and lice. A book called *Le Ménagier de Paris*, written in the late fourteenth century, advised a young wife to catch fleas using a sticky piece of bread placed on the floor, with a candle nearby to attract the insects to the light. It also suggested a white rug might attract the fleas and could then be shaken off outside the house. Anyone who has ever had fleas in their house can easily understand how ineffective these approaches were. Lice, as well, required removal by hand; family members probably groomed each other, while upper-class people were groomed by servants.

Internally, the most common human parasites were whipworm and roundworm, followed by beef, fish, and pork tapeworms. Both whipworm and roundworm are spread through contact with infected human feces, so if medieval households used human waste as fertilizer, they were increasing the chances of spreading parasites among their families and neighbors. Children who were infected with whipworm and roundworm could suffer intestinal problems, weight loss, and anemia. People of all classes seem to have had parasites, however; whipworm and other parasite eggs have been identified in the remains of King Richard III of England

(1452–1485), whose body was discovered under a parking lot in Leicester, United Kingdom, in 2013 (Anastasiou 2015, 210–215). The presence of different species of tapeworm likely stemmed from eating undercooked meat from infected animals. These are only a few of the human parasites that can be discovered archaeologically, and there were several others. A high burden of parasites may have contributed to the malnutrition and anemia observed in some medieval-era skeletons.

In some archaeological studies, scholars have noted that adult men seem to have outnumbered adult women in medieval society, sometimes even as high as 115 men per 100 women. This ratio is surprising given that scholars identify a natural ratio of 105–107 males per 100 females in a given population. There are many theories about the cause, ranging from female infanticide to different protection of children depending on their gender. It has been suggested that families may have shared food unequally, with females allotted a smaller share, which might have made them more susceptible to malnutrition or to diseases stemming from malnutrition. Environment may also have played a role—for example, constant exposure to cookfires inside houses with inadequate ventilation might have meant that females were more likely to suffer from respiratory illnesses. All these theories are defensible, particularly when used in combination with each other (Bardsley 2014).

CLASS AND STATUS

The Aristocracy

Medieval society divided people strictly according to the classes in which they were born. In the early Middle Ages, wealth and status coalesced around kings and their war bands, who became accustomed to exchanging military service for land or land tenure. These groups gradually formed into the medieval aristocracy, elites whose power came from the land they occupied and the unfree agricultural workers, or **serfs**, over whom they ruled. Elite men developed warrior cultures and technologies, such as armor, that enabled them to hold on to power. The mounted warrior, called the knight, chevalier, or knecht, was the dominant military force of the period. Elite women were also a key part of this equation, especially with regard to inheritance and childbearing (we will discuss elite women in chapter five). The social system that resulted

Upper-class women watch as two knights fight in a joust. (John L. Severance Fund/The Cleveland Museum of Art)

from these relationships expanded through the twelfth century as the population rose and more land came under cultivation.

Merchants and Townspeople

Changes in agricultural technology and rising populations helped contribute to the development of urban areas, where commerce became the central focus of the new urban society. The rise of a merchant class put pressure on nobles, whose job was theoretically making war, by diverting some of the funds that had previously supported their positions and using them for commerce. Over the course of the late Middle Ages, although the nobility continued to prosper, the supremacy of the mounted knight in battle was challenged, first by the longbow and eventually by the cannon. Equally importantly, the rise of towns and cities allowed urban people to lobby for rights of independence they previously did not have. Some towns secured agreements with noble overlords about their rights and debts that were recorded in documents called town charters. Town charters addressed such topics as taxation, **guild** membership, and the rights of those who lived in the town, who came to be called *burghers* or *bourgeois*—town dwellers. Serfs who escaped from manors to towns could sometimes be declared free of servitude if they stayed in a town for a year and a day. Runaway serfs may also have helped contribute to the populations of urban areas.

The Church

The people who made up the Roman Catholic Church hierarchy in the Middle Ages were largely drawn from the aristocracy and were shaped by, and helped shape, many of the aristocracy's beliefs and values. At the head of the church was the pope, an elected official who ruled—or tried to rule—over church institutions all over Europe. Below the pope was a large hierarchy of functionaries who administered the church and, below that, monks, nuns, and the parish priests who ministered to populations of ordinary people. Because of its elite origin and the command that every Christian should contribute to it regularly, the church was extremely wealthy in the Middle Ages. This wealth sometimes provoked criticism from those who believed in voluntary poverty as a way of pleasing God. The church also clashed with powerful kings and nobles who resented its power over their subjects. In the fourteenth century—which was already hard because of its famines and disease—political factions inside the church caused French-supported popes to move the papacy from Rome to the city of Avignon, near the border of France. The infighting that caused this schism deeply harmed the church in Europe. Ordinary people found themselves on either side of a disagreement they did not understand and had no part in. Worse, the disagreement was at its height just as the **bubonic plague** hit Europe, killing tens of millions of people and leaving the population stunned by the disaster. Confidence in the church dropped, and it began to lose some of its influence over everyday people.

Commoners

Common people, of course, made up the bulk of Europe's population throughout the Middle Ages. In the early Middle Ages, as much as 98 percent of the population lived by farming, either for themselves or for overlords. It has been estimated that 75 percent of these were **serfs**, whose labor belonged to the owner of the land they lived on. The poorest commoners struggled under a backbreaking system of labor that did not allow them more than subsistence. As the centuries passed, technology, such as better ploughs and a wider selection of crops, enabled some lower-class people to live a little better; as crop yields increased, fewer people needed to farm to keep the population fed. These changes left room for the growth of a middle and artisan class who lived by buying, selling, and producing goods for sale. As this group of people became wealthier, they demanded increasing power and influence from their governments and from the nobility. We will discuss this change further in chapter four.

Slavery

We should never forget that in addition to serfs, medieval Europe had **chattel** slaves—people who could be sold as property at any time by their owners. Slavery was present throughout the medieval period, whether as a result of warfare (very common in Rome and in the early Middle Ages) or as a feature of the increasingly complex trade in slaves that began around the Mediterranean in the ninth and tenth centuries and expanded into a thriving trade by the early fourteenth century. Scholars in the twentieth century noted that by the eleventh century, most Roman-style male slaves had become legally attached to the land and had become **serfs**. They incorrectly surmised that this was also true for women and children, but the pattern did not always hold. The enslavement of conquered enemies' women and children was a given in the early Middle Ages. Later on, a systematic trade in enslaved people developed as a result of demand from the Muslim world and trade between northern European peoples and the Levant. By the fifteenth century, enslaved people coming from many places, including the Black Sea, North Africa, and sub-Saharan Africa, could be easily bought in most Mediterranean cities. A high percentage of these people was female. Enslaved women were considered the sexual property of their masters and, in some locations, their children could be acknowledged as heirs by their fathers if there were no heirs born to a married couple. In other places, the children of enslaved women were also considered slaves, no matter who had fathered them. The sources for enslaved people are complex, and scholars have only recently begun to talk seriously about medieval slavery. When we think about the lives of everyday medieval women, we need to remember these enslaved people and their experiences (Barker 2021, 2; Rio 2017, 22–24).

RACE AND IDENTITY IN THE MIDDLE AGES

In the twenty-first-century United States, we consider skin color as part of identity, and we often talk about race in bifurcated terms: Black and white—although brown as a category has gained in recent years. We have to understand our own assumptions about what race means while we look at sources from the past. People in the Middle Ages thought about race partly as a function of language and religious affiliation, so an enslaved person in a document might be labeled a Saracen (a medieval word for an Arab Muslim), a Christian, or a Jew, or might be distinguished by his or her area of origin or language group—a Tatar, an Egyptian, and so forth. When free people described themselves, they were likely to refer to their families and places of origin, whether to an individual location such as an estate or a broader category, such as a town or kingdom.

It would be wrong, however, to say that people in the Middle Ages did not see color or that they did not make distinctions based on skin tone. They did. They used skin color as a way to distinguish ethnic groups, particularly in the context of slavery. Skin color was also used as a proxy for moral, physical, and religious virtue. The full development of the idea that "white" and "black" skin were easy ways to indicate the moral character of a person seems to have taken place in the thirteenth century. It is probably not an accident that the twelfth and thirteenth centuries were also the period of the first Crusades, when Europeans who did not live in the Mediterranean or the Levant had contact with darker-skinned people for the first time. For Europeans of this era, "whiteness" became equivocated with Christianity, while "blackness" was associated with non-Christian religions, especially with Islam. Some romances written in the later Middle Ages even had characters who began with black skin that suddenly turned white when they converted to Christianity. Writers also connected pale skin with female beauty; a peasant woman who was suntanned from her work in the fields was never going to be beautiful to upper-class people, who could afford to keep their skin pale by staying indoors (Heng 2018). Although ideas about race based on skin color did not operate in exactly the same way in the Middle Ages as they have later in history, ideas about race were still present and significant.

EVERYDAY CONCERNS

Money

In the early Middle Ages, money was rare in many rural areas, and payment for goods was often made *in kind*: trading one kind of product for another. Taxes and rents were also paid this way. Money became more common in the High Middle Ages when trade became an important part of local economies. European money took denominations inherited from Roman currency: silver **pounds**, silver **shillings**, and copper **pennies** (or livres, sous, and deniers in French). Twelve pennies made a shilling, and twenty shillings made a pound or livre (libra in Latin: this is the origin of the symbol for an English pound, £). Most commerce took place in shillings and pence. Coins became more complex along with growing economies. In England in the late thirteenth century, the **obol** or half-penny (at first, literally one half of a copper penny snipped with metal shears) and the **farthing** (one-quarter of a copper penny) provided much of the purchasing power in the purses of everyday people. One-pound coins also appeared in the thirteenth century, when rising trade made a larger coin more useful. Florence and Genoa, both major trading centers, were the first cities to issue gold coins to make trading in larger sums easier.

Coinage varied in size and design from place to place, as royal courts sought to control coin production, mints, and mines for precious metals. This caused the value of coins to fluctuate. For example, English pounds ("pounds sterling") were made of purer silver than the French livres, and so their value was higher. Merchants carried small scales to keep track of the relative weight of the coins they received. When royal courts sought to produce more money by adding inferior metals to coins, a practice called *debasing*, the value of those coins was less than if they were pure metal (Singman 1999, 65–67). Nowadays, the value of a coin is based on its face value, but in the Middle Ages, the value of coins could be debated in the course of a transaction.

Clothing

In the early Middle Ages, linen and wool provided most of the fiber for clothing. Linen, which is a cloth produced from the fiber of the flax plant, was soft, light, and easily washable, while wool was heavier and harder to clean and was more often reserved for outer garments. By the thirteenth century, wool had become a major export of the British Isles and the care and breeding of sheep had become a vital national industry. Cotton cloth was introduced into Europe through Muslim Sicily in the 1100s, after which Italy gradually developed a trade in cotton cloth. Cotton had been known to the Romans via trade from India, and the Mediterranean world valued cotton not only for its softness but its light weight. By the late Middle Ages, many Europeans had access to cotton fabric or to fustian, a combination of linen and cotton. Silk, too, made its way to the Roman empire but was only available in Europe by import until the twelfth century. Italian weavers then learned the secret of raising silkworms, spinning their thread and producing the cloth. Luxury fabrics were far more available in the later Middle Ages than they had been previously, and their use provoked not only economic competition but restrictive laws.

Linen undergarments were the foundation garments of both men and women during the Middle Ages. Men generally wore **braies**, or breeches, which were loose-fitting linen underwear to which they tied hose to cover their legs. In the early Middle Ages, men sometimes wrapped their lower limbs with cloth or leather. A linen shirt and then a wool tunic went on top. The tunic could be simple for a poor man or very elaborate for an upper-class man. Peasants generally wore hoods, while upper-class men wore elaborate hats that changed with the fashion. Most people probably had, at most, two or three sets of undergarments and perhaps a single tunic or two tunics to choose from. Undergarments were changed weekly, while outer garments were brushed. Soaking a garment in urine (discussed below) was one method of removing stains, but medieval people also used soap made from a combination of lye and animal fat cooked together.

Women's clothes were somewhat different from men's in that they do not seem to have normally worn **braies**, and their linen shirts and tunics were much longer, reaching near the ground. For this reason, their knitted stockings were shorter than men's and reached only to the knee. For menstruation, they probably wore something akin to **braies**, though there are no sources that explain the way everyday medieval women coped with menstruation (Singman 1999, 44–46). (We will talk more about the medieval view of the female body in chapter two.) Women also seem to have worn breastbands, which functioned much like bras, and there are a few examples of fifteenth-century linen undergarments from medieval Austria that approximate bras more directly (Nutz 2013). Married women almost always kept their heads covered with veils or wimples and, in general, wearing one's hair long and loose was a symbol of youth. (We will discuss fashionable clothing for upper-class women in chapter four.)

After children began to walk, their clothing was similar to their parents'. Newborns were generally swaddled in linen bands for the first two or three months of life. The practice was thought to keep the child's limbs safe and make them grow straight. As in our own era, children often began to walk between 14 and 18 months old. Archaeological samples have shown that children who were ready to walk wore long, loose gowns and shoes; some infants' shoes from York were equipped with drawstrings to make putting them on easier. They sometimes toddled on wooden walking frames with wheels. Older children wore more complex clothing, similar to the clothing of adults: underwear of linen, hose, and top garments that were long for girls and shorter for boys. Some children's outfits included belts with buckles and head coverings like caps and linen veils. They also appeared to have carried eating knives when they were old enough and to have worn belt pouches to serve as containers for small items. Pockets did not become widespread in clothing until the early modern period (Gilchrist 2012, 79–81).

When the people of the Middle Ages had opportunity to amass wealth, they displayed it through ostentatious displays of clothing—the equivalent, perhaps, of wearing expensive brand-name clothing today. Lower-class people stuck to similar fashions and garments over long periods of time. Clothing was neither easy enough to produce nor cheap enough to replace to be disposable. It was passed down in wills and resold by secondhand clothiers. After the **bubonic plague** outbreak of 1347–1351 and the rise of the merchant economy of the late Middle Ages, upper-class fashion changed much more rapidly and middle-class people were able to afford to dress more like the nobility. Not surprisingly, the nobility then began to enact **sumptuary laws** to curb noble spending and forbid commoners from wearing expensive, fashionable clothing and furs. (We will discuss fashionable clothing more in chapter four.)

Personal Hygiene: Bathing

Popular culture always portrays the world of the Middle Ages as dirty, and it is true that people in the Middle Ages did not bathe as often as we do in the twenty-first century (whether our standard of cleanliness should be the standard of perfection is a different question). But medieval people did bathe and wash themselves more often than is commonly believed. As in biblical times, washing a guest's feet was a frequent gesture of hospitality, and everyone washed their hands at medieval dining tables. In rural areas, those who lived near a water source could bathe and wash clothes outside in warm weather. The opportunity to bathe in cold weather was shaped by class: only upper-class people could afford servants to prepare indoor tubs filled with hot water for a winter bath.

Medieval towns and cities, however, often had public bathhouses where people could bathe in large tubs for a small amount of money. A few bathhouses originally built by the Romans continued serving customers into the medieval period. In the High Middle Ages, European communities built more and more public baths in different municipalities, sometimes as gifts of charity for the benefit of the poor. Bathhouses were also run privately for profit. Some bathhouses had good reputations and promised sex segregation and physical safety for women while in the bath. Other bathhouses had less strict sex segregation and were portrayed in literature and religious sermons as places for seduction and adultery. Some places actually were both bathhouses and houses of prostitution. (We will talk more about sex work in chapter six.)

Literary works often linked bathing and sex, particularly adulterous sex. The Old Testament story of David and Bathsheba was a frequent illustration in medieval Bibles, showing Bathsheba bathing outside while King David peeked at her. In "Equitan," one of the short narratives in *The Lais of Marie de France* (twelfth century), the title character conspired with his married lover to kill her husband by putting him into a bath of boiling water. The plan did not work; Equitan accidentally jumped into the bathtub and died, and the husband threw his adulterous wife into the fatal bath headfirst. In *Flamenca,* a thirteenth-century southern French romance, the wife of an abusive husband contrived to meet her lover by visiting the mineral baths. Bathing thus became an opportunity for unfaithfulness (Perez 2017). Nervous husbands of upper-class women may well have taken note of the dangers of visiting the bathhouse.

Mixed-sex bathing seems to have been the rule in Roman communities. Muslim rulers newly arrived to Spain in the eighth century were scandalized by the custom. They responded by strictly segregating bathhouses by sex and religious identity: particular days of the week were reserved for Christian men, women (of all faiths), Jews, and Muslims. The mixing of women from different faith traditions worried some medieval authors, who believed that too much contact between women would cause them to convert or even to conduct same-sex relationships. Elsewhere in Europe, Jews were not permitted to use public bathhouses at all, but were required to provide their own facilities. Custom varied around Europe as to how often and under what circumstances women visited bathhouses and whether they needed permission to do so.

King David spies upon Bathsheba while she bathes. (The New York Public Library)

One persistent myth about the Middle Ages is that the water was too dirty to drink. Medieval people drank, cooked with, and bathed in water. They understood that standing, brackish water was inferior to clear water and especially to running water, and they knew that pollution by human and animal waste was bad for health. Medical recipes from the Middle Ages often specified the kind of water that should be used in making up a medicinal bath, drink, or poultice. Health manuals and physicians prescribed bathing to keep healthy, particularly when the water was steeped with appropriate herbs. They also advised about the temperature of the water used. Paintings of people in baths—sometimes sex-segregated, often not—appeared in many medieval advice manuals on good health. The popular notion that the Middle Ages was full of people who never bathed is an error.

Personal Hygiene: Toilet Habits

All animals, including humans, produce waste, and we often imagine that the people of the Middle Ages did not manage their sanitation well. We can learn the most about actual medieval waste management and behavior from later medieval records, when towns and cities became so large that sanitation became a governmental concern. Archaeology has also provided evidence for the management of waste in medieval society. In general, the evidence shows that the world of the Middle Ages was dirty by our standards, but less dirty than today's popular culture would have us believe.

The Romans were accomplished sanitation engineers. Roman public areas in the Imperial period (first to fifth centuries CE) had public toilets, which were many-seated and often built either over running water or over a channel through which water was flushed to remove waste. As in bathhouses, the Romans seemed not to have been concerned about privacy when they needed to urinate or defecate, for there were no dividers between toilet seats and no separate accommodations for the sexes. These factors may have made public toilets all-male locations. It is probable that men used public toilets a great deal more than women and that modest upper-class women did not use them at all.

When they needed to urinate or defecate, most of the people of the early Middle Ages did what humans had always done: they simply went outside. Only the most expensive of rural villas had indoor toilets, which emptied either into water or into a cesspit. Otherwise, people who stayed inside used chamber pots largish clay vessels that held urine and feces and had to be emptied outside. Human waste could be used as fertilizer on gardens and was added to animal waste for that purpose. A given household might have a trench or hole for waste on its property that could be dug out for fertilizing. Dried animal dung could also be burned as fuel, especially important for those medieval peasants who were not allowed to gather firewood in their lords' forests. Feces represented a valuable resource.

Urine also had its own particular uses in the ancient and medieval world: it was used in the **fulling** of cloth and to clean garments, which were soaked in urine and then rinsed in water. The slight acidity of urine made it helpful for removing grease and stains. Some blacksmiths also seem to have used urine to quench tools and weapons they forged. The German monk and artist Theophilus Presbyter (ca. 1070–1125) even specified that the best urine for quenching steel was that of a small, red-haired boy, which he believed would result in a harder, more durable blade (Hawthorne and Smith 2012, 220). Fullers and artisans deliberately collected human urine for these purposes.

In the town or city, the situation was different. Urban areas did not have the space or resources to provide a latrine for every household or to manage the waste of the many animals—horses, oxen, dogs, cats—present in the city. Municipal governments did their best to provide facilities, especially in the late Middle Ages. Richard Whittington (d. 1423), who had been lord mayor of London, left behind enough funding to build a public latrine with sixty-four seats for men and sixty-four seats for women, divided from one another. London regulations provided rules against dumping waste onto the street, and the city paid for public latrines to be dug out periodically. Still, the level of waste contamination in London and other medieval cities must have been considerable. The court records of this period often cite complaints against people who defecated in the street, dumped their chamber pots out their windows, or befouled local waterways by building toilets out above them (Bayless 2012, 29–34). In Paris, householders could place their chamber pots outside the door, where *ouvriers des basse oeuvres*, or workers in low tasks, collected the waste in carts and carried it to public dumps outside the city walls. In twelfth-century Essex, England, a stream called the Shit Brook washed waste from the city into the river Exe (Bayless 2012, 37).

By the thirteenth century, indoor latrines that emptied into cesspits became the standard for new construction among the well-off. The name for these facilities was *privy*—from the French *privé* meaning private. French and English speakers also used the term **garderobe** as a euphemism for an indoor toilet. The concept of privacy itself began with the will to separate one's self or one's family from the outer world. Medieval people believed that the world was dangerous and immoral and also smelly and contaminated. They associated bad hygiene with sin and even with demonic power. Those who could attend to their toilet habits privately, therefore, perceived themselves to be not only cleaner but also morally superior.

Medieval people rich and poor still loved sexy, scatological humor. French poems called fabliaux, comic tales that used sexual adventures and toilet habits for humorous effect, survive from the twelfth to the fourteenth centuries. In one memorable tale, "The Knight who Conjured Voices," a poor knight and his squire came upon an enchanted fountain where they found three fairy women bathing. The squire stole their clothes to sell, but the knight insisted that the clothes be returned. Then the grateful fairies each gave the knight a magic gift. The first gift was simply that he would be welcomed, fed, and lodged wherever he went. The other two set up the bawdy theme for the main plot. The second fairy said the knight, when he wanted to hear the truth, could order any vagina—belonging to either a woman or a female animal—to speak to him. If, for some reason, the vagina could not answer, the third fairy gave him the same power over anuses. Not surprisingly, the knight then came to a wealthy manor where he won a lucrative bet against the lady of the manor by ordering her vagina and anus to speak (Hellman and O'Gorman 1965, 105–121). The story is a takeoff on more standard tales of knightly honor and chivalry, taking advantage of the giggles associated with taboo body parts and functions. Medieval people loved a good, raunchy laugh.

CONCLUSION

This book is an introduction to the everyday lives of medieval European women: how they ate and slept, what their work was like, and what factors shaped their experiences. We often have to contend with the problem that upper-class women are the easiest to access because they lived in the part of society that kept written records. The poorer and more marginalized women of medieval Europe require us to be more creative in selecting the sources that can reveal them, such as archaeology, court records, recipe books, songs, and stories. In the chapters that follow, we will take advantage of these kinds of sources to explore the experiences of women in medieval Europe.

CHRONOLOGY

ca. 420	Augustine, bishop of Hippo, writes *On Marriage and Concupiscence*, in which he outlines his views on the sins of contraception.
476	The Germanic king of the Ostrogoths, Odoacer, deposes the last emperor of Rome and creates a kingdom inside Italy.
495	The Frankish king Clovis converts to Roman Catholic Christianity and influences the peoples around him toward conversion as well.
ca. 547	Death of Benedict of Nursia, whose rule for monks and nuns influenced religious life in the Middle Ages and still does today.
566	Brunhilda, a Visigothic princess, marries Sigebert, King of Austrasia.
597	Death of Fredegund, regent of Neustria and ruthless politician.
ca. 600	Baudonivia writes the life of Saint Radegund, a Frankish queen turned saint.

800	Charlemagne, the king of the Franks, is crowned emperor of the Frankish empire.
841–843	Dhuoda dictates a book for her son William.
900s	Life of Hrosvitha of Gandersheim, the first female playwright in European history.
900s–1000s	Anglo-Saxon women record their wills and indicate their choices for bequests of their personal property.
ca. 1091	Death of Wallada bint al-Mustakfi, Spanish Muslim poet.
ca. 1100	Constance, a nun in Angers, France, corresponds with Bishop Baudry of Bourgueil.
1100s	Possible lifetime of Trota, a midwife and author of at least one medical manuscript in Salerno, Italy.
	Life of Qasmuna bint Isma'il ibn Bagdalah, a Jewish poet who wrote in Arabic.
	Life of Clemence of Barking, a nun who may have criticized a king in her translation of a saint's life.
	Life of Marie de France, author of several Arthurian romances.
1100s–1200s	Female poets known as the trobairitz write poetry to their lovers and to one another in southern France.
1155	Death of Christina of Markyate, who famously fled from her fiancé in order to live her life as an **anchoress**.
1164	Death of Héloïse d'Argenteuil, whose romance and marriage to her tutor Peter Abelard became a famous love story.
1179	Death of Hildegard von Bingen, a mystic, physician, composer, and political writer.
1195	Death of Herrad of Hohenburg, the author of an important book on theology written for the nuns she supervised.

1200s Nuns from the monastery of Helfta become some of Europe's leading mystical figures.

1204 Death of Eleanor of Aquitaine, queen of England and patron of many poets and writers.

1215 Death of Esclarmonde, countess of Foix, Cathar perfect and proud heretic.

Pope Innocent III forbids priests from presiding over an **ordeal**, eventually causing the ordeal to fall out of use.

1220–1229 The Albigensian Crusade is launched to root out the Cathar heresy from southern France and to bring the area back under the king's control.

1253 Death of Clare of Assisi, close companion of St. Francis of Assisi and founder of the monastic order called the Poor Clares.

1281 Death of Guglielma, daughter of the king of Bohemia and founder of her own religion.

1298 A church order from Pope Boniface VIII titled "Periculoso" ("dangerous") requires all Catholic nuns to live under **enclosure**.

1310 Marguerite Porete, a mystic and author, is executed by burning.

1322 Trial of Jacoba Felicie for practicing medicine in Paris.

1324 Trial of Alice Kyteler for witchcraft, the first example of a witch trial.

1347–1351 Outbreak of **bubonic plague** in Europe, killing between one-third and one-half Europe's population.

1371 French knight Geoffrey IV de la Tour Landry writes a book for his daughters that contains moral advice.

1380 Death of Catherine Benincasa of Siena, important mystic and extensive letter writer.

1392–1394 An unknown author writes *Le Ménagier de Paris*, or a book of advice and recipes for a fifteen-year-old wife.

1400s	Women of the Paston family of Norfolk, United Kingdom, exchange letters with each other and the people around them. The letters were discovered in 1735 in the basement of their manor.
1416	Death of mystic and **anchoress** Julian of Norwich.
1430	Death of poet and writer Christine de Pisan.
1431	Execution by burning of the French peasant saint Joan of Arc.
ca. 1439	Death of Margery Kempe, pilgrim, traveler, and mystic.
1440	Death of Bartolomea Riccoboni, nun and writer of a chronicle tracing Italian politics in the early fifteenth century.
1445	Foundation of the Ospedale degli Innocenti in Florence, the first municipal orphanage for abandoned children.
1470	Death of Helene Kottanner, who almost single-handedly bestowed the crown of Hungary on King Ladislaus V by completing a secret mission.
1486	Publication of the *Malleus Maleficarum*, the most **misogynistic** and most important anti-witchcraft text of the period.

1

MARRIAGE AND SEXUALITY

The great majority of women in the Middle Ages married at least once, and sometimes several times. Marriage was key to medieval understandings of sexuality, religious faith, and childbearing. In this chapter we will examine the major influences on the concepts of marriage and sexuality to understand how they shaped the everyday lives of medieval Christian and Jewish women.

Not surprisingly, religious writers disapproved of sex outside of marriage. The word they used for it was *fornication*, which was considered a serious sin throughout the Middle Ages. Fornication was a large category that covered a multitude of sexual behaviors, including premarital sex, adultery, homosexuality, masturbation, oral sex, and even "unnatural" sexual positions. Medieval authorities tried to control marriage, gender identity, sexual orientation, and extramarital sexual intercourse, arguing that the anger of God would be let loose upon the world if such behaviors were allowed to continue. Medieval writers—who were frequently men and women vowed to chastity and part of a small, educated elite—found it in their interest to suppress behaviors and people they considered to be sinful or aberrant. They also enforced strong binary categories in their understanding of medieval sexuality, so that they condemned those people who did not fall into approved gender roles for men or women.

LATE ANTIQUE AND EARLY MEDIEVAL MARRIAGE

Early medieval Christian writers based their understanding of marriage on the biblical book of Genesis. In Genesis chapter two, God created Adam (man) first, and then Eve (woman) second. The reason Adam needed Eve, according to the text, was that God thought Adam should not be alone: he needed a "helper" or "companion." God then created Eve out of one of Adam's ribs. After living for a time in the Garden of Eden, Adam and Eve chose to eat a fruit from the tree of the knowledge of good and evil, which God had forbidden them to eat. Therefore, they were cast out of Eden with harsh punishments: Adam was doomed to a life of hardship and manual labor, and Eve was cursed with pain and suffering during childbirth. She was also cursed to be subordinate to her husband and to be plagued by sexual desire: "To the woman he said, 'I will make your pains in childbearing very severe; with painful labor you will give birth to children. Your desire will be for your husband, and he will rule over you'" (Genesis 3:16).

The Genesis story formed the basis for the medieval Christian view of women and of marriage. One interpretation argued that the knowledge that Adam and Eve received after eating the forbidden fruit included knowledge of their own bodies and of sexual desire. Sexual desire, according to late antique and early medieval writers, was the result of this Original Sin, and, therefore, those who wanted to be completely faithful to God should abstain from sex. This belief fed into the growth of vows of **celibacy** by monks, nuns, and other **ascetics** in the period. Sex was permissible only within marriage, though marital sex was believed to be less virtuous than total abstinence. This positive view of celibacy came in part from the New Testament and the writings of Paul of Tarsus (ca. 4 BCE—ca. 64 CE), an important early Christian writer who believed that abstaining from sex was preferable to marriage because abstinence left Christian men and women free to contemplate and serve God. Paul was forced to admit, however, that if there were no sex and no marriage, then the faith would die out (1 Corinthians 7: 1–11), The tension between celibacy and the need to carry on the faith continued throughout the Middle Ages and influenced the way European Christian women understood their lives.

The tension also led to some sexual stereotypes. Male writers believed women to have stronger sexual desires than men and to be less able to resist sexual temptation. Men, so the reasoning went, were more intellectual and spiritual, and women more emotional and physical. For some religious writers among the early Christians, the Genesis story served as proof that Eve, and therefore all women, were guilty of the sin that had caused mankind to displease God and, by association, required the sacrifice of Jesus. This harsh view led to a strongly **misogynist** trend. The Christian writer Tertullian (155–240 CE) wrote a work in which he accused all women of being responsible for the death of Jesus because of their vanity and lustfulness: "Do you not know that you are Eve? . . . Because of what you deserve, that is, death, even the Son of God had to die" (Blamires 1992, 51).

The story of Adam, Eve, and the apple provided a deeply conflicted view of sexuality in the Catholic Church, and that conflict also affected the view of marriage among Church writers. But there were also examples from the Gospels to provide meaning to marriage. In a famous story from the Gospel according to John, Jesus attended a wedding in Cana of Galilee with his disciples and performed his first miracle by turning water into wine (John 2: 1–11). Christian writers took this to be an explicit message that God approved of marriage as long as it was undertaken in the proper religious spirit. Unfortunately, there was no example of a ceremony in Christian writ to give instructions for a standard ritual, so Christian marriage was largely patterned on marriage as practiced in local populations as they gradually converted to Christianity.

ROMAN MARRIAGE

One model for marriage came from ancient Rome. In republican Roman culture, a woman was considered to be under the legal control of either her husband or her father. The term for this was *in manu*, "in the hand." There were three types of ceremonies in which a woman moved from the control of her father to the control of her husband. The most common ritual required five adults to witness the groom handing a few symbolic bronze coins to the bride's father in return for the loss of his daughter. Afterward, the assembled guests accompanied the bride and groom to the groom's house. At that point, the bride was considered to be a part of her husband's family and not her own. Another, more elaborate ritual, reserved only for upper-class families, required the bride and groom to give bread as an offering to the god Jupiter before ten witnesses and a priest. Both types required the payment of a **dowry** from the bride's family to the groom's. Sometimes called the *falcidian quarter*, the dowry was defined as one-quarter of the bride's family's wealth and was equivalent to her inheritance from her family. It was also possible for a couple to have a common-law marriage: if a young woman cohabited with a man for a year and a day, she was considered to be married and in her husband's *manus*. A wife in a marriage *in manu* did not control her dowry or any of her personal possessions, and she could not divorce her husband. He could divorce her, in which case she returned to her father's *manus*.

A woman did have the option of staying in the *manus* of her family by contracting a "free" marriage. If she stayed at her father's house for three days every year, she could remain under her father's *manus*, and, therefore, her father would not give up control of her dowry. Some families likely chose this option to avoid giving too much control over their property to another family and to keep their daughters connected to their birth families. Women who were still in their fathers' *manus* when their fathers died could control their own property, so this "free" type of marriage had significant benefits for women. This type of marriage became very popular in the imperial period (ca. 100–400 CE) as some of the older types of marriage fell out of use (Herlihy 1985, 8–9).

GERMANIC MARRIAGE

The earliest description of Germanic marriage comes from the Roman writer Tacitus (ca. 50–126 CE) in his work *Germania*. He wrote approvingly that Germanic marriage customs were strict and military in character. "The wife does not bring a dower to the husband, but the husband to the wife . . . gifts not meant to suit a woman's taste, nor such as a bride would deck herself with, but oxen, a caparisoned steed, a shield, a lance and a sword" (Murray 2001, 11). Tacitus's work should be read with care because he was a Roman writing about customs that were not his own, but his observations give us our only clues as to what early Germanic peoples may have done.

By the fifth and sixth centuries, Germanic law codes provide us with more information. Like the Roman marriage, early medieval Germanic marriage customs had three aspects. The betrothal of the bride and groom was a festive occasion in which the families had a large dinner and drew up a formal contract for the marriage. The **dower**, or gifts to the bride and her family, made a second occasion. As in Roman marriages, there was an exchange of a few coins from the groom to the bride's father, but the most important part of the dower was the money and gifts given to the bride herself. By the eleventh century, she received not only an amount of money or possessions as a dower but also the ***Morgengabe***, a "morning gift" given the day after the wedding, after the marriage had been consummated. A wealthy bride could expect lavish gifts as her *Morgengabe*. The third occasion was the official transfer of the wife into the husband's home, similar to the Roman custom. A Germanic wife was subject to the *Munt*, or legal power, of her husband and could not divorce him, but he could divorce her if he issued a decree nullifying their marriage contract (Herlihy 1985, 49–51; Brundage 1987, 128). A year of marriage without conceiving a child was considered to be one reason to divorce (Brundage 1987, 131).

From the sixth to the tenth centuries, marriage was probably promoted in part by a family's ability to provide money to their son—sometimes as much as a quarter of the family wealth, depending on local custom. In the eleventh and twelfth centuries, however, the parts of Europe that gave the *Morgengabe* gradually changed over to the Roman dowry system, in part because of the new prominence of Roman law, and money began to flow from the bride's family to the groom's instead. This change affected the rights of women to their own property, because while a wife had complete control over her *Morgengabe*, the control of dowry property, although technically hers, often rested with her husband and his family. The Roman-style dowry system gradually spread throughout Europe between the twelfth and fifteenth centuries. By the end of the Middle Ages, the dowry had become a prominent feature of marriages all over Europe (Stuard 2013).

AGE AT FIRST MARRIAGE

We often imagine a medieval couple marrying very young by modern standards, and it is true that both the Catholic Church and Jewish law set the minimum ages of marriage at twelve for girls and fourteen for boys. However, ages of marriage varied according to custom and social and economic pressures. In the early Middle Ages, age at first marriage tended to in the teens for both husband and wife; the high risk of death to both children and mothers demanded that young women reproduce early and often to keep the population steady. After the year 1000, when the population stabilized, food supplies improved, and invasions ended, age at first marriage increased into the twenties, especially for peasants, who could now afford to marry later. Noble young women tended to marry early in most time periods to maximize their fertility, but upper-class young men often waited to marry until their fathers had died and they had become the heads of their own households. This often made them significantly older than their brides (Ferraro 2012, 61–62).

THE CHRISTIAN INFLUENCE ON EARLY MEDIEVAL MARRIAGE

The secular nature of traditional rituals, the common use of divorce, and the lack of concern over sexual mores in Roman and Germanic marriage customs left Christian writers dissatisfied. Over the first centuries of Christianity, they adopted Christian symbolism into the marriage ceremony by layering it on top of the ceremonies that communities already practiced. Augustine of Hippo (354–430 CE), a major writer of the fifth century, wrote that marriage had three great positive attributes, *fides*, *proles*, and *sacramentum*: faithfulness, children, and permanent union, a formulation that allowed Christian marriage to be linked to the practices of the time (Herlihy 1985, 11). Gradually, church officials formalized the rituals of marriage into a tripartite structure: engagement (which could be a formal betrothal), consent (usually a statement given in a ceremony with witnesses), and consummation (when the bride and groom had sex) (d'Avray 2008, 58). Christians kept a number of the old Roman and Germanic customs, the most important of which was the use of the **dowry**. Germanic communities continued to practice the **dower** and the *Morgengabe* until the eleventh century.

Over the course of the early Middle Ages, the church encouraged couples to exchange their consent to their marriages before groups of witnesses, either in or just outside a church. In Italy, most of these ceremonies took place on the steps of the church building before the bride and groom went to their new home. The French approach had the couple lie in bed together while the priest spoke a blessing over their marriage bed. In both cases, the consummation of the marriage was considered to complete the marriage and make it permanent (Brundage 1987, 88).

SEX IN MARRIAGE—FOURTH THROUGH ELEVENTH CENTURIES

Marital sex posed a problem for Catholic Church writers through the early Middle Ages because of the church's strong emphasis on virginity being desirable for the avoidance of sin and for right service to God. Ever since Adam and Eve had sinned sexually, they reasoned, it was almost impossible to have sexual intercourse without sinning, even within marriage. Virginity was, therefore, to be prized. Saint Jerome (ca. 347–420 CE) remarked bluntly, "I praise wedlock, I praise marriage, but only because they give me virgins" (Amt 2010, 17). As far as Jerome was concerned, marital sex should be limited to brief encounters that were strictly for procreation. Under his influence, later church authors began to place rules on when and how married couples could have sex without sinning. Caesarius of Arles (ca. 470–542 CE), an influential writer of rules for Christians, forbade couples to have sex during Lent (the forty days before Easter), on the vigils for feast days (the nights before religious holidays), on Sundays, and during menstrual periods and pregnancy (Brundage 1987, 91–92).

Ironically, this conflicted with another church prescription, the idea of the **marriage debt**, in which either spouse was required to have sex when asked, on the grounds that their bodies belonged to each other. Augustine of Hippo allowed husbands and wives to have sex without fear of sin, but other church writers were not so accommodating (Brundage 1987, 93). However, Augustine, one of the most important Christian writers of the period, was particularly harsh on the subject of birth control, because he believed that anyone who used birth control was engaging in sex for pleasure rather than procreation. Augustine's point of view provided the basis for the church's negative view of contraception throughout the Middle Ages.

Between the sixth and eleventh centuries, some Christian authors wrote handbooks to help the clergy understand when sexual sin had occurred and how to issue penance for it. These handbooks were called **penitentials**. Taking their cue from earlier writers, the writers of the penitentials took a very strict view of marital sex: not only did they restrict the days during the year on which married couples could licitly have sex, they also encouraged married couples to abstain from sex at regular intervals. Otherwise, they reasoned, the marriage was not a marriage at all, but a celebration of lust. Some writers even required newlyweds to wait three days after the wedding before having sex. Married couples were also to abstain during menstruation, pregnancy, childbirth, and lactation (nursing), as well as on particular days of the week: Wednesday, Friday, Saturday, and Sunday. Those couples who observed all these prohibitions would have been restricted to having sex only four or five times a month (Brundage 1987, 154–60). It is impossible to say, however, how closely married couples followed—or even knew about—all the restrictions of the penitential literature. The birth rate in the period, as far as can be told, does not reflect a strict use of the rules among married couples.

CONCUBINAGE AND POLYGYNY

Christian authorities in the early Middle Ages were particularly troubled by the Germanic acceptance of **polygyny** (having more than one wife). Germanic chieftains could have multiple wives and also kept **concubines**, women who were not wives but were recognized as legal consorts. Roman law also recognized a class of women who were not prostitutes but were not quite wives—frequently partners of a lower social class than the man—as *concubinae*, meaning "women who share the bedroom." The distinction between marriage and concubinage was not always clear, as the children of both wives and concubines could inherit property from their fathers (Brundage 1987, 135). From the early sixth century, when Germanic groups began to convert to Christianity, church officials worked to encourage the Germanic peoples to understand marriage as a permanent and exclusive arrangement. Germanic kings, however, continued to practice concubinage and multiple marriage. The Frankish king and later emperor Charlemagne (d. 814 CE) had many wives and concubines and a range of children by both. Although Charlemagne never had more than one wife at a time, he was never without at least one concubine, whose position in the royal household was expected to be slightly below his wife's. His biographer, Einhard, listed Charlemagne's children by both his wives and his concubines but confessed that he could not remember all the concubines' names—some evidence that there were many of them (Einhard and Notker the Stammerer 2008, 31).

Upper-class men continued to take concubines and mistresses throughout the Middle Ages, despite the church's strong disapproval of the practice. Such relationships were usually between wealthy men and women of a much lower social class. Church courts tried forcing men to give up their mistresses with only partial success. Count William IX of Aquitaine was excommunicated for his liaison with Dangereuse, the viscountess of Châtellerault, in the early twelfth century, but instead of repenting, he installed her in a tower at his castle in Poitiers and proceeded to live with her openly for many years (Flori 2007, 20–21). The laws of *Las Siete*

Partidas of Alfonso X of Leon and Castile (1221–1284 CE) even drew up regulations for the keeping of concubines. "Any man who is not hindered by membership in a religious order, or by marriage, can keep a concubine without fear of temporal punishment" (Amt 2010, 55).

Such laws provided that both parties would be legally protected, particularly if the man then wanted to marry someone else. In 1228, Countess Aurembiaix of Urgel made a contract with King James I of Aragon that detailed how they would own their property and how they would care for any children born of their union. It seems all that distinguished this contract from a marriage contract was that there was no marriage involved (Brundage 1987, 370).

Concubinage was also widespread among upper-class Jews in Spain. Even though Jewish religious law generally forbade men to keep concubines, the social practices of upper-class people permitted and even encouraged men to keep concubines or, in Muslim Spanish legal context, to take more than one wife. Some men who bought slaves to keep as concubines later freed and married them. Moses Maimonides (1138–1204), an important Jewish thinker in Spain and later in Egypt, ruled that freeing a concubine and marrying her was permitted, not because the practice was approved under Talmudic law, but because it was less sinful to marry a concubine than to have children with her out of wedlock (Grossman 2004, 137). Customs about what relationships were legal or illegal varied greatly depending on the social contexts in which they operated.

HIGH MEDIEVAL MARRIAGE AND SEXUALITY

Church Reform

In the eleventh century, the Catholic Church began a series of reforms that were aimed at consolidating the power of the church and emphasizing church law over the civil legal customs of the various nobilities of Europe. In doing so, the church incorporated much law taken from the Roman period, especially the laws compiled under the emperor Justinian (ca. 482–565 CE) and known as the *Justinianic Corpus*. Reforming popes such as Leo IX (pope 1049–1054 CE) and Gregory VII (pope 1073–1085 CE) sought to increase papal power and to reform those areas of the church that governed sexuality, particularly sexuality among the clergy (Brundage 1987, 178). Over the course of the twelfth century, papal power and Roman legal reasoning led to changes and adjustments in the understanding of marriage and sexuality. These changes led to new everyday expectations for medieval women.

Clerical Celibacy and Lay Marriage

Although the church's attitude toward virginity had always been approving, and taking vows of celibacy had long been a requirement for monks and nuns, the secular clergy—those priests and clerics who cared for the population—had never become entirely celibate, and many priests had even married or entered into out-of-wedlock relationships with women. Canonist reformers, experts in church law, of the eleventh century advocated a much stricter view of marital relationships that excluded all religious professionals, not just monks and nuns, from marriage and, therefore, from any kind of sexuality. The word *concubine* then changed to mean a woman in a sexual relationship with a man to whom she was not married, especially if that man was a priest. Sexuality, the reformers maintained, could only lawfully take place within marriage and only for the purpose of procreation. Joined to this was a much stricter definition of marriage: it was to be entirely monogamous, indissoluble, and freely contracted between the parties (Brundage 1987, 183). From the twelfth century on, the church was the chief arbiter of whether a marriage was legally valid.

Marriage throughout the Middle Ages, however, was not just the concern of the bride and groom: it was a contract between families and sometimes their secular lords and also concerned the church, which wanted the marriage to be as binding as possible. Historian Georges Duby, in a classic work, argued that between 1050 and 1300, two models of Christian marriage were taking shape that were fundamentally in conflict with one another. The first was a secular, family-based model that was primarily concerned with lineage and property. These marriages were often done without much attention to the opinions of the bride and groom but were rather predicated on what made the most sense in regard to land and allegiances. The second model was an ecclesiastical model in which the church's definition of marriage was primary. This model was not concerned with lineage or property but emphasized consent of the bride and groom over the consent of the family (Duby 1978). High medieval marriages eventually adopted a number of requirements to meet both the community's and the church's understanding of what made marriage valid. There were many local customs and practices, but the overall patterns were similar.

Here is an English example. A marriage usually began with the financial arrangement that led to the betrothal. A woman was expected to bring a **dowry** that represented her inheritance and claim to family property; sometimes that was land and sometimes goods and cash. She expected to maintain a claim to her dowry should she ever become widowed. A betrothal ceremony followed the financial settlement, often with many witnesses, in which the betrothed promised to marry one another in the future. After the betrothal, the **banns,** public proclamations of the coming wedding, should be called to make sure there were no legal impediments to the marriage. The wedding ceremony itself took place at the church door, where vows were exchanged, and the groom gave the bride a symbolic gift of money on a book or a shield to signify her **dower**. The groom also gave the bride a ring blessed by the priest. A mass followed inside the church, and then a wedding feast, after which the bridal bed and bedroom were blessed. The couple then got into bed together before witnesses (Leyser 1995, 107–109). A prayer from the Liturgy of Marriage in the Sarum missal, dating from the thirteenth century, blesses the woman in this way: "Let her be amiable to her husband like Rachel, wise like Rebecca, long-lived and faithful like Sara . . . May she be fruitful in child-bearing, excellent, and innocent" (Murray 2001, 267–268).

A royal bride and groom, escorted by attendants, are blessed by a bishop. (The British Library)

Consent and Sex

The combination of custom and church law made marriages from the twelfth century on more binding than they had ever been before. Although the church's definition of marriage emphasized consent, in general, European laypeople throughout the Middle Ages believed that consummation was one of the requirements for a valid marriage. Archbishop Hincmar of Reims (806–882 CE) described it this way in about 860 CE: a marriage was an agreement made between free persons, with parental consent, and was made valid with a dowry and sexual intercourse (Brundage 1987, 136). During the twelfth century, however, some church thinkers reconsidered this rule. Peter Lombard (ca. 1096–1160 CE), bishop of Paris, wrote in his work *The Sentences* that a marriage was complete when the bride and groom consented—that is, as soon as the bride and groom announced that it was their intention to be married. At that moment, they were married; sex was not required. The reason for this was theological. Peter Lombard and others worried that if marriages that were unconsummated were not real marriages, then the marriage of the Virgin Mary to Joseph would not have been valid, and neither would marriages in which the couples were unable or unwilling to have sex. His reasoning appealed to Pope Alexander III (Pope 1159–1189 CE), who encouraged others to adopt the view (Brundage 1987, 264).

Although this theological position solved the problem of Joseph and Mary, it posed a number of problems for families. Since consent could be given in private or in secret, valid marriages could be made without public betrothal or even the knowledge of the bride's and groom's families (Herlihy 1985, 81–82). This meant that families who were accustomed to having the last word in their children's choices of marriage partners could be undercut by a taking of vows in secret. During the Fourth Lateran Council of 1215, church authorities patched this loophole by requiring that the **banns** be called three times in the couple's parish church on successive Sundays or feast days before the wedding. The expectation was that if anyone in the community knew of a reason why the couple should not be married, such as incest or a previous marriage, they would have the opportunity to come forward. Thus, the marriage would have no reason to be contested later (Finch 1990, 190). Public consent continued to be a main requirement for a religiously valid marriage throughout the Middle Ages, and church courts called witnesses to attest that the taking of vows had occurred.

Indissolubility

During the twelfth century, church courts became the arbiters of marriage and its legitimacy. Pope Alexander III was responsible for the definition of marriage promulgated during that time. A valid marriage could be made by present consent, using words such as "I take thee as my husband," which meant that the parties were officially married. It could also be made by betrothal followed by sexual intercourse. Once the marriage was consummated, it was permanent. The reform canonists agreed that a marriage, once legally contracted in this way, could not be dissolved (Donahue 2007, 1–2), Divorce was forbidden, and **annulment**, the declaration that a marriage had never existed, was used rarely. Only a few instances provided consistent grounds for the separation of married couples: impotence (the inability to perform sexual intercourse); **consanguinity** (incest by blood relationship); and affinity (incest by marriage relationship). For some writers, such as Bishop Ivo of Chartres (bishop 1091–1116 CE), adultery also provided a reason for a separation. Separation, however, did not always mean divorce in the sense that the parties would be allowed to marry again: they were allowed to live apart (a practice called *divortium*, the root of our modern word *divorce*) but not to remarry, unless the marriage was declared annulled. Husbands and wives who decided to become monks or nuns were able to separate, but the spouses left behind could not remarry (Brundage 1987, 200–201, 334). Remarriage was often left to the few (usually noble) couples who were fortunate enough to petition for annulment in church courts that were less strict.

Impotence

The inability of a man to perform sexual intercourse was one factor that could lead to the annulment of a marriage. Since the Catholic Church defined marital sex in terms of procreation, the inability to procreate posed an intellectual problem. However, there was no one point of view on impotence in the early Middle Ages. In general, the canonists, such as the twelfth-century author Gratian, were of the opinion that impotence could cause a marriage to end (Rousseau 2014, 414). Church authorities worked on a case-by-case basis to determine whether impotence allowed for the dissolution of marriages. In the later Middle Ages, the church set a requirement that three years of impotence must be proven. If it was, the marriage could be declared annulled. Some courts required that the man who claimed impotence be tested by sex workers or matrons to see if he responded sexually to a woman who was not his wife. Women could also demand to be examined to prove that their marriages had never been consummated because of a husband's impotence. Lucrezia Borgia (1480–1519), the daughter of Pope Alexander VI, claimed in 1497 that her marriage to Giovanni Sforza had never been consummated and offered to be examined to prove that she was still a virgin. Sforza himself refused to be examined, so a church court under two cardinals declared the marriage invalid. Both parties later married again (McLaren 2007, 35–36).

Many medieval people believed that impotence could be caused by magic. Archbishop Hincmar of Reims (802–884 CE) suggested that any couples who were worried that magic might be at work in their relationship should immediately devote themselves to prayer and fasting so that the spell could be removed. Impotence by magic became a widely discussed public issue in 1193, when Philip Augustus, king of France (king 1180–1223 CE) married Princess Ingeborg of Denmark. Immediately after the marriage ceremony, Philip developed an aversion to Ingeborg and attempted to have the marriage annulled on the grounds of incest, because Ingeborg was related to his first wife. This was unsuccessful, so Philip claimed that he was unable to consummate the marriage because he was bewitched. Ingeborg, however, steadfastly argued that the marriage had been consummated. Philip appealed to Pope Innocent III (pope 1198–1216 CE), who advised him to wait the three years before attempting to end the marriage. In the end, the pope took Ingeborg's side, and Philip's attempt to annul the marriage did not work; his marriage to Ingeborg stood until 1223, Philip's own death (Rider 2006, 34, 72–74).

Consanguinity and Affinity

Church authorities were unanimous that a marriage made between people with **consanguinity**—sharing the same blood—was incest and, therefore, an impediment to a legal Christian marriage. This included those who were related by affinity, which came about through marriage; for example, it would be incest for a man to marry a close relative of his wife or his sister-in-law. In the early Middle Ages, to determine whether two people were too closely related to marry, a Germanic calculation was used: if the spouses were related within seven degrees of separation, they could not marry. Calculating the degrees of separation meant starting on a family tree at the first spouse, counting backward to the common ancestor, and then down to the second spouse, counting one for each person. If the number was less than seven, the marriage would be incestuous. Effectively, this meant that first cousins and even second cousins could not marry.

In the twelfth century, after the doctrine of indissolubility was taking hold, nobles could seek the dissolution of marriages on the grounds of consanguinity and be allowed to remarry. Since so many noble families were closely intermarried, it was often possible to discover a link between two married people either through their blood relatives or to one another's relatives by marriage. One well-known example of this strategy was at work in the end of the marriage of Eleanor, the duchess of Aquitaine, to the king of France, Louis VII, in the twelfth century. Louis and Eleanor were married for fifteen years and had two daughters but made the decision to seek annulment of their marriage on the grounds of their blood relationship, for which they had received papal permission when they married. It is likely that it was their lack of sons, instead, that drove the separation. The marriage was dissolved in March 1152 by a church council called for the purpose. Louis and Eleanor were both then allowed to remarry. Eleanor became the queen of England when she married Henry II in May of 1152, and Louis remarried two years later to his second wife, Constance of Castile (Flori 2007, 54–55). Louis and Eleanor's divorce is one example of how the doctrine of indissolubility did not always work out in practice. During the Fourth Lateran Council of 1215, the rule of consanguinity was reduced to four degrees, which reduced the number of marriages that would fall under prohibition, and such cases became rarer (Brundage 1987, 354).

SEX IN MARRIAGE—TWELFTH TO FIFTEENTH CENTURIES

In the High Middle Ages, the severe attitude of the Penitentials toward sex inside of marriage loosened a bit. Sex in marriage was permissible, as it paid the **marriage debt**, and it was not considered a sin if the intent of the couple was procreation. Moralists still advised that "immoderate" or "unnatural" sex positions were sinful, and so was having sex for pleasure, but sexual intercourse was still necessary for a valid marriage. Church courts even sentenced married couples to sex if their relationship was estranged. One court ordered a man "to pay the **conjugal debt** to the plaintiff [his wife] in her father's house one night each week" (Brundage 1987, 505). On the whole, church courts enforced the marriage debt as a way to ensure the morality of the faithful within marriage. The French bishop Jacques de Vitry (ca. 1160–1240 CE) cautioned married men to be sure that they kept their wives satisfied so they would have no excuse to stray. Women who were widowed were presumed to be sexually experienced and, therefore, more in danger of becoming wanton.

POSITIVE AND NEGATIVE VIEWS OF SEX

Outside of church jurisdiction, couples, we must suppose, continued to have sex without observing all the strict rules and regulations the church attempted to put in place. Two fourteenth-century English examples can demonstrate the difference between views of sex. Geoffrey Chaucer's *Canterbury Tales*, written between 1387 and 1400, introduced a character called the Wife of Bath, who had been married multiple times and was quite open about her love of sex: "My husband's going to have it night and day," she declared to her audience of astonished pilgrims (Blamires 1992, 203). The Wife's boast that she had married—and worn out—five husbands was intended to amuse, but the prologue to her tale was full of lusty praise for the "marriage debt."

In contrast, Margery Kempe, a middle-class woman who lived in England in the fourteenth century, was persuaded that abstention from sex was what God wanted and proposed to her husband that they have a celibate marriage. She was so horrified by marital sex (despite having borne fourteen children) that "she would rather have eaten or drunk the slime from the gutter than consent to any sexual contact, except out of obedience [to God]" (Bale 2015, 15). Eventually, Kempe persuaded her husband into taking a vow of chastity and went on a pilgrimage to Jerusalem. Kempe's view of marital sex was extreme for the period, but it illustrated the effect on everyday life of some of the religious teachings that were common at the time.

POSITIVE AND NEGATIVE VIEWS OF MARRIAGE AND WOMEN

Outside the realm of church law, popular texts sometimes spoke of marriage in negative terms for different reasons than the church writers. The basis for much anti-woman and anti-marriage writing in the Middle Ages was a work criticizing marriage by an author named Theophrastus, which was quoted at length in Saint Jerome's fourth-century work *Against Jovinian*. Theophrastus criticized both women in general and wives in particular:

"To support a poor wife is hard; to put up with a rich one is torture . . . If she has a bad temper or is a fool, if she has a blemish or is proud, or has bad breath, whatever her fault may be—all this we learn after marriage" (Blamires 1992, 71).

Theophrastus may have been arguing satirically, but Jerome took him seriously. In an effort to convince his readers that celibacy was better than marriage, he used Theophrastus's points: wives were a financial drain; a wife was liable to be a bad bargain because she could not be "tried" before marriage; and all women were so lustful that they would be unfaithful, whether they were beautiful or ugly. Those points appeared over and over in anti-marriage and anti-woman literature throughout the Middle Ages. Notably, the same points were used in Jean de Meun's section of the fourteenth-century *Roman de la Rose*, a work in which all the stereotypes of marriage were used to great effect. De Meun had a character called the "Jealous Husband" lament: "Would that I Theophrastus had believed and never wed!" (de Lorris and de Meun 1962, 173).

De Meun's section includes a diatribe in which the Jealous Husband railed about his wife's love of luxury, her wanton behavior, and her lack of regard for his desires or comforts. These criticisms were part of an overall negative stereotype of women in the Middle Ages: they were portrayed with a desire for wealth, fine clothes, and jewels; lustfulness; and love of talking. Such stereotypes were often deployed humorously to tease women, to tease men about their wives, or to mock the desire to marry, but they were also used to support and proliferate negative stereotypes of women and wives.

Not all writers, however, had such a dim view of married life. The anonymous fourteenth-century author of the *Ménagier de Paris* wrote a work for a young wife in which he extolled the benefits of marriage and educated her about her duties and cares in her married life. "Certainly," he wrote, "a man, no matter what his position, noble or not, can have no better treasure than a wife who is virtuous and wise" (Bayard 2001, 45). The twelfth-century bishop and poet Marbode of Rennes (ca. 1035–1123) agreed: "Of all the things which are seen to have been bestowed through God's gift to the advantage of humanity, we consider nothing to be more beautiful or better than a good woman, who is part of our own flesh, and we part of her flesh" (Blamires 1992, 228).

Authors who wrote positively about marriage, almost without exception, emphasized chastity as part of the good wife's virtues, but what they meant was faithfulness to her husband rather than celibacy. The author of the *Ménagier de Paris* was unwilling to go into much detail about married sex, but he made it clear that a wife should guard her chastity very carefully: "It is certain that all good things forsake a girl or woman who is found wanting in virginity, continence, and chastity. Nothing—neither riches, beauty, wisdom, high birth, nor any other asset—can erase talk of the contrary fault" (Bayard 2001, 45). A reputation for sexual continence was key to keeping a respectable social position in a medieval community.

JEWISH MARRIAGE AND SEXUALITY

In European Jewish communities, a slightly different set of customs prevailed for marriage. Jewish parents arranged marriages for their children as Christian parents did, at similar ages, and the couple's wishes were not a factor in the arrangement, although a bride did have the right to refuse a marriage. Husbands paid a bride-price, or *mohar*, to the bride's family, and the bride also contributed a **dowry,** often consisting of jewelry and household items. Although religious interpretations varied across the Jewish communities of Europe, some customs applied across national boundaries. The marriage was made by the signing of a legal document called a ketubah. As in Christian ceremonies, the wedding ceremony often took place outdoors. Sometimes a prayer shawl (called a tallith) was draped over the bride and groom as a sort of tent, the ancestor of the modern huppah (canopy). A rabbi chanted prayers and blessings while the bride received a ring on her right hand. At the end of the ceremony, the bride and groom each took a ceremonial drink from a cup of wine. Sometime in the Middle Ages, the custom began of breaking the cup from which the wine was drunk. A week's worth of feasting and celebration then occurred, depending on the resources available to the families.

As in Christian law, Jewish law prohibited sex outside of marriage, but sexual intercourse within marriage was not shaped by the ambivalence that characterized Christian thought. Jewish law generally recognized that marital sex should be fulfilling and satisfying for both parties and that mutual affection should be required. A woman might, in some communities, declare that she found her husband repugnant and ask for a divorce. Divorce was also possible in cases of infidelity, though some rabbis insisted that a woman could not be divorced without her consent. Although not all relationships were successful, Jewish law did provide a woman with security through her ketubah for many marital problems. Abuse was not tolerated and could be grounds for divorce; forcing a woman to move houses without her consent was also prohibited. On the whole, Jewish women were provided with more recourses in the case of an unhappy marriage than their Christian counterparts (Roth 2005, 43–54). Unfortunately, the sources do not survive to give us comparable information about Muslim women at the same time.

RAPE AND SEXUAL VIOLENCE

Writing the history of rape and sexual violence is difficult, because our modern ideas about rape and about the ownership of the body are very different from the ideas of the past. Particularly complex is the use of the word *raptus*, which has come into English as the word *rape*, but which could also mean *abduction* in historical texts. Both Romans and Germanic peoples in the early Middle Ages recognized marriage by abduction, which the Romans called *raptus* and Germans called *Raubehe* (Brundage 1987, 129). Both involved the kidnapping of a woman and (presumably) her sexual assault, which was considered to function as the consummation of the marriage.

In some situations, the penalties for abduction and rape were severe but largely financial. The Burgundian Code, written in the fifth century, assessed the penalty for abduction as a fine of nine times the woman's normal **wergild** to her family and a fine of twelve ***shillings*** to the king, an amount so high that it would seem impossible for anyone to pay it. If, however, her kidnapper did not rape her and she was returned unharmed, the wergild was only multiplied by six. If the man could not pay the sums of money involved, the law handed him over to the girl's parents "that they may have the power of doing to him whatever they choose" (Drew 1972, 31). Although these laws were clearly written to discourage rape, they also recognized the possibility that women might choose to marry without their families' permission. If a woman chose to have sex with a man willingly, he only owed three times her **wergild** to the person who held her *Munt* (Drew 1972, 31). A woman who married by elopement in this way did not transfer her *Munt* to her husband but kept it within her own family (Brundage 1987, 129). Similarly, in Frankish culture, the sixth-century Salic law provided the same penalty for "stealing" a wife as for killing a man, which was 200 *solidi* (Wemple 1981, 34). Large as these amounts may seem, it is worth remembering that the monetary compensation was not paid to the woman herself but to her family and was adjusted to reflect her overall worth in the society according to her age, fertility, and sexual status.

It is often difficult to tell when, how, and for what reason different punishments were promulgated, how often they were used, and whether the laws that were written about rape and abduction actually reflected how medieval people responded when confronted with a case of rape. Aelfred's laws, an Anglo-Saxon compilation from the ninth century, gave these instructions: five shillings' compensation was due to a lower-class woman for a touch on her breast, while a rape demanded a compensation of sixty shillings. The law went on to say, "If another man has lain with her before, the compensation is then to be half that"—that is, 30 shillings (Saunders 2001, 40). It is important to notice the role that social class played in the laws: the woman was to be compensated according to her status in society. It is also clear that the woman who was raped was expected to be a virgin. If she was not, the compensation dropped by half. Much of the burden of proof, therefore, lay on the victim. In the late-twelfth-century English law code called *Glanvill*, the law gave very strict instructions for a rape victim: "A woman who suffers in this way must go, soon after the deed is done, to the nearest vill and there show to trustworthy men the injury done to her, and any effusion of blood there may be and any tearing of her clothes" (Saunders 2001, 53). The injuries of the victim, the emphasis on her chastity, and her social level were all frequently used to evaluate the victim's claims of having been raped.

Rape figures prominently in popular stories about the Middle Ages. Many movies and books include a custom called jus primae noctis, or the right of the first night, in which a medieval lord had the right to have sex with the bride of one of his men before her husband did. Scholarship has firmly proven that this right did not exist. Writers refer to it to show that the people of the Middle Ages were barbaric and cruel in comparison with the customs of their own time and place. Fiction writers have persistently used the right of the first night for dramatic plots. It should be noted, however, that although there was no law allowing a lord to have sex with his vassal's new wife, we know that such rapes certainly could and did occur. Gregory of Tours (538–594), a historian and bishop, recorded an interesting example in his *History of the Franks*. A nobleman named Amalo lusted after a young freeborn girl. He ordered his men to bring her to him, and he beat her before attempting to rape her. The girl got free long enough to draw Amalo's sword and kill him. She then escaped and made a difficult thirty-five-mile journey to Chalons-sur-Saône to beg the king for mercy. Impressed, the king not only granted her forgiveness but ordered Amalo's family not to seek revenge against her. Gregory wrote that he was happy to learn that "with God to guard her she did not lose her virginity at the hands of her brutal ravisher" (Thorpe 1974, 514). Gregory's point of view was that the young girl's escape was a miracle; that, in itself, may suggest to us that such rapes took place in sixth-century France.

Some high medieval laws prescribed very harsh punishments for rape, even making it a capital crime. The twelfth-century laws of Henry I of England (1068–1135) listed rape under the heading of crimes that were so bad that compensation could not be paid for them, which eventually came to be called felonies. The chronicler William of Malmesbury (ca. 1095–1143) remarked approvingly that "[Henry I] followed his father's example . . . ordaining that convicted offenders should lose their eyes and testicles" (Saunders 2001, 50). Some laws imposed blinding, castration, flogging, or the death penalty on rapists. Even so, we have few examples of these punishments being put into practice. The woman's family connections negotiated any punishment or settlement, if any, that happened afterward. The most common punishments were flogging and fines. In some places, women could be married to their rapists as part of the settlement (Scarborough 2012).

Bringing a charge of rape could also be dangerous. It was not considered possible, because of the **marriage debt,** for a woman to be raped by her husband, as she was expected to provide sex on demand. Furthermore, women who were raped were sometimes judged even more harshly than their attackers. In 1391 France, Bertin Quenet raped Alicia, widow of Jean Hoquet, after breaking into her house. When they appeared before the local court at Cerisy, Bertin was fined only five sous, but Alicia was fined fifteen sous for having sex out of wedlock. Conversely, records from the seignorial court at Saint-Martin-des-Champs in Paris told the story of how, in 1337, a tailor named Jean Agnes raped two twelve-year-old girls and was dragged through the streets before being hanged (Gravdal 1991, 127, 129).

The chronicler Jean Froissart (ca. 1333–1400) told the story of a knight's wife who was raped by another knight while her husband was away. Her husband and family pursued the case to the highest court in France, which ruled that, because the two parties had no evidence to prove guilt or innocence, the matter could only be decided by an **ordeal** by combat, or a duel. The lady's husband dueled the accused man while the lady waited, dressed in black. Froissart wrote, "You will understand that she was in great anxiety . . . for if her husband got the worst of it, the sentence was that he should be hanged and she burnt without appeal." The lady's husband won the battle. It is easy to see, however, why even noble women might have decided not to pursue rape charges, if death by burning was a possibility. Froissart wrote pensively, "I do not know . . . whether she had not often regretted having gone so far with the matter that she and her husband were in such grave danger" (Brereton 1978, 314).

The differences between these cases illustrate the challenges of understanding medieval rape: were the cases different because of their locations, the social classes of those involved, different laws, or something less tangible? Custom and local practice are probably at least part of the answer to these questions. Rape was situational: a woman's marital status, virginity, religious vows, or property ownership shaped whether she could bring a charge of rape. Altogether, rape cases tried in courts show "a long-standing tradition of indifference to male violation of a woman's sexuality and legal personality" (Gravdal 1991, 131). When a woman was married, however, her status as the dependent of her husband challenged this indifference. We will discuss adultery and its relationship to rape more closely in chapter six.

DOMESTIC ABUSE

Many modern people are familiar with a practice known as the **rule of thumb**—the belief that sometime in the past, husbands were allowed to beat their wives with a stick, as long as the stick was no thicker than the husband's thumb. This, however, appears to have been a myth that was popularized in the eighteenth or early nineteenth century. There are no medieval records that reflect such a practice (Kelly 1994). Still, medieval society generally accepted that some level of physical abuse between husband and wife would take place. Violence supported the hierarchy of men over women and was, at times, overtly encouraged in literature. Medieval women were taught that their husbands were masters over their everyday concerns and activities and that obedience was always required (more discussion of obedience is in chapter four).

Geoffrey Chaucer's (ca. 1340–1400) famous "Wife of Bath's Tale," part of his larger work the *Canterbury Tales*, featured an introduction in which the character of the Wife of Bath described her own experiences during her five marriages. She recounted a physical fight in which her fifth husband rendered her deaf in one ear with a blow. There was a later fight during which she was struck to the ground. The whole episode, however, was played for laughs. The message was that the wife deserved to be beaten and that her husband—whom she manipulated into apologizing to her—had not been keeping her under control as he should. The Wife even added that she loved her fifth husband more than any of the others because she dominated him, a statement that would have made Chaucer's audience laugh with appreciation for its absurdity (Weisl 1998).

In court records from late medieval Europe, when the record keeping is better than in earlier periods, there are sometimes visible cases of domestic violence. Altogether, such cases show that women were only able to call on courts for help after particularly violent or bloody incidents in which the husband was the aggressor. Otherwise, medieval laws recognized the husband's right to beat his wife. The *Glossa Ordinaria* of the early thirteenth century cautioned the husband that he was allowed to beat his wife "only insofar as the law allowed," however far that might be. Otherwise, he might be fined up to one-third of his marital property. An upper-class woman might also bring a case of marital cruelty to a church court in an effort to seek a legal separation, or *divortium*. A separated couple was not required to live together, but they could not marry again (Brundage 2000, 187).

Husbands were frequently the defendants when women were murdered, although no study is possible on overall rates across Europe. In cases of female homicide, gleaned from late medieval Bolognese courts, a "small but significant" number of wife murders was a constant across the fourteenth century (Dean 2004, 529). When women harmed their husbands, medieval courts were harsh. In 1352, an English law covering treason defined women's murder of their husbands as a form of treason, similar to a subject attempting to kill a king or a servant their master. The punishment for these crimes was execution: men were hanged, drawn, and quartered, while women were burned at the stake (Hanawalt 2000, 197).

Women accused of murdering their husbands were often charged with using poison, magic, or both (we will discuss magic more in chapter seven). In 1394 Provence, a woman named Margarida de Portu was accused of having poisoned her husband, Johan Damponcii. He died after eating a stew she had prepared for their lunch. He complained of not feeling well while working in the field and returned home, only to crawl into his bed and die. His brother, a local notary, insisted that Margarida, who was very young and suffered from epilepsy, had either poisoned his brother or killed him with sorcery. Epilepsy was regarded as a suspicious, partially supernatural disease. Margarida's family and friends countered by calling witnesses to attest that the entire family had eaten the stew together. Her brother-in-law tried repeatedly to have her questioned under torture, but, fortunately, the court would not agree. Eventually Margarida was acquitted of murder, and she countered with a suit for defamation, for which we do not know the verdict (Bednarski 2014). This case is unusually well documented, but it follows the pattern of other, less well documented cases in which the support of the family and their connections enabled the accused person to win acquittal.

Accusations of physical violence by women against men also occurred. In a case from Bologna in July 1398, a woman named Ursolina was charged with beating her husband, Carlo, to death. Since there were no witnesses, the court called neighbors to prove that Ursolina was likely to commit such a crime because of her violent personality. The neighbors summoned to testify in the case, six women and two men, asserted that the couple had a volatile relationship in which Ursolina often shouted at and beat her husband. The two male witnesses testified that Carlo had told them both that his wife hated him and wanted to kill him. Witnesses summoned by the defense, however, stated that Carlo had really died of a fever and had no bruises or marks on his body when he was laid out to be buried. Furthermore, it was "not the custom of wives to hit their husbands" (Dean 2004, 537). This line of reasoning led to Ursolina's acquittal.

CONCLUSION

Most of the relationships that shaped the lives of medieval women were based in the family: women were mothers, daughters, aunts, and especially wives. Marriage was not only a place where companionship and reproduction were shared, but ideas about marriage regulated sexuality, property ownership, social status, and law. In the next chapter, we will explore how reproduction and child-rearing also shaped women's everyday lives.

2

CHILDBIRTH, CHILD REARING, AND THE LIFE CYCLE

Reproduction is always central to discussions about historical women, and that was also true in the Middle Ages. This chapter discusses several aspects of medieval thought: the scientific view of women's bodies and fertility, the care of the pregnant, and living through life's different stages, all of which affected the daily lives of medieval women.

UNDERSTANDING THE FEMALE BODY

Scholars in the Middle Ages wanted to understand the female body and the reasons why a woman could or could not have children. Four liquid substances, called **humors**, were believed to make up the human body in the same way as the four elements (earth, water, air, and fire) made up the physical world. These humors were blood, black bile, yellow bile, and phlegm. Each humor was associated with qualities: wet or dry, and cold or warm. The processes of the body, from respiration to digestion, were believed to be affected by the balance of the four humors. If the humors were out of balance, a person became ill: for example, a high fever and flushed forehead could mean an imbalance of blood, the hottest and wettest of the humors. Treatment for such illnesses included baths, carefully chosen food, and sometimes an intervention such as bleeding a small amount of blood from a vein.

Humorally, men and women were believed to be polar opposites. Men were most healthy when they were hot and dry, and women were most healthy when they were cold and moist. This contrast was necessary for procreation. A man had to be sufficiently hot and dry to produce semen, and a woman had to be cold and moist enough to produce menstrual blood. Women's bodies were believed to be so moist that the flesh was spongy and wet, which made production of menstrual blood possible (Dean-Jones 1994, 55–58). Monthly purges of menstrual blood were necessary to rid the body of impurities. Lack of menstruation in a young woman, therefore, demanded a medical intervention, usually via changes to her diet or treatment with herbal remedies.

We know nothing about how medieval women dealt with their periods, though we know they understood that fertility depended on regular menstruation. We can guess that they probably used cloth of some kind to catch the flow; perhaps each individual woman had a set of rags that she kept for that purpose. Since we know that healers used herbal tampons called **pessaries** for medical purposes, it is also possible that they used some sort of tampon for menstruation. Medical works contain many remedies that were used to bring on a period if it were delayed. Some of these remedies were **abortifacients** that might have been used as a sort of contraceptive. Other than that, the sources are silent. This is an area in which we cannot hear the voices of everyday women speaking to each other. (We will discuss contraception further below.)

Menstrual blood itself was thought to be extremely unclean, an inheritance both from Jewish law and from ancient attitudes about menstruation. Pope Innocent III (1160–1216), in a work called *On the Misery of the Human Condition*, wrote, "This blood is said to be so abominable and foul that contact with it causes seeds not to germinate and vineyards to dry up, grass to die, trees to drop their fruit, and if dogs eat it they become rabid." These views were inherited from a Roman author, Pliny (Skinner and van Houts 2011, 95). Some authors believed that having sex with a woman who was menstruating caused **leprosy** or led to children with birth defects. Despite such beliefs, women were not forbidden to attend church while menstruating, although they were not allowed to attend after childbirth until a prescribed amount of time had passed.

Scientific writers continued to be curious about female anatomy. Galen (d. ca. 216 CE), whose writings on anatomy became very influential in the high Middle Ages, conceptualized the sex organs of men and women as mirror images of each other: the shape of the vagina and the penis, and the ovaries and the testicles, provided him with a justification for seeing the female system as an inversion of the male. Yet there was no place in this conceptualization for the clitoris, which was almost entirely misunderstood by medieval thinkers. Some theorized that the clitoris functioned to keep the vagina closed, or that it protected the vagina from the touch of the air. One exception was Pietro d'Abano (ca. 1257–1316 CE), who noted that women became sexually aroused when the clitoris was rubbed: "For the pleasure that can be obtained from this part of the body is comparable to that obtained from the tip of the penis" (Jacquart and Thomasset 1988, 46).

Perhaps as a result of lack of knowledge about the clitoris and perhaps because of the preoccupation with fertility, the womb or uterus became the focal point for the medieval intellectual understanding of female sexuality, and by extension, beliefs about fertility and infertility. The womb was believed to be like a living creature that, lacking the moisture necessary for pregnancy, could move around the body and cause various ailments such as shortness of breath and choking, sometimes termed "suffocation of the womb" or "wandering womb." Sexual intercourse was one of the treatments for this problem, because it was believed to move the uterus back down where it belonged and to restore its moisture via a man's semen. The condition could also be treated with an application of sweet smoke to the woman's vagina and foul-smelling smoke to her nose in order to attract the womb back into its place. Her flesh was so spongy that it could be affected by odor remedies, according to medical writers (Thomasset 1992, 48).

The medieval system of understanding the body fit perfectly with the understanding posed by Christian writers. Not only were women believed to be less moral than men, their very physical bodies were less perfect (because they were less hot and dry), and their bodies were intended entirely for procreation; otherwise, why would the womb be so greedy and troublesome? The female body, which required sexual intercourse regardless of situational morality and produced unclean substances like menstrual blood, was an object of great uneasiness to Christian thinkers. As a result, medieval women who were exposed to these points of view understood their own bodies and biological natures as dangerously sinful.

PREGNANCY

We often imagine that medieval women gave birth to many children in quick succession, but that may not have been the case. Nutrition was often poor. A successful pregnancy requires a woman to have specific nutrients in order to carry a child to term. Since the diets of medieval women varied greatly with social standing, lower-class women may have had trouble conceiving and giving birth. A diet consisting primarily of grains may not have provided women the amount of folic acid that allowed for the development of the neural tube in a fetus, and children born with a neural tube defect such as spina bifida would not have survived. Many people in the Middle Ages also suffered from anemia, the lack of iron, which causes problems with the blood and bones. Very poor women may also not have had sufficient sources of calcium to strengthen their own bones and to build the bones of their infants. Osteoporosis, which is caused by the lack of calcium, has been identified in some early medieval Frankish women who were as young as thirty (Garver 2012, 228–229). (For the bone markers of poor nutrition, see the introduction.)

Medieval writers understood that good food was necessary for conception and pregnancy, and writers of medical literature were quite specific in their dietary advice for women who wanted to conceive. Medieval thinkers imagined that conception occurred when a man's semen acted upon the menstrual blood in the woman's uterus. Some writers even used the analogy that the menstrual blood functioned as wood and the semen the tools that were used to work it. There was debate, based on the works of Aristotle and Galen, about whether the woman emitted "seed" during orgasm or whether her only contribution to conception was to provide the menstrual blood that the man's semen then turned into a fetus. Aristotle had argued that the female parent could contribute only one material, the menstrual blood, to conception. Galen, however, argued that women did emit seed at orgasm (Jacquart and Thomasset 1988, 61–62). This discussion influenced the question of whether female orgasm was necessary for conception and, if so, what role the female seed played in the development of the embryo. William of Conches (ca. 1080–1154), writer of an influential encyclopedia, claimed that the female seed was necessary for conception. Unfortunately, however, he also argued that women who conceived from rape must have experienced pleasure from the violation to become pregnant. (Read more about sexual violence in chapter one.) Other writers did not go that far but suggested that the female sperm was weaker and might not be involved in the formation of the fetus at all, but perhaps formed the amniotic sac or chorion (Thomasset 1992, 56–57).

Medieval thinkers also had a humoral explanation for the formation of infants of either sex. The influential medical text called the *Pantegni* was a translation of the Arab writer Ali ibn al-Abbas al-Majusi (d. ca. 994) by the great eleventh-century translator Constantine the African (ca. 1020–1087). The *Pantegni* described the womb this way: "The womb is like the bladder in shape, for both of them are very deep, but it is different in its two extensions which are similar to horns" (Jacquart and Thomasset 1988, 23). The development of male and female fetuses was thought to depend on the relative heat of the sides of the womb and what side of the uterus the child was conceived within. The right side of the uterus, which was closer to the liver, was thought to be warmer than the left side and, therefore, the site of the conception of a male, while a female embryo, which was cooler and moister than her brother, would rest on the left side of the uterus.

The calculation got more complex when the dissection of pigs revealed that sows have a bicornate (two-horned) uterus, which was assumed to also be true for human women, since human dissection was not allowed until the very late Middle Ages. Medieval thinkers eventually adapted sow's anatomy to mean that the human uterus had seven chambers. In this conception, the three cells on the right side of the womb would produce boys, the three on the left produce girls, and hermaphrodites would be conceived in the middle chamber (Thomasset 1992, 59). Hildegard of Bingen (1098–1179 CE), a German mystic and scientific writer, took the idea of the action of warmth and strength on the embryo even further by attaching the love felt by the child's parents to the later moral development of their child. She wrote that two parents in love produced virtuous, happy children; if either of them lacked love for the other, they produced bitter offspring (Cadden 1984, 155).

Understandably, infertility caused medieval couples a great deal of concern. Women had a broad tradition of charms, prayers, and objects to turn to when they had trouble conceiving. A ritual written in the margin of a text by a medieval physician named Gilbertus Anglicus (ca. 1180–1250 CE) gives the following instructions: A man of twenty years old or more should gather comfrey and daisy roots, make a juice with them, and write a prayer using the juice on a piece of parchment. That parchment was to be worn around the neck of the man, if a boy baby was desired, or the woman, if a girl was desired, during sexual intercourse. The manuscript called this charm "A remedy that never fails" (Jones and Olsan 2015, 412–413). Women sometimes carried amulets and other objects that were intended to enhance fertility. One popular item, handed down from mother to daughter, was a string of coral beads that were thought to "make fruit multiply." Amulets dedicated to Saint Margaret, the patron saint of childbirth, or to the Agnus Dei, the Lamb of God, were also common gifts (French 2016, 129). Once a pregnancy was achieved, just as people do today, medieval people wanted to guess the sex of the fetus before he or she was born. An Anglo-Saxon text advised, "Observe how the woman walks. If she touches the ground more with her heels she will bear a boy; if she touches the ground only with her toes she will bring forth a girl" (Larrington 1995, 92).

Pregnancy could be very stressful for medieval women because of their natural fears that something could go wrong (Gilchrist 2012, 219). Charms and prayers have survived, which indicate a concern with the success of pregnancy. An Anglo-Saxon charm against miscarriage advises the pregnant woman this way: "The woman who cannot bring her child to maturity must go to the grave of a dead man, step three times over the grave and say these words three times: 'This as my help against the evil late birth; this as my help against the grievous dismal birth; this as my help against the evil lame birth'" (Larrington 1995, 91). Frequently, such charms were accompanied by prayers. Such semimagical practices may have helped to reassure women who were worried about the outcome of their pregnancies.

Saints were sometimes credited with a longed-for pregnancy after couples made vows. As we will discuss further in chapter six, medieval people saw visiting the **relics** of saints—objects including personal belongings or even bones or hair—as ways of accessing the powers of the saint to help with life problems. Families might take a vow to go on pilgrimage to particular shrines or to give particular gifts to the saints. In the early fourteenth century, an Italian couple whose names were Guido and Margarita testified before a church inquiry into the sainthood of Louis of Toulouse that they had been childless for twelve years of marriage. They vowed to take the saint a waxen image the same length and weight as any child they might bear. Margarita then became pregnant with a son who was about eight years old when the papal board of inquiry wrote down evidence of the miracle (Finucane 1997, 19).

Women who conceived often visited saints' shrines to ask for safe childbirth and good health for mother and child. Specific **relics** had reputations for being good for mothers and children. The cathedrals of Chartres and Aachen claimed to have pieces of the Virgin Mary's robe, the *Sancta Camisia,* which attracted many pilgrims. The churches of Rocamadour, in southern France, and Walsingham, in northern England, both had statues of the Virgin Mary that were reputed to be miraculous. People who visited the shrines to these **relics** could purchase small pilgrim's badges, which were usually made of an alloy of lead and tin, and pictures and candles. Such objects were touched to the shrine to connect them with the holiness of the saints' relics (Gilchrist 2012, 135). Devotees also left their own objects, which are known as votives, at saints' shrines as thanks for favors or for healing; wax votives of body parts were common, as were gifts or money or other symbolic objects.

CHILDBIRTH

Once labor began, there were many charms and rituals designed to help with the pains and fears of childbirth, some of them for women to use and some to be done by a priest. One particularly long-lived charm consisted of a list of mothers from the Bible followed by an exorcising prayer and a command to the infant to come out, like Lazarus from the tomb (John 11:43). This particular charm was to be written on wax and applied to the woman's right foot during labor (Jones and Olsan 2015, 415–416). Charms like this one were sometimes written on parchment or wax and applied to the body. One interesting example from the fourteenth century had a series of prayers to be written on three communion wafers, which the woman was then to eat to aid in birth (Jones and Olsan 2015, 423). Holy **relics**, too, could be used in childbirth to help the laboring mother. Westminster Abbey in London claimed to hold the girdle or belt of the Virgin Mary, and Elizabeth, the daughter of Edward I and the countess of Hereford and Essex, made a special pilgrimage to Westminster in 1303 in order to borrow the girdle for her upcoming delivery. The girdle may have been tied around her waist as she labored to help her give birth (French 2016, 133). Another birthing girdle, made of parchment 180 centimeters long (approximately 5′ 11″) to simulate the height

This medieval birth scene shows a woman in bed while female birth attendants wash the new baby. (The Metropolitan Museum of Art)

of Jesus, still survives in the collection of the Wellcome Library in London (Leyser 1995, 129).

Miracle stories from the records of various saints' shrines give examples of how frantic family members might react to complications of childbirth, especially stillbirth. Newborns who did not breathe immediately after birth were sometimes thought to be dead, provoking prayers and vows from the women present and from the men in the family. Often, the newborn was taken to the nearest shrine in hopes that the saint would resuscitate the infant. A coin might be bent over the body of the child and the coin vowed to a particular saint, or the child might be "measured" with a piece of string that was later incorporated into wax as an offering (Finucane 1997, 11).

The birth experiences of medieval women were different from our own, since all births took place at home rather than in a hospital. It was common for birth attendants to try to keep the woman upright while she delivered her baby, encouraging her to walk around as labor progressed and then, when birth was imminent, placing her on a birthing stool. There are surviving examples of these stools from the late Middle Ages and early modern period, but evidence for them dates as far back as the ancient world. They often had three legs and were structured to provide the woman support as she delivered. The design of birthing stools and chairs remained fairly consistent across the centuries. Their greatest benefit was to allow the laboring woman to sit as upright as possible, using natural gravity to help her give birth (Banks 1999, 3–15).

There is no way to know how often medieval women gave birth successfully and how often they died in childbirth, because record keeping was scant in most areas until well after the end of the medieval period. Certainly, the number was higher than in the present day, and probably higher than it was one hundred to two hundred years ago, even before the advent of antibiotic drugs and the surgical delivery of babies. Because most people married and because the rate of contraception use was probably very low, most women from their first marriages to the end of their period of fertility were at risk of dying in childbirth. A study of Swedish parish registers in the eighteenth century put the maternal mortality rate at eleven per thousand births around 1760; this is significantly higher than the most recent statistics for the United States, in which the maternal mortality rate in 2015 was fourteen per hundred thousand births (Schofield 1986, 237). Although the eighteenth-century statistics cannot be directly connected to the Middle Ages, the contrast between the eighteenth century and today suggests how different women of the past's expectations for maternal mortality might be.

Similarly, even after a successful birth, medieval children were still at risk. Infant and child mortality were high throughout the Middle Ages, perhaps as high as 20 to 30 percent among children under seven. The trauma of birth and childhood diseases combined to make early childhood very dangerous indeed. Cemetery examples sometimes reflect this reality: in Frösön, Sweden, a cemetery used between 1050 and 1350 yielded a sample in which half of all skeletons were children under seven (Youngs 2006, 24, 26). The deaths of small children left unsupervised often feature in the coroner's rolls of medieval England, the children dying by "misadventure" when their parents were not home: falling into fire, drowning, or being attacked by domestic animals.

The **Black Death**, the epidemic of the **bubonic plague** that began in the mid-fourteenth century, was particularly hard on children. Children made up 88 percent of all the deaths from plague at the Dominican cemetery in Siena, Italy, in 1383. Without effective medical interventions, children's deaths struck both rich and poor families. At one time, medieval historians wondered whether ancient and medieval parents had the same kind of love for their children that modern parents do today. They argued that frequent infant and child death might have made medieval parents less attached to their children at birth because they died so often. But we cannot imagine the levels of sorrow that must have attended mothers and fathers who lost several children, whether one at a time or all at once. Our evidence for the period indicates that medieval parents loved their children with the same fervor as our more fortunate society today (Crawford 1999, 2–4). The fourteenth-century Welsh poet Llywelyn Fychan mourned his children who were killed by the plague in a poem called *The Pestilence*. "I was left, feeling betrayed and stunned, barely alive in a harsh world" (Johnston 1993, 50–53).

BIRTH ATTENDANTS AND MIDWIVES

Although they are sometimes difficult to find in medieval sources, we must assume that midwives (the word means "with women") provided the bulk of the birth assistance throughout the Middle Ages. Historians of childbirth have argued that birth, in most instances, was female business and that men waited for news of the birth at a distance (Harris-Stoertz 2012, 263). But we know surprisingly little about normal childbirth from medical texts; most of the medical literature of the period addressed problems in childbirth but not the course of a normal birth. An author named Trota, possibly a midwife, who lived in the twelfth century in or near Salerno, Italy, wrote a work called *On Treatments for Women*. This work was the second section of a compound work that became known as the *Trotula*, three short works on women's health compiled in the twelfth century. Despite the title, there is very little in *On Treatments for Women* about normal childbirth, though the work contains detailed prescriptions for such complications as blood loss during birth and uterine prolapse (Green 2001, 124–125). (Read more about Trota in chapter eight.)

Equally sparse is our information about who attended normal births. Early literature on childbirth from the Roman period was written expressly for professional midwives. Soranus, a second-century Greek physician who wrote a work called the *Gynecology*, explicitly directed his advice to them in the expectation that midwives would be present at most births. The documents then fell silent for several centuries as ancient authors were copied and recopied, and documents about the profession of midwifery disappeared. Since most of what women knew about and did during childbirth is lost to us because women taught one another verbally, we must rely on sources written almost entirely by men. From the thirteenth century onward, male physicians increasingly considered fertility and childbirth to be within their purview, and often criticized or disparaged midwives as ineffective and ignorant (Green 2013, 347). The men who studied childbirth in this period sought to understand the "secrets of women"—meaning the vagina and uterus. Such "secrets" were not written down for women to learn about their own bodies, but so that men in their families could ensure their fertility.

What women who attended births did or did not know about the female body is unavailable to us from the sources, so we are forced to look at the few examples that remain to construct some ideas about how and when they worked. Bartholomeus Anglicus, an encyclopedist writing in the thirteenth century, detailed the midwife's activity this way: she rubbed balm on the mother in labor, tied the infant's navel cord, washed the child, and wrapped him in cloths. She was "a woman that hath craft to help a woman that travaileth [labors] of child, that she bear and bring forth her child with the less woe and sorrow" (Orme 2001, 17).

The church gave midwives an important concession in the thirteenth century: if a midwife felt a child was in imminent danger of death, she could baptize the child to ensure that he or she would go to heaven if it did not survive. Beginning at this time, church officials preached the doctrine that the souls of unbaptized babies could not go to heaven but went to a corner of hell called limbo, where they did not suffer punishment but were unable to gain the bliss of heaven (Lynch 1992, 278). A fifteenth-century writer cautioned that the midwife should make sure the child was baptized, "for she bears more responsibility than all the other women" who attended the birth for ensuring the child went to heaven (Green 2013, 352).

Concern about keeping babies from going to hell or limbo provoked a number of practices in the later Middle Ages. These included what we now call cesarean section, which was called a *sectio in mortua* (Latin for "a cutting of a dead woman"). If a mother died during birth and the attendants believed the child might still be alive, the mother's body would be cut open to extract the child for the purpose of baptism if nothing else. The first surgical author to describe a cesarean section was Bernard de Gordon (ca. 1270–1330 CE). Unfortunately, we have no evidence as to whether the practice was widespread and little evidence as to who performed the procedure: there are only twelve examples of the procedure in medieval documents, and we do not know if they were successful. One is an Italian case from 1473 in which a notary recorded the removal of a child from Caterino, the deceased wife of Nicoulau Fabri. When he learned that his wife was dead, Fabri petitioned the local bailiff for permission to perform the operation. The bailiff consented, but we do not know whether Caterino's baby survived (Bednarski and Courtemanche 2011). Although it was probable that there were midwives present at the birth, the document that preserves the story does not mention them. It is possible that the midwives at Caterino's birth provided care before and during the birth but that they did not participate in the *sectio in mortua*.

Stories of complex births from saints' miracles reveal midwives worked in shifts to help suffering mothers who were undergoing complications. In a particularly sad example from the late thirteenth century, a woman named Dulceta, who was seventeen years old, could not deliver her child after four days of labor. A series of midwives tried to help, but none was effective until a woman named Guillelma helped her deliver the partially decomposed fetus. Dulceta was badly hurt by the birth and suffered tremendously for two years from what she thought was a bone lodged in her vagina. A surgeon was called in, but before the procedure, Dulceta made a vow to St. Louis of Marseilles, who caused the object to fall from her body painlessly the next day. Dulceta begged for enough money from parishioners at the church to offer a wax candle to St. Louis and swept out the church as often as she could to show her appreciation to the saint (Finucane 1997, 31–32). In this story, the writer emphasized that a group of midwives and even a surgeon could not measure up to the standard of a saint when it came to healing.

Midwives suffered in the later Middle Ages not only from criticism but also from outright accusations of wrongdoing. The *Malleus Maleficarum*, or "Hammer of Witches," a work written in 1486–1487 by two Dominican inquisitors, Heinrich Kramer and Jacob Sprenger, accused midwives of sorcery and committing the souls of the infants in their care to hell. This work is infamous for its misogynistic rhetoric, but midwives received particular vitriol from the two authors, perhaps because of their permission to baptize babies. Instead of baptizing babies, Kramer and Sprenger argued, midwives frequently cursed them. "Even when they [midwives] do not kill babies, they offer them to the demons by devoting them with a curse" (Mackay 2009, 369). We will address witchcraft further in chapter six, but this example shows that some views of midwives were marked by uneasiness about their power to affect the spiritual status of newborns.

CONTRACEPTION, ABORTION, AND INFANTICIDE

Augustine of Hippo (354–430 CE), the authoritative Christian writer of the early fifth century, laid down the Catholic Church's strict view of contraception: any sexual activity that was not intended to achieve conception was a sin, regardless of whether the couple was married (Brundage 1987, 89). Writers of the twelfth and thirteenth centuries equated the use of contraceptives to adultery and regarded it as deserving comparable severity. They did not elaborate on the specifics of what they considered to be contraceptive, and it is likely that what they were prohibiting was coitus interruptus, or withdrawing before ejaculation so as to prevent pregnancy (Brundage 1987, 358). Coitus interruptus was a widespread, but often unsuccessful, technique for preventing pregnancy throughout the ancient and medieval periods, and church authors took care to forbid it. The eighth-century *Canons of Theodore* called the practice "uncleanness or a detestable sin, whence we read that Onan, the son of Juda, was struck by God after entering into his wife and spilling his seed on the ground." "Wasting" the semen was a sin that violated God's purpose for sex (Payer 1984, 57).

Despite these prohibitions, knowledge of contraception did exist and was used in medieval Europe. It is not known whether barrier methods of contraception were used, but early medieval Europe certainly inherited knowledge of herbal preparations that could cause abortion, or **abortifacients**. Some of these herbal remedies came from traditional or ancient sources, and some from the Muslim world. In medieval Islamic law, a woman might use contraception or abort a fetus before 120 days' gestation (a limit set by the Prophet Muhammad). In the great era of the translation of Muslim medical works into Latin for use by medical practitioners, sections of works describing contraception and abortion became available to European readers. Particularly important were Abu Bakr Muhammad ibn Zakariyya al-Razi (called Rhazes in Latin, ca.

865–925), and Abu Ali al-Husayn ibn Sina (in Latin, Avicenna, 980–1037), both of whose works were translated into Latin by Gerard of Cremona in the twelfth century. Al-Razi prescribed a contraceptive tampon, which contained the juice of the herb rue and pepper, to be inserted after intercourse. Ibn Sina cited such plants as juniper, cyclamen, and birthwort as causing a spontaneous abortion when brewed into a drink (Riddle 1992, 127, 130–134).

It is difficult to determine when or how often such remedies were used, not only because of a lack of data but also because they often appear in manuscripts as **emmenagogues**—that is, drugs that would bring on the menstrual period, since women who did not menstruate regularly were thought to be in poor health. The herbal drugs were often given orally or administered in a **pessary**, an herbal tampon that was inserted into the vagina. Modern research has established that many of the remedies were not effective, but herbs such as rue and pennyroyal can cause abortion when ingested in high enough doses (though in the case of these herbs, the toxicity can be dangerous to the mother) (Riddle 1992, 53–54).

An Old English recipe from the *Leechbook III*, written in the mid-tenth century, prescribed that a woman whose period was delayed should first drink an herb called brooklime (*Veronica beccabunga*) boiled in ale, and then bathe in a hot bath. When she rose from the bath, she was supposed to use a poultice made of barley meal (*Hordeum vulgare)*, green mugwort (*Artemisia vulgaris*), and wild celery (*Apium graveolens*) on her genitals and also drink some of that mixture. The recipe added that all this should be done at the time when the woman would normally have had her period. The treatment could be repeated, if necessary, if it was not effective the first time (Osborn 2008, 154–157). Brooklime, mugwort. and wild celery all contain chemicals that can provoke menstruation. Between drinking this potion and applying a poultice, a woman who used this remedy might actually have succeeded in starting her period.

There is no way to know how often, or whether, medieval women used such preparations or whether they had other remedies available to them that do not appear in the sources. We do know that they used quasimagical preparations, such as amulets and charms, for contraception, which could not have been effective but are very interesting. The *Trotula*, a collection of texts on women's medicine from the twelfth century, listed a number of such charms, including: "If a woman does not wish to conceive, let her carry against her nude flesh the womb of a goat which has never had offspring." Perhaps mindful of religious rules against contraception, the work went on to explain that a woman might have "been badly torn in birth and afterward from fear of death does not wish to conceive any more" (Green 2001, 96–99). Medieval people understood that nursing could slow down conception, and upper-class mothers often chose not to nurse their children themselves so that they could conceive again more quickly. Church authorities deplored the practice and tried to encourage noble mothers to breastfeed their infants themselves. We will discuss nursing more completely below.

Both secular and sacred law threatened parents with serious punishments if they sought an abortion or killed a child after birth. In Carolingian Europe, the penances demanded of women who had abortions depended on the development of the fetus. Once the fetus had "quickened"—meaning the mother could feel it moving in her uterus—the penalty was much higher, because the church held that after forty days in the womb, the fetus was given a soul (Garver 2012, 230–231). Penances could range from a few years to a lifetime, depending on the religious authority. The penitential writer Theodulf of Orléans (ca. 750–821) would not allow a woman who had killed a child to enter a church for ten years. Similarly, some Spanish authors of the time sentenced a child-killer to lifetime **excommunication** for the double crime of adultery and murder. Paul the Deacon, writing in the eighth century, called a prostitute who drowned her children "more cruel than all wild beasts" (Atkinson 1991, 92–93).

Desperate families who had unwanted children might have turned to infanticide, though the direct evidence for infanticide is sparse. The Romans certainly practiced infanticide, and there is evidence that girl babies were killed more often than boys, but there is little evidence for infanticide of either sex in medieval cemeteries. Infant bones do not survive well archaeologically, so this may be one reason why samples are rare (Crawford et al. 2010, 62). Infants were sometimes buried, however, under the floors or by the walls of houses; it is not clear whether these infant burials were the result of infanticide or stillbirth, or if they were infants who did not survive and whose parents could not bear the expense of a funeral or who had not been baptized before death. Examples occur from the twelfth to the sixteenth centuries (Gilchrist 2012, 220–221). There are also stories in documentary sources. In one story from a saint's life, a notary named Berard recorded how in around 1300, his wife had given birth to a stillborn boy whom they planned to bury in the house, since he was not baptized. Fortunately, the child revived long enough to be baptized and was buried at the church (Finucane

1997, 45). In Ireland, some small unconsecrated spaces, called *cíllíns* or killeens, became places for unbaptized babies to be buried. Since they were not baptized, these children were denied burial in sacred ground. They were often buried in the shadow of ruined ring forts or unused churches. Although the spaces were not consecrated, the burials of infants in them often included grave cloths and small trinkets, indicating that the parents of the infants wanted to bury their children with love (Finlay 2000, 408–409).

What about children who were born with physical or developmental impairments? Children with catastrophic medical conditions were unlikely to survive, but some people with disabilities certainly did survive and grow up. The many miracle stories that tell of healing indicate that people with disabilities were present in medieval society and that they actively sought miraculous interventions. In fact, one study has estimated that over 90 percent of the miracles recorded between 1201 and 1300 were miracles of healing. Parents often carried or transported their disabled children to saints' shrines, hoping for divine intervention. Blindness, deafness, and muteness frequently appear in these stories, accompanied by physical difficulties such as paralysis or wasting. These stories provide evidence not only that people with disabilities lived, but that they were valued and cared for.

Medical writers cautioned mothers that a range of factors might cause them to give birth to children who were physically or mentally impaired. Children conceived from sex during menstruation or lactation were widely believed to be deformed or even afflicted with **leprosy**. Creative sexual positions, labeled "unnatural," could also harm children. Medieval mothers were cautioned not to think about ugly things during sex because they might imprint such deformities onto the children they conceived; some writers went so far as to encourage women to look at portraits of beautiful people during sex. Pregnant women were cautioned about what and when to eat. The blame for a child born with a disability was most often placed on the mother, with the assumption that something she had done had caused the problem (Metzler 2006, 85–89).

ILLEGITIMACY AND ABANDONMENT

Although the necessity of having married parents was less emphasized in the early Middle Ages than it was later on, by the twelfth century, the church defined a legitimate birth as one that occurred only to married parents. Those born out of wedlock were not allowed to inherit property or claim other inheritances from their parents and were not allowed to become priests without special permission from church authorities. The rate of illegitimate births was very low, but medieval people strictly distinguished between legitimate and illegitimate births. They invented such words as "bastard," "horcop" ("whore's head"), and "leir-child" ("child of the leir or lying") to refer to the illegitimate (Orme 2001, 56–57).

As the Middle Ages passed, children born out of wedlock had fewer and fewer claims on their parents' property. On occasion, the church legitimated children born out of wedlock if their parents later were married. One well-known example is of John of Gaunt (1340–1399 CE), duke of Lancaster, and his third wife Katherine Swynford (ca. 1350–1403 CE), whose four children, born while he was married to other women, were declared legitimate after the couple married in 1396. However, most illegitimate children were not children of the aristocracy and could not access such consideration.

Some parents of unwanted children simply abandoned them, frequently into the care of the church, by the late Middle Ages. The practice of abandonment, for many, was preferable to killing a child by placing it outside or "exposing" it, which had been a recognized option in ancient Rome. In 1274, a church council at Bordeaux stated that women who abandoned their children were "wicked" but also added, "They should be told that if, God forbid, they are going to do this, they should use salt as a sign that the child has already been baptized" (Boswell 1990, 324). Later, church councils recommended that a priest who found an abandoned child at a church should check to see if salt had been left with him or her. In the late Middle Ages, rising rates of child abandonment, perhaps linked to economic pressures, led to the founding of orphanages or foundling homes, the first of which was the Ospedale degli Innocenti in Florence, founded in 1445. The rate of death for infants placed in such homes was astronomically high. There were more infants in need than could possibly be served and not enough **wet nurses** to supply milk (Sperling 2013, 11).

Selling children into servitude or slavery was also an option in some areas for parents who were desperate. The laws of Castile called *Las Siete Partidas*, promulgated for King Alfonso the Wise (1221–1284 CE), recognized such terrible possibilities: "A father who is oppressed with great hunger or such utter poverty that he has no other recourse can sell or pawn his children in order to obtain food" (Boswell 1990, 328). Such laws reflect the many ways in which poor people in medieval Europe skirted the boundary between being free and being enslaved.

THE AGES OF MAN

We turn now to the stages of medieval life and the different experiences of women during such stages. Writers in the Middle Ages recognized that human lives had different, developing phases, but they conceptualized the phases for men and women differently. Isidore of Seville (ca. 560–636 CE) a bishop and prolific writer of the early seventh century, laid out what he understood to be the phases of a man's life cycle, divided into terms of seven years. It began with infancy up to seven years old and continued with *pueritia*, childhood, which lasted until fourteen years. Adolescent males, up to the twenty-eighth year, were ready to become fathers. A man then entered the time of youth, which lasted until the fiftieth year. The mature period lasted until the age of seventy, at which point the man entered the age of senescence, or old age, ending with *senium*, the period right before death (Sears 2019, 61).

Descriptions of women's ages were more general. A Middle English text described the ages of women as congruent with the seasons: spring was a young girl, summer a beautiful bride, autumn a matron, and winter "a decrepit old woman" (Hanawalt 2007, 35–36). From society's point of view, a woman was defined by her marital status and her ability to produce children, which lasted over half the metaphorical year, or half her life. One indication of the importance of women's reproductive capacities can be found in early medieval law codes, which assessed harsh fines for harm to a fetus or a pregnant woman. The Salic law, which dates from around 500 CE in France, assessed a **wergild** for a woman of child-bearing age at 600 **solidi**, which is three times the wergild for an adult man; her wergild dropped to 200 solidi, the same as a man, when she reached menopause. In some law codes, half the mother's wergild was also assessed for the death of a fetus still in utero. The sums demanded were highest when the woman was still fertile (Harris-Stoertz 2012, 267).

STAGES OF LIFE: THE FAMILY

We often imagine the medieval family as being large and extended, in contrast to the modern first-world model of the nuclear family. Archaeological evidence, however, suggests that most medieval households were fairly small and consisted mainly of a married couple with their children. One reason for the small size of many families may be the shortened average life span of adults in some regions: if only 10 percent of adults lived past forty-five years of age, as in parts of Anglo-Saxon England, it is not surprising that few grandparents lived with their extended families. On the other hand, the availability of land for settlement made a difference in how families developed. In places where there was little land available, households became larger simply because there was nowhere else for grown children to go. Such households might have had multiple nuclear families sharing the same house and land. Social class also had an impact on household size: wealthier households supported servants and others outside the nuclear family and occupied larger homes and pieces of land (Crawford 1999, 10–12). Most children likely grew up in communities of connected families. Godparents were considered part of the family, and some people used the term *godsibs* ("God siblings") to describe one another (the root of our word "gossip"). The relationship was taken very seriously. Marrying into the family of a godparent was considered incest and was forbidden (Orme 2001, 25).

STAGES OF LIFE: INFANCY

As we have seen above, parents were concerned about making sure their babies were baptized in a timely manner in order to assure them a blessed afterlife. By 1300, most infants were baptized quickly, within three days of birth, although wealthy families sometimes waited a little longer to baptize healthy infants so that a grand ceremony could be planned. The mother of the baby normally did not attend the baptism, as she could not enter the church until she was declared ritually clean from the childbirth, or "churched." This term of waiting was normally forty days, much longer than families wanted to wait to ensure their children's spiritual safety. Instead, the father and chosen godparents took the infant to the church. They answered ritual questions posed in Latin, and the priest anointed the child with oil. The baby was immersed in holy water three times and anointed again with chrism, a mixture of blessed oil and balm. Then the child was wrapped in a cloth called a **chrisom**, which was intended to keep the oil and balm in place. The priest warned the biological parents that they should guard the child from harm and directed the godparents to see to the child's education in the prayers and teachings of the church. The **chrisom** was a religious item and so had to be returned to the church at the mother's churching, although some babies who died early were buried in their chrisom cloths (Orme 2001, 28–29).

The child was also formally named at the baptismal ceremony. The practices for choosing names varied across Europe. In England and France, the child was often named for one of the godparents; in Italy, the father generally chose the child's name. Names might also be chosen to honor particular saints, especially the saint whose feast day fell on the day of the baptism or a saint who had particular meaning for the family (Youngs 2006, 47). Just as they do today, families passed down names from older relatives; for example, in the lineage of the counts of Anjou in the eleventh century, all the first- and second-born sons were named either Fulk or Geoffrey. Girls' names often varied more than boys' names, arguably because they were not the focus of the lineage the way their brothers were.

Care of infants fell, for the most part, to mothers and female caregivers in the home. Most infants were exclusively breastfed in the Middle Ages, frequently to the age of two or three years old. Lower- and middle-class mothers nursed their own infants, but upper-class women often employed **wet nurses** to nurse their children in order to enable the mothers to return to daily activities more quickly. As a result, there was a type of literature advising families on the choice of a wet nurse. The literature about wet nursing originated in the ancient world with a writer named Soranus (second century CE), who set out a lengthy series of qualifications for a wet nurse. He assumed that a woman who had already had children would be healthier and better able to nurse. "One should choose a wet nurse not younger than twenty nor older than forty years, who has already given birth twice or thrice. . . . Her breasts should be of medium size, lax, soft and unwrinkled, the nipples neither too big nor too small and neither too compact nor too porous and discharging milk overabundantly" (Soranus of Ephesus 1956, 90–91). Breasts that were too large, Soranus explained, would increase the chance that leftover milk could spoil in the wet nurse's breasts and harm the child. Sexual intercourse was also thought to "spoil" breast milk, so wet nurses were paid in part to remain celibate while feeding someone else's child. Medical writers also told fathers to be sure to hire wet nurses who were not drunks, as an excess of alcohol might harm the child. In Renaissance Italy, studies have shown that there was a difference between the treatment of male and female babies in wet-nursing; boys were nursed at home by live-in nurses more often than girls, who were more likely to be sent out to live with a wet nurse in the town or country. This may have contributed to a higher rate of infant mortality for girl babies in places where this was the practice (Ferraro 2012, 66). Infant feeding could also be done through artificial means. One method was to fit a hollow cow's horn with a sponge or cloth and allow the infant to suck on it. Infant feeders were also made of pottery, either with a small hole for feeding or with long spouts designed to admit very little milk at one time. We do not know how often or how successfully such items may have been used (Gilchrist 2012, 155).

Some writers in the Middle Ages, such as the Italian politician Francesco Barbaro (1390–1454 CE), in a treatise called *On Wifely Duties*, urged noble mothers to breastfeed their own infants, citing the belief that the nurse's personal traits and qualities were passed to the infant with the breastmilk (Youngs 2006, 48). The belief was both long-lasting and widespread. In an Old French song about the life of Godfrey of Bouillon (1060–1100), who became the ruler of Jerusalem during the First Crusade, the author commented that Duke Godfrey's youngest brother, Eustace, had once been breast-fed by another woman, despite strict instructions from his mother, Countess Ida of Boulogne. The angry countess shook the baby until he vomited the other woman's milk, but the poem states that she was too late: the foreign milk had done its work, and Eustace never measured up to his brothers in later life (Labarge 1986, 77).

Between birth and age seven, medieval children were considered to be too young to be at fault for their actions, and writers put great emphasis on the need for a good upbringing to make children into good adults. Children at this time were sometimes compared to clay or wax, that would take the impression of any lessons learned from parents. *Las Siete Partidas* specified that younger children were the responsibility of their mother, and older (presumably male) children of their father: "Mothers should nourish and bring up their children while they are under three years of age, and their fathers those who have passed that age" (Amt 2010, 55). Children began work and chores at young ages; children at four or five could be set to watch infant brothers and sisters, pull weeds or herd livestock, and young girls could learn the rudiments of spinning and sewing. Children seem to have been left unattended much more than we would think wise today and to have taken on responsibility earlier.

Around the age of seven, parents often made decisions about their children's long-term futures. Boys would go to work in the fields or be sent to apprentice for a trade or train in other skills, while girls were becoming responsible for the skills that would enable them to marry and be successful wives and mothers within their own classes. Lower-class girls went out to the fields early, while upper-class young women were kept close to home and taught the skills that would

Mothers were responsible for the education of daughters. This miniature painting shows St. Anne teaching the Virgin Mary to read. (The British Library)

make them attractive partners. In wealthy households, where there could be multiple sons and daughters, the greatest attention was paid to the boy who would inherit the bulk of the property and to girls intended for marriage; extra sons and daughters could end up in monasteries, even as early as aged eight or nine (Ferraro 2012, 63–64).

Though work began early for medieval children by our standards, there were still games and fun. Despite its sad origin, a lament for a dead son by the fifteenth-century Welsh poet Lewys Glyn Cothi gives us a few hints about children's games: a wooden sword, a bow made of a branch, and dice were a few of his son's favorite toys (Johnston 1993, 102–103). Infant rattles, tops, and dolls are some of the toys mentioned in other medieval sources. The fifteenth-century poem "Ratis Raving," written by a Scottish man for his young son, mentions that children "will always with flowers for to jape and play" (Orme 2001, 176).

STAGES OF LIFE: ADOLESCENCE

According to Isidore of Seville's calculations, adolescence was the time in which young people were able to become parents, and in many places, young people married early by our standards. The church set the minimum age for marriage at twelve for girls and fourteen for boys, and there are certainly examples of women who were married early: a case in point is Lady Margaret Beaufort (1443–1509), mother of Henry VII of England, who was married at twelve in 1455 and gave birth to the future king at thirteen (Phillips 2003, 38–39). Adolescent mothers were not uncommon. Hildegard, wife of Charlemagne, died at age twenty-five in 783, already having had nine children (Garver 2012, 233). Archaeological evidence also supports some early marriages. In an Anglo-Saxon grave from Abingdon, Berkshire, archaeologists discovered the body of a young woman, fifteen or sixteen years of age, who had clearly been pregnant when she died. She was buried with brooches, beads, and other tokens of class and wealth, suggesting that she had been buried with affection and respect (Crawford 1999, 48).

Medieval artists often illustrated the education of the Virgin Mary. Here, she learns to read with her mother, St. Anne. (Gift of G. J. Demotte. The Cleveland Museum of Art)

In many places, however, puberty was not automatically thought to be the best time to marry, because most women were not ready at twelve or fourteen to take on the duties of a fully grown married woman, even though they were capable of bearing children. Economic pressures shaped age at first marriage. In the Carolingian period in the early Middle Ages, when farmland was passed down from fathers to children, couples married in their twenties, and the ages at first marriage for men and women were fairly close (Herlihy 1985, 77). Economic and social pressures forced the age of first marriage back for upper-class women beginning in the central Middle Ages. The Italian poet Dante Alighieri (ca. 1265–1321 CE) criticized the people of his time for early marriages, and the moralist Desiderius Erasmus (1466–1536 CE) wrote, "It isn't rare to see, especially among the French, a girl hardly ten years old married, and a mother at eleven" (Herlihy 1985, 104–105). For English princesses in the late Middle Ages, the approximate mean age at first marriage was sixteen. The period before marriage has been described as a time of "maidenhood" for late medieval English women, between twelve and fifteen, in which the responsibilities of adult life were stayed until they were old enough for full marriage and childbearing (Phillips 2003, 39). The age of maidenhood was a time of beauty and desirability: young women wore their hair down, suggesting both their sexuality and their virginity.

STAGES OF LIFE: ADULTHOOD

Although maidenhood was privileged as a time of beauty, adulthood was a time when grown women could assert their places and responsibilities in society. To "come of age" in this period meant to be old enough to inherit property or to fulfill the demands of a profession. For women, it meant being old enough to marry, give birth, and run a household or workshop. The word adult, from the Latin word *adolescere*, means "grown up." Young people did not necessarily become adult all at once. The narrator of the *Ménagier de Paris*, a middle-aged man writing to his fifteen-year-old wife, advised that she had time to enjoy her adolescence. "Know that I take delight rather than displeasure in your cultivating rose bushes, caring for violets, and making chaplets, and also in your dancing and singing . . . for it is only right and just that you should thus pass the days of your maidenly youth" (Bayard 2001, 27–28). The Ménagier planned for a new wife to learn the chores of her married life gradually under her husband's instruction. We generally look askance at couples for whom the age difference is so great today, but it was not unusual in the Middle Ages for an older man to take a young wife.

STAGES OF LIFE: WIDOWHOOD

Christine de Pisan (1360–1430), writing in the fourteenth century and herself a widow, spoke frankly to widows about what they could expect in her *Book of the Three Virtues*. "Rich women are in trouble because people try generally to rob them, and poor and less wealthy women because no one will show pity toward them" (Blumenfeld-Kosinski 1997, 169). In societies where wives were generally younger than their husbands, their chances of being widowed were greater. **Dower** property was reserved for widows after their husbands died, but it was not always easy to get the husbands' heirs to release the property for the widows' use.

Some widows certainly chose to remarry, though the number and ratio of those who remarried is unclear. Anecdotally, the sources suggest some level of remarriage in most places. The author of the *Ménagier of Paris* fully expected that a young wife would remarry after her husband died and made frequent reference to it. Not surprisingly, age made a difference: a study of Florentine women indicated that among that population, two-thirds of widows under twenty remarried, but only 11 percent of widows in their thirties did. The difference may partly be a reflection of fertility (Klapisch-Zuber 1985, 120). Money and property also played significant parts in women's decision making about remarriage, because there were outside pressures from family and from society. Some husbands who left wills specified that their wives were entitled to certain monetary or property benefits only so long as they remained unmarried and "of good reputation." Other families pressured widows, especially young widows, to remarry as soon as possible (Youngs 2006, 151–152).

In her study of peasants in fourteenth and fifteenth-century England, Barbara Hanawalt points out that for some women, widowhood meant financial and personal independence: "A widow could enter into land contracts on her own, could decide on marriage alliances for children, could make her own decisions about remarriage and whom she would marry" (Hanawalt 1986, 220). Many widows maintained the tenure of their lands for themselves and for their minor children. One example is Agnes de la Lande, who held her family's tenancy for twenty years, from 1286 to 1306, until her son Richard turned twenty-one and could manage the land himself. She then received a third of the property as her **dower**. Other widows negotiated rights for themselves from grown children if the children already managed the family holdings. These included rooms in the house, the use of dower property, and sometimes sums of money or amounts of food (Hanawalt 1986, 222–223).

Widows also provided for their heirs through wills. Anglo-Saxon wills from the tenth and eleventh centuries show widows disposing of both land and belongings. In her tenth-century will, a wealthy matriarch named Wynflaed left land and jewelry to her daughter Aethelflaed, made numerous bequests to churches, and freed at least ten slaves. Aethelflaed was the greatest beneficiary of her mother's will. The testament ends with this catch-all: "Then she makes a gift to Aetheflaed of everything which is unbequeathed, books and such small things, and she trusts that she will be mindful of her soul" (Amt 2010, 116).

STAGES OF LIFE: OLD AGE

The image of elderly women in sources from the Middle Ages is uniformly negative. After the menopause, which was thought to occur at around fifty years old, medieval writers spotlighted declining physical and mental health. Loss of fertility, too, reduced a woman's value in society, both metaphorically and literally (Youngs 2006, 167). In the *Danse Macabre des Femmes*, a fifteenth-century French work in which various women meet Death, the character of the old woman complained, "I'm not worth two silver coins" (Harrison and Hindman 1994, 94). Medically, moreover, women who were no longer menstruating were thought to contain all their bodily impurities inside them, which posed a danger to others, especially children, who could be harmed by the "evil eye." An anonymous author known as Pseudo-Albertus Magnus wrote in the late twelfth century that "The retention of menses engenders many evil humors" (Metzler 2006, 114). Elderly women could be treated as though they were worthless, or worse, feared because they were toxic.

Writers of the Middle Ages sometimes followed a pattern known as the *vituperium in vetulam* ("insult against an old woman"). The insult could be in any medium—prose, poetry, song, etc. Authors dwelled on the unattractiveness of the elderly female body—baldness, toothlessness, and physical infirmity—and equated the old woman's ugliness with indecent sexuality. One Italian poem from the fourteenth or fifteenth century addressed the old woman as an "annoying sow" and wished that she would have "asps, and frogs, and scorpions" attack her body. Such literature describes elderly women in the worst language possible—probably a form of medieval humor that we would prefer to forget (Alfie 2017, 396).

Regardless of bad press, some elderly people in the Middle Ages succeeded in securing a sort of retirement for themselves through negotiation with landlords or even with their own children. Corodies were arrangements made between elderly people and monasteries in which the owners of land handed it over to the monastery in exchange for food, drink, and clothing for life. They could be used as a sort of pension and, in many places, could be purchased to ensure a steady living in old age. In 1322, for example, Hainrich Klucke and his wife agreed to turn over their land to the hospital at Villingen in return for maintenance (Metzler 2006, 124). Contractual agreements could also be drawn up between elderly people and their children or elderly people and those not related to them. In 1327, a woman of Great Waltham, Essex, named Estrilda Nenour complained to the court that she had agreed with her daughter to turn over her landholding in exchange for food, clothing, and a place to live, but that her daughter had not fulfilled the contract. The court awarded her a sum of money for the breach of contract, and Estrilda found another couple to support her (Youngs 2006, 177).

Retiring to a religious house was also possible for those women who could afford it. A number of medieval queens, such as Eleanor of Aquitaine, retired to convents in their later years, but retiring to a monastery or nunnery was also widespread among people lower on the social scale than nobility, though not among the poor. Families sometimes gave gifts to nunneries to ensure that their elderly relatives had a place to go when they wished. Two widows from Châteaugontier, France, Raingardis and Maria, gave their land to the monastery of Le Ronceray d'Angers in the eleventh century to allow them to profess as nuns. Anselm of Châteaugontier and his wife, Elizabeth, also gave Le Ronceray a large donation of land and goods, with the expectation that Elizabeth would enter the nunnery if she was widowed (Marchegay 1854, 3:87–88).

If a devoted noble patron died a distance away from the place she wished to be buried, she might arrange to have her heart sent back to the site rather than her entire body. Hildegarde, countess of Anjou in the early eleventh century, died in 1046 while on pilgrimage to Jerusalem. Her heart was sent back to France to be buried at the nunnery she and her husband founded in 1028. Hearts and intestines might be preserved so that a wealthy patron could be buried in more than one place. Isabel of Clare was buried next to her second husband in 1239, but her heart was placed next to her first husband, Gilbert, in a different cemetery.

Outside of the wealthier classes, the fate of elderly women in the Middle Ages was often a difficult one. **Guild** regulations sometimes provided for the widows of members, especially if they were infirm and unable to work. Charitable bequests to the elderly occurred in many medieval wills. Joan Cotyngham, a widow with property in York in the 1450s, left another widow named Joan Day "my russet gown lined with buckskin and a chemise of linen cloth." This would have been a coarse garment made of the rough brown or gray wool cloth called *russet*. Emma, another widow from York, left all the widows in her area three pennies each, "total by estimation, 10 s. 9 d" (Goldberg 1995, 162–163). English coroner's rolls, which record deaths, give other pictures of women in poverty and desperation. In Bedfordshire in 1274, "Emma of Hatch came from Beeston, where she had been begging bread from door to door, and towards vespers she returned towards Beeston to seek lodging . . . . [She] was overcome by cold and died by misadventure" (Goldberg 1995, 165). Such cases remind us that although wealthy women might have considerable control over their decisions, poor women might live on the edge of starvation.

STAGES OF LIFE: A GOOD DEATH

Medieval people hoped for a "good death," a death in which a person was surrounded by family and died peacefully without pain, having confessed all their sins and ensuring a good afterlife in heaven. Dying people in the late Middle Ages were encouraged to meditate on the death of Christ as they approached their own ends. Deathbed scenes appeared in books of hours illustrating prayers for the dead, reminding the readers both to pray for their loved ones and to be aware of their own mortality. Yet although aristocratic women often commissioned and used books of hours, most of the dying people portrayed in these images are men, surrounded by female caregivers. Illustrations of what is called the "dormition" of the Virgin Mary, however, are also included in books of hours. (Theologically, Mary did not die but was assumed bodily into heaven.) She is usually shown surrounded by the apostles and lying on a bed. Sometimes the image includes Jesus as he summons her to heaven, carrying Mary's soul in his arms. Women who were devoted to Mary may very well have imagined their own deathbeds as similar to hers.

This carved altarpiece depicts the dormition ("sleeping") of the Virgin Mary, surrounded by the Apostles. (The Cloisters Collection, 1973. The Metropolitan Museum of Art.)

CONCLUSION

Social and medical authorities concentrated on women's fertility in the Middle Ages because fertility, in the face of infant and maternal mortality, affected the well-being of all of society. Women's relationship to fertility as they grew up and aged shaped their interactions with their families and their society. It may also have shaped how they understood their purpose in the world. Not all events in women's lives were related to fertility, however. In the next chapter, we will look at women's other work, both inside and outside the home.

3

WORKING WOMEN

In this chapter, we will explore the working lives of women in the Middle Ages. Although for many women their primary work was keeping a household, some women worked for wages outside their homes and participated in trades, crafts, and other economic activities. We will see that work outside the home was far more common than has been believed for women of all classes except the elite. We will also see how daily life was shaped by the labor-intensive work of cooking and keeping the house.

LIVING AND WORKING IN THE COUNTRYSIDE: SERFS AND PEASANTS

By far, the largest group of workers in the Middle Ages were those who farmed and produced food. The prosperity of the upper class was based on a large population of agricultural workers, many of whom were unfree men and women. There were many types of servitude and many different ways for peasant workers to be exploited by the upper classes. For example, in France in the eleventh century, a **serf** (*servus* in Latin, the root of our English word *servant*), was bound to his or her own land and could be bought and sold along with the land. A *colonus* was not bound to the land but owed regular labor to the landowner, and a *lidus* was a person whose rights fell between the two. Servile status was hereditary and descended through the mother, a system many historians believe was a holdover from Roman-style slavery. Serfs could be freed, and it was also possible for free people to deliberately take servile status. It was even possible for a free person to become a serf as a punishment for a crime or for not paying one's duties to the lord (Tierney 1999, 183).

Many serfs and unfree peasants lived on agricultural estates called manors, which were under the control of a particular lord. A serf generally could not change houses or leave the estate without the lord's permission. Serfs and other low-status people owed their landlords payment in kind for their rents. If a peasant farmed, he and his family owed his lord a substantial portion of his crop; if he grazed his pigs in the lord's forest, he owed some pork. The lord also had considerable power over his peasants' daily lives. Serfs owed the lord fees such as a chevage or head tax, paid yearly; the *corvée*, which was a requirement that they work on the lord's land several days per week; the *formariage* or *marchet*, a sum of money for permission to marry; and the *mortmain*, money paid when they inherited their relatives' lands or privileges. The lord could order all his tenants to have their grain ground at his mill, which also required a fee. He ran the law courts on his land as well, so any crimes that were committed were tried and fined under his control (Tierney 1999, 182–183). The bond between a lord and his serfs was difficult to break. One wealthy abbot described a serf of his monastery as "mine from the soles of his feet to the top of his head" (Bloch 1975, 58).

Serfs and other poor and unfree people are often hard to see in historical documents because they were illiterate, and upper-class people seldom saw fit to record specifics about them. One exception is that some monasteries kept records when they obtained people as part of a land transaction; another is when such people were freed. In one example from the twelfth century, the monks of the French abbey of Marmoutier's priory in Blois witnessed the freeing of a female serf named Haiilde and all her offspring on behalf of the lords of Fréteval, Hugh and Eudo. The wealthy brothers freed Haiilde and her children as an act of piety, hoping to gain spiritual benefits for their loved ones who had died (Métais 1889, 124). In another, a knight gave the monks of Marmoutier a miller, his wife, and their three daughters as a donation (Salmon 1864, 54). When women were given "with their offspring," it meant both those already born and those not yet born. A free man who married an unfree woman also became unfree, so servile status was passable through marriage. Manumission, the freeing of serfs, was rare, and once an individual was declared to be of servile status, it was usually permanent.

In the poorest of peasant families, both men and women had to shoulder the burdens of farming. Families were generally nuclear, consisting of a husband and wife and their children, and high rates of infant mortality and lifetime hardship meant that their lives were statistically short (see the section on nutrition in the introduction). Their housing was primitive by modern standards. It often consisted of a **wattle and daub** hut roofed with straw **thatch**, built around a hearth. Thatch was cheap, light, and waterproof and was easy to repair if damaged. The smallest of houses were simple one-room houses, perhaps sixteen by twelve feet, or two-room houses that were longer, with an enclosure at the end to house the animals. They often had clay or earthen floors; stone floors were also used in places where stone was plentiful. Floors were covered with straw or rushes to make a soft surface underfoot. When these became dirty, the housewife swept them out and replaced them with fresh straw. Many houses had horse and cattle pens attached to them, both to protect valuable animals and to take advantage of as much warmth as possible. In the simplest dwellings, people and animals shared the inside space. In more prosperous households, however, a separate room or building might be built for the animals. During winter, the whole family worked to stay warm and fed. During warmer weather, husband, wife, and children worked to get their land planted, cultivated, and harvested (Leyser 1995, 142–43; Hanawalt 1986, 32–33).

It is difficult to know just how much land and how much grain would have been required to support a peasant family at subsistence level. One calculation estimates that a holding of twenty acres would provide about 153 bushels of barley, oats, and wheat—enough for a yearly income of 35 shillings fourpence. A one- or two-acre holding with a garden was generally thought to be sufficient to support one person, but another estimate states that thirty-six bushels of grain (of whatever type) were needed to feed a family for a year, which would require at least five acres under cultivation. When crops failed, as in the famines of the early fourteenth century, some of the seed corn would need to be eaten, which would leave the following harvest short as well (Hammond 1993, 27–28).

Styles of cultivation varied across Europe and influenced the way that medieval peasants conducted their labor. In places

A peasant couple cutting and stacking hay. (Spencer Collection, The New York Public Library. "Full-page miniature of haymaking, in June." New York Public Library Digital Collections.)

with poor soil, farmsteads were typically spread far apart. Single homesteads were surrounded by their land. The land closest to the house was fertilized by the household animals and could be planted continuously year-round. Other plots were farmed until they were no longer fertile. In places with better soil, households gathered into villages, and villages had a different system. In regions in the northern part of Europe, this system was called *open-field* farming. Fields were divided into strips, each strip belonging to a different house, and each house held several strips mixed in with the strips belonging to their neighbors. The open-field system demanded that all the people in the village work together, since their plots of land were close together. Half the strips of land in a given year were allowed to lie fallow to rest the soil from cultivation. In the southern part of Europe, village houses had rectangular plots that were also rested every other year (Tierney 1999, 176–77). In the early Middle Ages, peasant women worked alongside men in the fields, until better farming technology in the High Middle Ages permitted them to give more time to the household or to selling their goods or produce for money.

Occasionally, women peasants are visible in monastery records. In one document from the women's monastery of Ronceray in

Angers, France, a woman named Bohilia rented one quarter of an **arpent** of land (an arpent is approximately 0.85 acre or 0.34 hectare) from the nuns, and her neighbor Ausendis held one-half arpent (Marchegay 1854, 3:201). At another property, a woman named Albegia, wife of Morehen, paid 5 **pennies** for her yearly rent (Marchegay 1854, 3:250). Tenants of very small and very cheap plots of land must have lived at subsistence level. Some of them were probably widows who were permitted to keep living on the land left by their husbands. Women like these might do many kinds of manual labor if they were strong enough: haymaking, thatching roofs, breaking rocks, or reaping in return for food (Leyser 1995, 148). They could also be hired as servants or as laborers in other contexts.

Servants

There were also wealthier people, of course, who owned their own land, and some employed lower-status people as servants and workers. Many young peasant women worked for wages in these more well-off households. These kinds of jobs attracted young women (beginning at about age twelve) who wanted to save up for a **dowry**. Descriptions of what kind of work young rural women did for wages give us clues about what kinds of work medieval society expected women to perform. In a thirteenth-century text called the *Seneschaucy*, the anonymous author described the work of a dairymaid in great detail, writing, "The dairymaid ought to be loyal, of good repute, and clean; she ought to know her work and what relates to it . . . . She ought to know the day on which to begin making cheese and of what weight." She also had many other duties, including winnowing grain and supervising the care of poultry (Amt 2010, 150–151). Overseeing the servants was part of the housewife's job. "How the Good Wife Taught Her Daughter," an English poem of the fifteenth century, reminded the housewife to manage her servants carefully and not to be "too bitter or too debonaire" with them (Furnivall and Rickert 1908, 36).

Young women could be bound over as servants permanently, either as **chattel** slaves, who could be bought and sold, or a kind of indentured servitude in which the term of service and pay were designated through contracts. In 1090 in Amalfi, a widow named Asterada bound her daughter Sica over to a household where she promised to serve until the deaths of her employers. In return, they owed her clothing, shoes, and food, and a sum of money to be paid from their wills (Skinner and van Houts 2011, 57–58).

Keeping the Peasant Household

When they married, free young women commonly did not continue to work for wages but switched to the tasks needed by their own households. This might include the care of livestock and poultry, spinning and weaving, sheep shearing, growing vegetables and herbs, and of course caring for children (Leyser 1995, 145). The household was the place where a woman's leadership was most visible, even if female leadership was not normally praised outside of the house. A fifteenth-century poem called the *Ballad of the Tyrannical Husband* tells the amusing story of a husband who challenges his wife to undertake his work plowing the field while he does the housework. He complains that his wife has nothing to do all day and spends her time gossiping. Although the end of the poem is lost, the wife's list of her duties remains: caring for the children, milking the cows, churning the butter, feeding the chickens and geese, baking, brewing, working both flax and wool, and feeding the household (Larrington 1995, 110–11).

Care of cows and sheep was also a primarily female occupation during the Middle Ages (Herlihy 1990, 53). Extra production of milk and cheese could be sold at the market. Women could also be paid to work during the harvests. The wage was one penny a day, often paid in grain. Making soap, by boiling wood ashes into lye and then adding animal fat, was another common household chore. Medieval women often did their washing by taking clothes to a river and beating and scrubbing them with sticks or rocks. Lye or human urine might be used as a stain remover.

In the later Middle Ages, women also performed many duties for their local churches in addition to their own households: cleaning, providing wax candles or cloth for vestments and hangings, sewing and mending, or providing other necessary supplies. In this way, ordinary women could express piety through the use of skills they acquired through housework, and express it in ways that were reflective of their household roles (French 2008, 18–20).

Living and Sleeping in Town

Archaeological evidence has shown that urban cemeteries have greater percentages of female than male skeletons, suggesting that a large migration of women to cities and towns occurred in the High Middle Ages. This challenges the long-held scholarly supposition that migrants to urban areas were predominantly male. Urban women tended to marry later than their counterparts in the country, perhaps because they had to earn enough money for a **dowry**. Since such women married later, they were also threatened by childbirth mortality later than country women and, therefore, skew older in urban cemeteries in contrast to rural ones (Kowaleski 2014, 586–589).

The basic design of the house of a well-off peasant or town dweller of the later Middle Ages was in place by ca. 1250 CE. In general, the house was divided into three sections, with a central hall that functioned as living space and which contained the hearth, a private sleeping chamber for the family at one end, and a pantry and other storage space at the other end. If livestock were quartered in these houses, they were in a space of their own at the pantry end. In towns, where there was more competition for space, some houses added a second story (Gilchrist 2012, 117–119). Excavations of such houses have allowed us to understand a number of characteristics of housework of the period. The hearth was often in the middle of the floor, covered at night with a ceramic lid called a *curfew*. At Wharram Percy in Yorkshire, a village abandoned in 1500, many women's skeletons displayed a condition that occurs when the individual has been squatting for long periods of time, perhaps cooking on a similar hearth (Gilchrist 2012, 60). Floors were of beaten earth, chalk, or clay, covered with rushes. Window openings were small to conserve heat and covered with horn or oiled parchment, which let in the light (glass windows were uncommon until the very end of the medieval period). Artificial light was possible through lamps and candles, but the medieval house must have been quite dark by our standards, especially after night fell. Most households used lights made from animal fat, or tallow. Wealthier households could afford beeswax, which cost about three times as much.

Furniture seems to have been fairly sparse: a bed, a few chairs, a chest for storing clothes and linens, and perhaps a trestle table for eating, were common examples. The most valuable possession in the medieval household may have been the bed. Not only were the wooden parts of the bed expensive, but wool or (from the fourteenth century on) down-stuffed mattresses, curtains, and bed linens were also frequently passed down in medieval wills. In early medieval manor houses where the entire household slept in one large room, bed curtains provided extra warmth and privacy.

Since the bed was also the location for sex, birth, and death (think of our words *childbed* and *deathbed*), it possessed significant cultural meanings. The household had a few eating utensils mostly made of wood and clay pots to cook the food in. A young wife's most treasured possession might well have been the chest she used to hold her belongings; the remains of small chests or coffers are very common archaeological discoveries (Gilchrist 2012, 121). Tending to all these aspects of the household, as we have seen, was a central task of married women. Maintaining these important properties and possessions so they could be passed to future generations was a significant chore.

EVERYDAY FOOD

The staple of the medieval kitchen was bread, which varied from a white, wheat-based loaf eaten by upper-class people to the brown or black, thick rye, or barley bread more common to the lower classes. For the most impoverished, a sort of bread could be made of bean flour and the siftings of wheat. Bread provided about 82 percent of peasants' daily caloric intake: a one-pound loaf of bread provided about one thousand calories, as well as various major nutrients (Scott 2010, 5–6). Unleavened bread such as flatbread could be cooked on the home hearth by using a clay pot heated in the ashes, but leavened bread required an oven, a luxury for many people. Some villages had communal ovens for bread baking. By the late Middle Ages, professional bakers baked much of the bread in town settings (Montanari 2012, 60). In some parts of Europe in the late Middle Ages, women were professional bakers, as well as millers: female bakers are mentioned in the records of Constance, Troyes, Frankfurt am Main, and Cologne, among others (Uitz 1988, 57). In towns, women often sold bread by moving through the town as itinerant sellers.

Producing bread was a laborious process. Raw grain harvested from the field had to be separated from its chaff, or inedible covering, by beating it with an instrument called a flail. The grain then needed to be winnowed to remove any excess chaff, which required shaking it in a basket so that the lighter chaff would rise to the top and blow away. Then the grain could be taken to the mill to be ground into flour. This flour could be made into bread with yeast, salt, and water; its quality determined whether the loaf would be light and fluffy or heavy and hearty. Bread was so important to the medieval diet that from the thirteenth century onward, many places in Europe passed laws that regulated the cost of a loaf of bread. Although the cost of a loaf was kept steady, the size and weight of the loaf varied according to the price of grain (Davis 2004, 466). Heavy, dark bread made up the bulk of many medieval diets.

Peasant diets were supplemented by vegetables, especially peas and beans, when the weather was warm. Peas and beans had the advantage of being easily stored for winter, when they could be boiled up into a thick porridge called a pottage. In the summer, fruits and berries could be had, and, in the fall, poor women and children were often allowed to glean nuts and grain that were left behind during the harvest. Able-bodied men were not allowed to glean (Hanawalt 1986, 54–55). Eggs and milk also provided some of the protein available to peasant families, and many households kept hens. To stop milk from spoiling, it had to be made into cheese or butter, which was made regularly to stay fresh. The butter was made from the cream skimmed off the top of the milk, and the left-over milk was made into cheese. Types of cheese varied from the hard cheeses that were aged before consumption to "green" cheese that could be made in a day.

Vegetables and fruits, widely available in rural areas, were also produced for sale in urban areas. In London in the fourteenth century, produce was brought into town from neighboring counties, but gardens in the city also supplied the markets. Town dwellers with enough money to buy produce had a wide choice: they could find tree fruits, such as apples and pears; vegetables with strong flavors, such as onions and leeks; and root crops like carrots and beets. Various herbs that flavored food or that functioned as medicine were available. Grapes were pressed not only to make wine but also verjuice (a green grape juice that was not fermented, used in many medieval recipes). Town markets were scheduled regularly and were often arranged by merchandise—fish, meat, poultry, and produce. Town governments did their best to regulate this commerce, to tax it, and to make sure that outsiders did not try to undercut the market prices (Hammond 1993, 42–43).

Archaeological sites have produced various animal bones that show what meat was available to medieval people. In the High Middle Ages, meat was regarded as the best and most nourishing food for good health. Aldobrandino da Siena (d. ca. 1296), a medical writer who wrote a health manual for elite medieval diners, wrote that "among all the things that nourish man, meat is the one that nourishes him best, fattens him, and gives him strength" (Montanari 2012, 64). Pork and chicken seem to have been the meats of choice for peasants. Pig bones are scarce in archaeological digs because their bones deteriorate quickly when boiled, so it is difficult to judge how much pork was available to high medieval diners. It was very likely a significant amount, because pigs are adaptable, reproduce well, and are easy to raise in a modestly sized space. In the Middle Ages, pigs were fattened with scraps and by letting them gorge on acorns in forests, and forests were assessed for taxes by the number of pigs that they could support, a sum called *pasnage* (Montanari 2012, 63). Similarly, chickens could be raised with very little extra expense and provided not only eggs but meat.

Upper-class medieval people certainly also ate beef (slaughtered when the animal was two years old), mutton (sheep's meat), and poultry such as ducks and chickens. In the earlier Middle Ages, upper-class people favored fresh meat, especially wild game, to be served at the table: bear, stag, and wild boar were considered to taste rich and give strength for fighting battles. The emperor Charlemagne (d. 814 CE) was fond of roasted meat served to him at the table on spits so that he could cut off a portion with his knife. By the High Middle Ages, domesticated meat made up most of the meat served at wealthy tables. Upper-class people preferred veal, especially milk-fed veal; various kinds of mutton, especially lamb; and wild poultry such as pheasant and quail. These "lighter" and more expensive foods were understood to be appropriate for people of higher birth and greater refinement, interested more in court functions than in battles (Montanari 2012, 70).

During Lent, the forty-day period before Easter when eating meat was forbidden, and during religious holidays, households turned to fish to supply their diet. Some of this fish came from the coast, where saltwater fishing was commonplace, and some from local freshwater sources (Hanawalt 1986, 52–53). Data from the early Middle Ages in Britain suggests that only those who lived near the coast had saltwater fish in their diets, but by the eleventh and twelfth centuries, commercial fishing made it possible for people inland to supplement their diets with saltwater fish such as cod. It was packed into barrels with salt to be shipped, and then soaked to remove the salt before cooking (Müldner 2016, 241). Salting and drying meat was an easy way to preserve it for the long term, though salt had to be purchased and was not cheap. The sources of salt in the early Middle Ages were usually salt pans or mines where salt crystals could be dug from the ground. In the later Middle Ages, salt produced by evaporating seawater became more common, and prices dropped.

Everyday Drink

Medieval people were quite aware that polluted water sources were bad for drinking from. Hildegard of Bingen (1098–1179), a

German abbess of the twelfth century, advised that well water was preferred to spring water, while water from rivers and swamps should be boiled before use. Accessing clean water for drinking was a more difficult problem for people in towns and cities than people in rural areas, but all medieval Europeans contended with obtaining and carrying water for their household needs. Much like traditional societies today, in rural areas, fetching the water was a chore for women and girls. Women carried water in cities as well, but there were also male water carriers who were paid to provide water to affluent households. Many medieval towns and cities built aqueducts and fountains for public use, some of which were theoretically intended for drinking water and some for washing clothes and watering animals. The number of fines and punishments in the laws about the fountains, however, show that many people ignored the rules. In general, city governments discouraged commercial interests from using public fountains, but they often did so, particularly brewers, who needed large amounts of water to brew beer. How medieval people felt about drinking water may be suggested by a teaching work written by a monk named Aelfric (955–ca. 1012), who lived in England. Asked what he liked to drink, one of the young monks replied, "Beer if I have it, but water if I don't have beer" (Magnusson 2001, 134).

Brewing was an important chore for medieval women. Before the introduction of hops in the fourteenth century, the drink of choice in much of northern Europe was ale made from barley. This ale spoiled quickly and had to be made every few days to keep a fresh supply. Many women made ale at home, like the woman above in the *Ballad of the Tyrannical Husband*, and included it in their regular household chores. A few put together commercial enterprises. Denise Marlere of Bridgewater, England, who died in 1401, had a brewing business that was prosperous enough to leave her daughter and servant all the accoutrements of a thriving trade: numerous leaden vats and sacks of malt, along with silver cups and luxury bedlinens. However, Marlere was not typical among the brewers of her day, who were becoming increasingly commercialized. As in weaving, once the technology to make longer-lasting beer replaced the ale trade, brewing gradually came under the purview of men (Bennett 1996, 14).

Wine was also produced around Europe. Between the eleventh and fourteenth centuries, a slight climate change made it possible to grow vineyards as far as northern France. At the same time, the population of Europe was increasing significantly, and demand for wine grew with the population (Phillips 2016, 34–35). Women are visible in the records as vineyard workers and as owners or renters of vineyards. A 1264 list of renters from the Cistercian abbey of Saint-Antoine, northwest of Paris, shows several women renting land from the nuns for viticulture. These women were likely to have been widows, and some were labeled with their husbands' names rather than their own. The rents ranged from very cheap—from half a **penny** for one-quarter **arpent** of vineyard, about half an acre—to very expensive, 300 pennies for one-third of an arpent of established vines. The property rented to women was generally on the cheaper side, one or two pennies (Berman 2018, 1–3).

Wine was widely traded around Europe, so townswomen would probably have been able to buy it readily. It was usually drunk new and was not kept for long because it rapidly turned acidic and sour, especially when exposed to air. The *Ménagier de Paris*, writing to a young wife, suggested a method for opening a wine cask without letting in enough air to sour it and also gave her instructions on what to do if wine went bad. Exactly what made wine "bad" for the medieval palate is unclear, but it suggested adding bags of spices to overcome the strong odor (Hammond 1993, 57–58). If wine turned into vinegar, it had many uses in the medieval household, including wound dressing, cooking, and cleaning.

UPPER-CLASS FOOD AND FEASTS

In large noble houses, feeding the family, retainers, and staff was a major production. Cooks ran large staffs and oversaw many people, and were more often men than women. The household accounts of Dame Alice de Bryene in 1412–1413 reveal a complex, expensive system that served as many as three hundred people at one time. Dame Alice was born in the late fourteenth century at the **manor** of Acton in Suffolk, England, and died in 1435. Through her marriage and the inheritance of property left by her mother and grandmother, she controlled around six thousand acres altogether and had an income of around £400 a year (around $576,000, in 2022 money) (Nye 2022). The accounts show that she spent about 40 percent of this income on maintaining the household, and 65 percent of that amount on food and drink. A usual meal at Alice de Bryene's house consisted of a two-pound loaf of bread for each guest and three and a half pints of ale. The estate at Acton maintained its own bakery and brewery. More important guests received wine instead of ale. To this was added meat, shellfish, fresh and dried fish, cheese, and vegetables. On special occasions, when a very important person was present, Dame Alice added such delicacies

Servants prepare a large feast in the margins of a medieval Book of Psalms. (The British Library/StockphotoPro)

as suckling pigs. High-ranking guests might come from neighboring **manors** for celebrations, while on the lower end of the social-class spectrum, the estate often paid laborers and artisans in food (Carlin and Rosenthal 2003, 135–136).

At an aristocratic medieval feast, everyone ate together in a large space, usually the great hall of a **manor** house or castle. The highest-ranking guests sat together at a table at one end of the hall. This table was covered by one or more linen cloths, smoothed with a rod to lie flat, and was sometimes physically raised up from the rest of the room by a dais. Each guest received a large, flat piece of bread called a trencher that served as a plate. The finest crust of this bread was reserved for the lord—the "upper crust." (Peasants often used trenchers made of wood, since they did not have the luxury of trencher-style bread.) Utensils consisted of a spoon, a napkin, and a knife, often the diner's personal eating knife (forks were not used until the sixteenth century). The next luxury item was the salt cellar, which was often a large, ornamental vessel that was placed near the lord before being passed down the table. Guests washed their hands with scented warm water and dried them carefully before the first course was served. During the meal, servants watched closely to remove trenchers that had become wet or food that the diners had finished, because what was left would be given to the poor. At the end of the meal, they served fruit and cheese, small sweet or savory cakes, and sometimes a spiced wine called hippocras. The guests then washed their hands again (Hammond 1993, 109–117).

Since diners at medieval tables often shared dishes and cups, the manners required were also elaborate. Courtesy books, beginning in the thirteenth century, specified how guests were to act at the table and differentiated the upper class from the lower. The higher-ranked guests were, the closer they sat to the high table, and the more elaborate the dishes they were given to eat. Diners were offered water and a towel to wash their hands before the meal. Since most people shared dishes with others, it was considered rude to take the nicest bits, and overfilling the mouth, speaking with the mouth full, and spitting were denounced. Diners were told not to wipe their knives on the tablecloth or blow their noses into their napkins. When taking salt, the diner was to take the salt and put it on the trencher before dipping meat into it. Sticking one's finger into nose or mouth, naturally, was forbidden (Hammond 1993, 116–119). Such manners were not only more hygienic but emphasized the social differences between the well-bred and the ordinary.

Recipe books from this period were written for the convenience of cooks in noble houses and usually contained instructions for making elaborate ceremonial dishes rather than everyday food. Medieval recipes were not as formal and uniform as modern recipes, with few measurements or complete instructions listed. These recipes used large numbers of expensive ingredients. Sugar, which was considered a spice in the Middle Ages, appeared along with pepper, ginger, cinnamon, grains of paradise (a pepper substitute related to ginger), and many others that would have been imported and purchased at a premium price. Officials in the noble kitchen also had the responsibility of producing huge edible sculptures made of bread, cake, or marzipan called "subtleties," which were served between courses. Sometimes such sculptures illustrated famous stories or religious subjects (Hammond 1993, 130, 142–143).

CLOTH PRODUCTION

Piers Plowman, a poetic work from the fourteenth century, advised: "Wives and widows, spin wool and flax" (Larrington 1995, 89). The work of women is often symbolized by the image of a woman spinning; images of a woman with a **spindle** and a **distaff** (a stick holding fiber that was ready to be spun) are in medieval manuscripts. The image of the spinning woman was so pervasive that it has survived in figurative language: a "spinster" is an old word for an unmarried woman, and the female side of a family tree is still called the "distaff side." For much of the Middle Ages, housewives spent considerable time spinning thread to be woven into cloth and carried their spindles and distaffs with them as they did other chores. The instrument of spinning was called a drop **spindle**. It was a wooden rod with a whorl on the end that was spun quickly at the end of the fiber, twisting the wool or flax into thread or yarn.

Cloth production as a part of women's work developed over time but was consistently present. There is clear evidence that textile workshops, called gynaecea (**gynaeceum** in the singular), from the Greek word *gyne*, woman, persisted from the ancient world and were common on large estates in the early Middle Ages. Workers were quartered in long, narrow buildings where the women both lived and worked. One example of such a building from Germany was twenty-nine meters long (about 95 feet) and six meters (about nineteen feet) wide, suggesting a capacity of twenty-two to twenty-four women. Gynaecea often owed their owners or landlords specific amounts of thread or cloth. In some instances, rents were even paid with cloth (Uitz 1988, 16–17).

In excavations from early England in the fifth and sixth centuries, loom weights are often discovered on the floors of houses, meaning some cloth was made at home. The rows of loom weights are long enough that archaeologists have suggested that weaving involved more than one person at a time. As the industry became more complex during the seventh to ninth centuries, female slaves worked at the production of wool and linen cloth in larger workshops. There is evidence, however, that upper-class women were still required to know the basics of cloth production and that spinning, weaving, and sewing still took place at home (Henry 2005, 51–55). The emperor Charlemagne (763–814 CE) forbade his female workers from working at chores on Sunday, such as washing clothes, shearing sheep, and cutting out patterns to sew—everyday chores in the household and the gynaeceum (Herlihy 1990, 34). His biographer, Einhard, also stated that the emperor made his daughters learn to spin, weave and work wool so that they might avoid idleness (Einhard and Notker the Stammerer 2008, 32).

As towns became larger and more important locations for production of cloth, textile production became more specialized. Women still did the majority of the spinning, even in towns, where individual households might contract with weavers to produce a certain amount of thread. After the spinning wheel was introduced

This fourteenth-century embroidered purse depicts scenes from the popular medieval story "Patient Griselda." Here the noble Count rides away with Griselda after their marriage. (Gift of Mrs. Edward S. Harkness, 1927. The Metropolitan Museum of Art.)

in the thirteenth century, spinning became a more sedentary activity but remained women's work. Weaving, however, gradually became a male profession. In the eleventh century, the invention of the horizontal treadle loom allowed for longer pieces of cloth to be produced. It was significantly faster than the vertical looms of the earlier centuries. Rabbi Rashi of Troyes (1040–1105) distinguished between women's vertical looms and the horizontal looms that two men at a time worked with their feet, which suggests that both women and men worked in weaving, but that men used the heavier commercial treadle loom (Henry 2005, 55). This heavy loom was more effective in producing larger lengths of cloth that could be exported. By the late Middle Ages, just as brewing had become a commercial business, weaving was professionalized and became mostly a man's job.

Beginning in the eleventh century, better quality, softer fabric became available in England as a result of sheep breeding. The

The Bayeux Embroidery, stitched by unknown artists in the eleventh century, is likely to have been produced by women. (Jorisvo/Dreamstime.com)

new breeds of sheep had wool that was longer in fibers and softer once spun. These soft fibers, combined with the treadle loom, made luxury fabrics available for export, and a cloth called scarlet became the standard for luxury around Europe. Scarlet was woven tightly, fulled (a process to make the fabric become felt), brushed, and trimmed to make a velvet-like consistency. It was customarily dyed bright red, which is where our word *scarlet* originates. Materials and techniques for dyeing cloth also developed beginning in the eleventh century. In addition to the bright red or "sanguine" color of scarlet, it was possible for most well-off people to have garments dyed blue or green with woad (a plant from the cabbage family used for its dark blue color). By the end of the Middle Ages, the most popular colors were dark blue, green, and black. Women were certainly central to the development of such dyes, though documentary evidence is scarce for the period (Piponnier and Mane 1997, 15–17).

Fine needlework such as embroidery was considered to be a virtuous pastime for upper-class women throughout the medieval period. In the biographies of two future abbesses, Herlindis and Renula, a Carolingian-era author wrote of their education in fine work, including sewing gold thread and pearls, so that "they turned into artisans accomplished in extraordinary methods." Unlike the lower-class women who provided basic linens, women who did such skilled work produced the vestments and luxury items used in churches (Garver 2009, 224). The most famous piece of medieval needlework is the Bayeux Embroidery (sometimes incorrectly called a tapestry), stitched by unknown artisans in the late eleventh century to commemorate the conquest of England by William of Normandy. There are many theories about who made the embroidery, but considering that needlework was uniformly women's work, it is likely to have been the work of women.

TOWN WORK IN THE MIDDLE AGES

Women in towns were, of course, obliged to do many of the same tasks as their counterparts in rural areas, and in the early Middle Ages, there was very little difference between them. As towns became larger and more focused on trade and commerce in the later Middle Ages, the roles women were able to take within them changed, just as in weaving and in brewing. The most important economic innovations of this period were the trade organizations called **guilds**. Guilds provided for the apprenticeship of children to guild members to train up new members of the organization, like the guild of goldsmiths or weavers, and guaranteed the quality of the items produced by guild members. Guilds controlled the apprenticeship system, in which children were legally transferred to a workshop to learn a craft or trade under the guidance of a master. Upon being released from their apprenticeships about ten years later, they could petition to join the guild as masters themselves, or they could be required to spend some years as a journeyman, or wage laborer, until eligible to apply for membership (Tierney 1999, 280). Guild membership, however, was often restricted to men, except in cases where the craft was thought to be women's work, like embroidery. In many places, women could have only limited access to the advantages of the organizations except through their husbands. The context of their work was often the household rather than the guild hall.

Guild rules sometimes allowed widows to continue to run their husbands' businesses as guild members and to train up their children and other apprentices (Uitz 1988, 51). In town charters, some lords guaranteed the rights of children and widows to inherit the goods and privileges of their husbands and fathers without paying an inheritance tax. For example, in the twelfth century, Duke Conrad of Zähringen guaranteed the inhabitants of Freiburg im

Breisgau that "If one of my burghers dies, his wife and children should inherit everything: everything her husband leaves behind belongs to them and cannot be sequestered by others" (Uitz 1988, 20). These widows had rights to guild advantages that were not often extended to other women.

Craftswomen do show up in the sources. The Paris tax registers (*livres de la taille*) of 1300 show women working as flax beaters (preparing flax for spinning by beating and carding the fibers) and as wool spinners. The largest trade for women in fourteenth-century Paris was silk spinning, which was divided into two types of thread that were spun on different sized spindles. Those craftswomen who spun on larger spindles were completely independent and could train apprentices and their children, including their husbands' children from previous marriages; those who spun on smaller spindles did not have the same rights. There were thirty-six female silk-spinning masters in the 1300 tax roll. Silk weaving was also a primarily female occupation, as was purse-making; in fact, in the total of 321 professions listed in the Paris documents for the second half of the thirteenth and early fourteenth centuries, 108 named female workers in a broad variety of roles, including master (Uitz 1988, 52). Although men dominated the most high-status jobs in the silk industry such as gold beating, women silk workers were high status compared to other working women. Women artisans made gold thread by wrapping beaten metal foil around a wool center and worked at twisting silk fibers together into yarn, a process called "throwing" (Farmer 2017, 111). A lower-level "throwster" might still be very poor, for many of them did piece work only as they could and made very little money. In contrast, a female mercer, or cloth seller, could make herself very rich.

Paris, however, was a unique example, because its high population increased demand for luxury goods and may have increased opportunities for women to be involved in trades such as silk production (Uitz 1988, 53). Paris had five female-dominated guilds, but London did not have any. Membership in the Paris guilds for women was fairly easy to obtain because the level of expertise required was not very high; the statutes of the silk thrower's guild, for example, included only the requirement that the craftswoman be willing to follow guild rules. By contrast, the men's guild of makers of silk cloth and velvet specified that all practitioners had to be experts in the craft. This included not only an examination by the masters of the craft in Paris but also a sum of money paid to the guild and to the king for the privilege of operating (Farmer 2017, 115).

For women in England, the ability to engage in trade and to conduct business was governed by laws that placed married women as dependents of their husbands. A woman who did business under this law was called a *feme covert* (literally, a "covered woman"), who was legally under her husband's control and finances. A *feme sole*, on the other hand, was a woman who did business under her own control. Such women were often unmarried, but English law also allowed married women to operate as *femes soles* when they practiced a craft separate from that of their husbands, like brewing or silk work. London custom also allowed a widow one-third of her husband's property after his death, which she could take with her into a new marriage or a craft as a *feme sole* (Hanawalt 2007, 6–7).

CREATING AND TRANSMITTING KNOWLEDGE: BOOK PRODUCTION

Although women lagged behind men in literacy in the Middle Ages, there is considerable evidence that women worked as scribes. In the early Middle Ages, literate nuns copied religious manuscripts for themselves and for each other and continued to do so once vernacular (non-Latin) books became more common in the later period. Apart from those famous nuns who wrote their own works, like Hildegard of Bingen and Herrad of Hohenburg (see chapter seven), these writers copied major works for both inside and outside the monastery. In the late eighth to early ninth centuries, the nuns of Chelles, a Benedictine monastery in northern France, were widely acknowledged for their ability at copying. They produced a six-volume set of Augustine of Hippo's *Commentary on the Psalms* for Archchancellor Hildebold of Cologne, along with many other works. The handwriting of the nuns of Chelles was so distinctive that some Chelles manuscripts are identified in libraries simply by the script. Many other nunneries had resident copyists. The nuns of the Benedictine monastery at Admont and the Premonstratensian house of Schäftlarn in twelfth-century Bavaria collaborated with the men in their double monasteries to copy numerous works and also authored new works on their own (Beach 2000).

When a particularly important person died in a monastery, some monasteries (male and female) sent messengers to travel between churches and monasteries to ask for prayers for the dead person's soul. Such messengers carried documents called mortuary rolls. Each place they visited added written prayers to the original document that carried the announcement of the death. When they ran out of parchment at the bottom, they sewed on another piece, so that the rolls became very long—some as long as thirty meters. One particularly fine example is the mortuary roll of Abbess Matilda of Holy Trinity, Caen (d. 1113), which is about twenty-two meters long (about 72 feet) (Leslie 1993, 116–124). The testimonies added to the parchment roll from women's monasteries are likely to have been the work of the nuns.

Outside the cloister, as literacy and vernacular literature became more common, laywomen also copied manuscripts for themselves and each other. The Findern Manuscript (Cambridge University Library MS Ff.1.6), which contains the handwriting of over forty scribes, is an interesting example compiled in the late fifteenth and early sixteenth centuries. The manuscript belonged to an English gentry family, and several women were closely involved with its compilation. It contains poetry, romances, and some well-known works from famous authors such as Geoffrey Chaucer (ca. 1340–1400) and John Lydgate (ca. 1370–1450), but it also has unique examples of poetry. Some characteristics of the manuscript, such as the feminine pronouns used, give hints that the women revised and edited texts along with copying them. Four women's names also appear in the manuscript, but it is not clear whether they were copying someone else's work or setting down their own (Hanson-Smith 1979).

CAREGIVING AND HEALING

Women worked as caregivers and healers both as part of household labor and in public. Although the sources are far fewer for the early period than for the late Middle Ages, in the household the primary healer was always female. Healing lent itself to the daily activity of the household, as the preparations of foods and medicines were often identical and took place in the same kitchens. Herbs brewed or preserved by themselves, called "simples," were given for everyday illnesses from sore throats to joint pain and could be eaten or drunk, plastered on with a bandage, rubbed on as an oil, or added to bathwater. They could also be combined together for more complicated medications.

Prayers and incantations were often used in healing. An early example of a medical text, the Anglo-Saxon *Lacnunga* (tenth century), includes charms that instruct the healer to concoct a number of herbs over a fire into a thick soup called a pottage, and then to say a prayer over the pottage before giving it to the sick person to eat. The prayers in the *Lacnunga* are mostly Christian, but there are many phrases that we would consider magical; in fact, the distinction between religious and magical language seems to have been irrelevant to the people who used the remedies. The text does not specify who was doing the cooking and praying, leaving open the possibility that women were a central part of this healing process.

Women learned recipes and caregiving techniques from other women in their communities, particularly from their own families. In the later Middle Ages, aristocratic women wrote to one another about health issues and exchanged recipes that still survive. Such letters also tell us that upper-class women sometimes stayed in one another's households for medical care, especially when an illness was prolonged or if they were widowed and did not have other family to take care of them. Although the passing of medical recipes from one woman to another has to have been largely oral rather than written, the letter evidence shows a strong network between aristocratic women that must mirror the exchange everyday women did on a daily basis. Some recipes may have had very long lives, as they were passed from mother to daughter and from neighbor to neighbor. Among them were cosmetic recipes as well—often to whiten the skin or make the hair more blond (Cabré 2008, 38, 48).

The most visible place to find female healers was certainly in women's health and fertility. Pregnancy and childbirth were women's business throughout the Middle Ages, although the university-trained medical community—all male—attempted to exercise increasing control over the process as the period progressed. (See chapter three for more information about midwifery.) The twelfth-century compilation known as the *Trotula,* one part of which was probably written by a female healer named Trota, gives numerous remedies for childbirth complications. The recipe evidence also suggests women healers continued to provide pregnancy and childbirth care throughout the period. (See chapter two for more information about the *Trotula,* and chapter seven for more information about Trota.)

An interesting example of a female healer survives in a court case that the medical faculty of the University of Paris brought against a woman named Jacoba Felicie in the fourteenth century. Jacoba had been practicing medicine, including examining patients' urine and prescribing drugs, in and around Paris for some time. University-trained physicians, all men, were suing her to make her stop practicing. Numerous witnesses attested to Jacoba's success in treating their illnesses. Some of the witnesses had even consulted professional physicians before consulting her. Jacoba argued before the court that not only had she been successful in treating the sick but also that her sex allowed her to visit and heal women who were too modest to show their illnesses to strange men. She also suggested that allowing her to practice medicine was a lesser evil than letting such modest women die of their illnesses (Wallis 2010, 366–369). The court did not agree: Jacoba was excommunicated and forbidden to practice medicine. Her story, however, may show us that some medieval people were comfortable with female healers and sought them out for treatment.

CONCLUSION

The work that medieval women certainly conformed to some of our modern expectations: cooking, child care, and household management were the central occupation of many. Managing the household, however, did not necessarily mean that a woman worked only at household tasks. Many women worked at least partly outside of the home, and a few became successful professional women. The gender binary of the Middle Ages restricted their ability to participate in some trades, but the wives and daughters of guildsmen were involved in making the household's livelihood work. In the next chapter, we will explore the lives of upper-class women, who also performed important functions both inside and outside the home.

4

NOBLE WOMEN

This chapter's purpose is to discuss the everyday lives of upper-class and elite women in the European Middle Ages. We know more about noble women than we do about women of lower social status because upper-class women feature in documents from the period more often. Such documents have allowed historians to look for the places in which women exercised everyday power, controlled property, and exerted influence on their communities. Their power depended on either their birth families or the families into which they married. Some aristocratic women had only a small circle of influence, but other elite women and queens convened royal courts, carried out the duties of lordship, and influenced the larger society and culture around them. When we think about upper-class women in the Middle Ages today, we may be tempted to be distracted by the privileges they enjoyed. However, dynastic demands, fertility, and the responsibilities of ruling could all pose difficult problems for medieval aristocratic women.

Until recently, scholars argued that the early Middle Ages offered more opportunities for noble women to exercise power than the later Middle Ages. They noted that noble women controlled property and took public roles more often and with greater impact before the rise of centralizing state institutions in the twelfth century gradually excluded women from positions of power. Recently, however, scholarship has begun to understand women's power as a normal part of upper-class rule throughout the Middle Ages. Kings in the Middle Ages relied heavily on their queens, who sometimes represented the most loyal and consistent of political allies (Jestice 2018, 3). Later medieval queens and noblewomen, over whom their husbands and the church had more control, also exercised power over both people and property. Individual aristocratic women could play important roles in their communities by using their personal property and influence to form relationships, but women also ruled directly over territories, controlled armies, and made laws.

MARRIAGES AND CHILDREN

From the time an upper-class girl was born, the most significant question for her family was whom she might marry. Marriages among upper-class people were formed in large part by dynastic and political concerns: young women from noble families were valuable resources for their kin in making alliances and forging relationships. Thus, a young woman entered marriage not only on her own behalf but also as the representative of her lineage and its power and influence. Women brought property, prestige, and political weight into marriages.

Royal marriages in particular, according to commentators of the period, were designed to extend the control of the monarch over other territories and fulfill dynastic expectations. Kings looked for potential brides who had control over specific lands or who offered connections to desirable lineages. Royal brides sometimes came from very far away. The second wife of the German emperor Otto II (955–983) was a Greek princess from Constantinople named Theophanu; his father, Otto I, had been married to an Anglo-Saxon princess, Edgitha. Closer to home, territorial ambitions might provoke marriage negotiations. Anne of Brittany (1477–1514) was married first to Charles VIII of France and then, after his death, to his younger brother Louis XII. Anne's attraction for the monarchy was her status as the heir to Duke Francis of Brittany, a territory coveted by the French crown (Williams and Echols 1994, 184). Neither Anne nor the two princes were consulted more than perfunctorily about their marriages. Upper-class young people did not expect to choose their own spouses, and love matches were nearly nonexistent.

Young noble girls were sometimes betrothed as small children when politics or family dynastic concerns made it desirable. Some young, betrothed women went to live with their future husbands' families to learn the language and customs of their new homes. Eleanor, one of the daughters of Henry II of England and Eleanor of Aquitaine, journeyed to Spain in 1170, when she was nine, to grow up at the court of her future husband, the king of Castile. Inviting a young bride to come to her future husband's home country allowed her to become at home there. It also weakened the family ties to her birth family, making her more dependent on her husband's family and removing outside influences—advantages that her in-laws might find attractive.

Betrothal at a young age did not necessarily mean that young women would be sexually active young as well, though we have already seen the example of Margaret Beaufort, who was married at twelve and a mother at thirteen. Dynastic pressures and political alliances were the most common motivators for trading young girls between noble houses. If the children were too young for canonical marriage (twelve for girls, fourteen for boys), a betrothal could hold an alliance together until the children were old enough for marriage.

It was not unusual in the Middle Ages for aristocratic women and men to be married multiple times. High rates of death in childbirth meant that upper-class men married younger women repeatedly in search of a fertile relationship. A woman who was widowed, controlled property in her own right, and was still young enough to bear children could experience intense pressure from her family to remarry. Many upper-class women had stories not unlike that of Elizabeth of Clare, Lady deBurgh, who was born in 1295 and had been married and widowed three times before she was twenty-seven. One of three sisters, she spent much of her time dealing with noble infighting and lawsuits over the inheritance she was owed from her father, the earl of Gloucester. She was even briefly imprisoned at the abbey of Barking and at York Castle while fighting against her brothers-in-law for control of her patrimony. It is perhaps not surprising that after her tumultuous early career and third widowhood, Elizabeth of Clare decided to remain unmarried and lived on for more than thirty years, performing good works and eventually endowing a college at Cambridge, Clare College (Labarge 1986, 89–91).

Aristocratic women who married were expected to produce children, and they did, sometimes in numbers that surprise us today. Blanche of Castile, queen of France (1188–1252), had twelve children by her husband Louis VIII, eight of whom survived to adulthood; her daughter-in-law Marguerite of Provence (1221–1295) had eleven. When there were few sons, dynastic interests could be complicated. Queen Matilda of Scotland, wife of King Henry I of England (ca. 1080–1118), had only two children; after her son died in a shipwreck in 1120, his sister, also named Matilda, claimed the English throne against her cousin Stephen, and threw England into a civil war that lasted from 1135 until 1154 (Labarge 1986, 49).

Childless queens and aristocratic women were faced with political and personal difficulties, including repudiation by their husbands. Emperor Henry II of Germany (973–1024) surprised his nobles when he refused to annul his marriage to his wife Kunigunde (975–1040) despite her childlessness. Later stories about Kunigunde explained that the emperor and empress had taken a vow of chastity; according to legend, Kunigunde even walked across red-hot plow blades to prove she was not guilty of adultery. Both emperor and empress later were venerated as saints by the Roman Catholic church. When Henry died in 1024, however, the imperial crown went to a new bloodline with the election of Conrad II in 1027—an explanation of why, perhaps, the critics of Kunigunde had wanted Henry to repudiate her.

DOWRY, DOWER, AND INHERITANCE

One way in which we can understand the particular roles and expectations of medieval aristocratic women is to examine their connection to property: whether they owned property in their own right and could freely sell or give it away or whether their property concerns were owned and managed by male relatives. Medieval elite women had much greater power over property than historians once thought, though their control of property was often dictated by the various customs that covered **dowry**, **dower**, and inheritance.

As discussed in chapter two, aristocratic families in the High Middle Ages provided dowries that went with their daughters into marriage. Dowry property could be land, but it often also included personal possessions such as furniture and clothing or simply money. This property was the woman's personal property and, in theory, could not be alienated (bought or sold) without her permission. In some places, the dowry was supplemented by dower property from the groom's family, which often represented around one-quarter to one-half of the groom's possessions or future inheritance. Husband and wife often managed these properties together, though in some places and times, the husband was responsible for managing the property for as long as he lived. Dowry and dower property were kept to guarantee the woman's security if she were widowed. Depending on the local laws and customs surrounding widows, she might then pass to the guardianship of another male relative or be able to administer the property on her own behalf.

Women often passed dowry property and personal belongings to their daughters. It is perhaps not surprising that furniture and other personal property would be passed down through female heirs (what was a son to do with a chest full of dresses?) but landed property also could be passed from mother to daughter, a method by which family land could be maintained down the matrilineal side. The viscounty of Mareuil-sur-Ay, in the Champagne region of France, was passed down through three generations of women in the twelfth century (Evergates 1999, 92). Some historians have noted a pattern in which families passed land to sons but money and movables to daughters. In Salerno, Italy, in the twelfth century, for example, daughters received money in greater amounts than sons, while sons inherited landed property more often than daughters (Bennett and Karras 2013, 334).

Widows could also exercise freedom to control personal property, even in those regions that demanded that women be under guardianship. The *Customs of Amalfi*, an Italian legal code from the thirteenth century, stated that a married woman had custody of her husband's property to manage for the children as long as she remained unmarried. "A married woman after the death of her husband is lady and mistress of the property of her husband . . . . That is, if she does not marry nor go to a second marriage" (Bennett and Karras 2013, 335–336). Although the widow in this circumstance had to have approval from a judge to sell any of her husband's property, she was able to do so if her living expenses required it. Widows in such cases were expected to maintain the living expenses of their husband's heirs, whether they were her own children or not, from that property.

As in the example above, husbands sometimes specified in wills that their wives could enjoy the marital property only so long as they remained unmarried. Dower property was supposed to provide for widowhood without such a restriction. Even so, widowed women sometimes had trouble gaining control of property, especially when they clashed with their husbands' heirs. Clemence of Burgundy (ca. 1078–1133), wife of Count Robert II of Burgundy, had several children by Robert, who died in 1111. She remained influential throughout the reign of her son Baldwin VII. When Clemence wanted to exert control over her dower property, however, her son balked, not wanting his inheritance to be reduced by his mother's claims. Clemence demanded that her son turn over the land or face a lawsuit. Bishop Lambert of Arras intervened by sending a letter to Baldwin to urge him to comply with his mother's wishes. "We ask of your excellency so as not to provoke your mother to rage, but [follow] the command of our Lord who said, 'Honor your father and your mother.'" Baldwin was forced to agree. Clemence continued her control and influence over Flanders well after Baldwin VII's death in 1119, retiring to her dower lands toward the end of her life (Nicholas 1999, 118–119).

ROYAL POWER AND REGENCY

In the Middle Ages, noble mothers were expected to oversee their children's interests while their children were still young. In the Merovingian period in the sixth and seventh centuries, the various Frankish kingdoms were often in conflict with each other, and some Frankish kings had both multiple wives and concubines. The noble women of this period jockeyed for position within the courts and against one another to take advantage of the access to power that such positions could give them. The most notorious of these Frankish queens was Fredegund (d. 597), who began as a servant to Audovera, the wife of King Chilperic I of Neustria (ca. 539–584). She persuaded Chilperic to put aside the queen in her favor and, eventually, to put aside his sons by Audovera in favor of her own children. When Chilperic died in 584, Fredegund took over the administration of Neustria on behalf of her infant son, Clothar, and maintained her power as **regent** until her death in 597, when Clothar was thirteen years old. The Frankish bishop who wrote about Fredegund, Gregory of Tours, deplored her ruthlessness, which even extended to deliberate assassinations of her political rivals, including Chilperic's other sons (Wemple 1981, 64–65).

Medieval queens sometimes also took on the office of **regent** when their husbands were incapacitated or when the monarch was very young. When the Emperor Otto II of Germany (955–983) died at the age of twenty-eight, he left a minor heir, his three-year-old son, Otto III (980–1002). After a brief conflict, Otto III's mother, Theophanu (ca. 955–990), stepped into the role of regent for her young son. When she died in 990, Otto III was still only nine years old, and the power of the regency was taken by his grandmother, Adelheid (931–999), who managed the German kingdom for her grandson until he came of age in 995. Both Theophanu and Adelheid used their power over the high-ranking nobles and churchmen of the period to maintain their control over the sprawling German empire.

During the era of the Crusades, some queens and noblewomen took on the tasks of governing their lands on behalf of husbands or sons who had gone to fight in the Middle East. Blanche of Castile managed France while her son Louis VIII (1187–1226) was a child and, after he died, on behalf of his younger brother, Louis IX (1214–1270). Blanche's regency over Louis IX lasted eight years, until he reached his majority. During that time, she personally led armies to bring some of Louis's most difficult nobles into agreements with the French crown. Afterward, then in her sixties, she ruled France while Louis IX went on Crusade. He was captured and held for ransom by the Egyptian army in 1250, and Blanche was responsible for raising the astronomical sum of four hundred thousand **livres** tournois to release him. Blanche died in 1252 at the Cistercian abbey of Maubuisson. Guillaume de Nangis, one of the chroniclers of the period, described her: "She was the wisest of all women of her time, and all good things came to the realm of France while she was alive" (Labarge 1986, 52–55).

Despite the considerable evidence for royal women actively exerting power in their own right in the Middle Ages, the literature that these women probably read or had access to was firmly in favor of the submission of women to men. Standards for women's conduct were different from men's, and corresponded to a stereotype of a good, gentle, amiable, and ultimately subordinate woman. We will go through and discuss a few.

CONDUCT OF AN ARISTOCRATIC LADY: IDEALS

Noblewomen were encouraged to pursue many of the same virtues as women of the lower classes, but there were also virtues specifically advised for aristocratic women. A fourteenth-century French knight, Geoffrey de la Tour Landry, wrote a book for his two daughters to advise them on good behavior that is known as the *Book of the Knight of the Tower.* The book was copied many times: twenty-one manuscripts are still extant, with numerous early printed copies in German and English, as well as its original French. Like the *Book of the Three Virtues* by Christine de Pisan and the *Ménagier de Paris*, this book encourages women to pay attention to the careful maintenance of their souls, as well as giving romantic advice, good housekeeping tips, and a guide to making a respectable marriage.

In his book, Sir Geoffrey told his daughters a story about a young woman whom he rejected for his own wife because she was too flirtatious when they met. He emphasized meekness, chastity, fasting, and prayer. He was particularly hard on women for what he considered frivolous vanity and love of fine clothing: "Such fancy clothing could be compared to the spider who makes his net to take flies" (Barnhouse 2006, 122). He cautioned his daughters not to pluck their eyebrows, not to use cosmetics, and not to treat their hair with anything that would change its color. Beauty, by Geoffrey's definition, encouraged pride, which led to more sins, several of which he covered explicitly in sections of his book. By his account, the pride and fashionable clothing of women had been one of the factors that had led to the Great Flood in the Old Testament.

Pride and Humility

In the High Middle Ages preachers cautioned their parishioners to avoid seven "deadly sins": lust, gluttony, avarice (greed), envy, pride, wrath, and sloth (laziness). According to some writers, pride was the worst of the seven deadly sins because it could lead to any of the other sins; a woman who was prideful, the Knight of the Tower suggested, could cause divine justice to come down on her community. Similarly, in Christine de Pisan's *Book of the Three Virtues*, written around 1405, Christine admonished a wealthy lady not to give in to pride: "When the princess or high-born lady wakes up from her sleep in the morning and finds herself lying in her bed between soft sheets . . . with ladies and maids-in-waiting around her, intent on catering to her every need . . . temptation may often assail her, singing this song: 'Dear God! Is there in this world a lady greater than you, or more worthy?'" (Blumenfeld-Kosinski 1997, 158). Christine advised the princess to meditate on religious subjects in order to resist the temptations that would assail her as she went about her day.

Christine de Pisan's advice for the upper-class woman also included instructions for practicing prudence and sobriety, two qualities that "are especially necessary for a princess and any noble lady, indeed for any woman who desires honor." The prudent noblewoman would keep her emotions in check, speak softly and politely, and disassociate herself from anything coarse or vulgar. She would also forgive her husband when he was "perverse, rude and unloving" to her and be obedient and loving to him at all times (Blumenfeld-Kosinski 1997, 166). The double standard that allowed upper-class men to have multiple sexual relationships often forced noble wives to accept the mistresses and concubines of their husbands.

Obedience

Geoffrey Chaucer (ca. 1340–1400) and Giovanni Boccaccio (1313–1375), two influential writers of the fourteenth century, both told the story known as "Patient Griselda" in their major works, the *Canterbury Tales* and *The Decameron*. In the story, a wealthy count chose a poor woman named Griselda to be his wife but then decided to put her through a series of tests to prove her worthiness. The tests included taking away her children and telling her that he had them executed and commanding her to prepare his household for another bride who would take her place. Griselda bore all of this suffering without complaining, even though the nobles at the court considered her husband to be wicked and cruel. At the end of the story, the husband returned both the children, revealing that the "new bride" he had commanded her to serve was, in fact, their daughter. Griselda and her husband were reunited, and everyone rejoiced that Griselda's obedience and patience had been rewarded. Reading this story in a modern context is complicated. The count's actions seem arbitrary and unfair, but many people in the Middle Ages read the story as an allegory. Griselda represented a human soul who was being tested by God rather than by her husband, and the story's message was the patient bearing of suffering in the face of divine will.

Despite this interpretation, the character of Griselda featured in a number of messages preached to medieval women, and the story was told and retold in numerous languages and contexts. There is even a fourteenth-century purse embroidered with scenes from the story in the Metropolitan Museum of Art in New York. The author of the *Ménagier de Paris*, writing around 1393, encouraged a young wife to emulate Griselda because he believed obedience was the key to having a husband's love (Greco and Rose 2009, 119). Elite women were also admonished to imitate Griselda in obedience to their husbands in everyday life. Writers who preached to women argued that even if noble women had power and influence, they were to refrain from exerting that power contrary to their husbands' wishes. How often women refrained from using power, for whatever reason, is impossible to tell.

Peacemaking

In practice, power relationships between couples were often complex. Christine de Pisan admonished the wise princess to be a peacemaker, "thinking of the great evil and infinite cruelties, losses, deaths, and destruction of land and people that result from war whose outcome is often terrible" (Blumenfeld-Koskinski 1997, 163). Christine contrasted the possible outcomes of quarrels between hot-headed princes with the princess's God-given desire to make peace between her lord and others. Queens of the early Middle Ages often advocated for poor and powerless people before their more martial and less sympathetic husbands. The queen's role as a purveyor of mercy continued throughout the medieval period. In a famous example, Philippa of Hainault, Queen of England (ca. 1314–1369), saved the lives of several merchants from Calais. The chronicler Jean Froissart wrote that despite being heavily pregnant, Philippa fell on her knees and begged her husband, Edward III, not to execute the men, who had offered themselves as hostages for the safety of the city. Watching his pregnant wife kneel at his feet overcame King Edward: Philippa convinced him, and she was given custody of the six men, whom she fed, clothed, and then released (Brereton 1978, 109). Her pregnancy made Philippa's intercession particularly powerful. Having fulfilled her requirement to bear a child, she could exercise influence over her husband and his decisions.

Some noblewomen took more active roles in peacemaking. Matilda of Canossa, countess of Tuscany (1046–1115), was a key figure in the eleventh-century Investiture Controversy, in which Emperor Henry IV pitted himself against Pope Gregory VII in a struggle over church authority. Matilda, who supported the papacy in the conflict, arranged for the pope and king to meet at her castle of Canossa in 1073 as a way of ending the conflict before it turned to all-out war. When their agreement fell apart, however, she also became a major player in the ensuing war, even leading troops of her own.

Piety

Every book of advice for noblewomen recommended religious devotion as central to a good and praiseworthy life. In the early Middle Ages, several Merovingian queens were venerated as saints for their piety and for their efforts to convert their non-Christian husbands. Queen Clothilde (ca. 474–545 CE), according to her biographer, "softened the hearts of a pagan and ferocious people, namely the Franks," including her husband Clovis, through her works of piety. It took a battlefield miracle to convince Clovis that Clothilde's god was worthy of his worship; however, when he called on Jesus during a battle, his enemies turned and ran the opposite direction (McNamara, Halborg, and Whatley 1992, 47). Clothilde's biography, written in the Carolingian era (eighth to ninth centuries), portrays her piety as a key facet of her public persona and of her personal power.

Women also chose to forego social position to adopt religious lifestyles. One aristocratic woman, Delphine of Glandèves (1284–1358), pursued a religious life while married to Elzéar, Count of Ariano (1285–1323). Married when they were thirteen and fifteen, respectively, the young couple took vows of chastity. Both spouses were deeply influenced by the Franciscan order (see the next chapter) and wished to live a life of poverty, but their aristocratic lineages demanded that they remain both wealthy and married. After her husband died, Delphine did everything she could to give away her substantial personal property, and took a vow of poverty that led her to recruit her sisters and ladies-in-waiting for a new monastery (Vauchez 1993, 76–77). She understood her own life, which had to be a public one because of her rank, as an opportunity to save the souls of the faithful.

The private devotions of upper-class women in the high and late Middle Ages provoked the production of books of hours, books of prayers that were designed to be read at specific intervals throughout the day. Such books often appear in illustrations of women, including the Virgin Mary, whom artists often portrayed as reading when the angel Gabriel arrived for the Annunciation. Aristocratic women patronized artists who copied and illustrated prayer books. Prayer books were passed down through families, and they were also given as wedding gifts to upper-class brides. Some of these works were heavily and expensively decorated, and some even had portraits of the people who commissioned them. In the *Hours of Catherine of Cleves*, painted in the early fifteenth century, Catherine kneels before the Virgin and Child in the margin of a page covered with her coat of arms, vines and branches, angels, and an owl. Some **books of hours** designed for particular queens had imagery that associated the queen's prayers with her fertility; since fertility was required of every queen, even prayer had an orientation toward childbearing.

DAILY LIFE FOR UPPER-CLASS WOMEN

The Castle

Early castles were principally fortresses, used for defense against attackers, and the great age for castles of this type was the eleventh century. In these castles, everyone slept in one large room, with the best places near the fire kept for the highest-ranking people. By the thirteenth century, however, castles had developed into large stone keeps that featured separate living quarters for the nobles who owned them, their families, and their servants. Such castles frequently had a great hall or chamber, which was used for daily living, dining, and other activities; some servants slept there at night in case they were needed. The noble family had private bedchambers of their own—husbands and wives usually had their own bedrooms—with fireplaces for warmth and privies for convenience. Aristocratic women sometimes had a room with plentiful windows called a solar, a place to work on appropriate projects and to receive guests.

The great hall was the center for meals and daily activities. It usually contained trestle tables that could be moved around to accommodate large or small groups of people for the two meals of the day, dinner at noon and supper around seven o'clock, depending on the season. It also functioned as an office for the nobleman and his wife, and an aristocratic lady might spend most of her day there. The great hall, as well as the bedchambers, could be plastered and brightly painted as a symbol of status, and sometimes woven tapestries were hung on the walls. From this vantage point, the aristocratic woman could supervise all the activities of the household that were her responsibility (Singman 1999, 150–151).

Care of the Aristocratic Household

In the later Middle Ages, documents give us a chance to see much more of the duties and activities of medieval aristocratic women. Much of a medieval elite woman's day could be spent attending to the administration of a property that might be very large and that included servants, artisans, cultivated land, and extensive farms and outbuildings. Feeding, clothing, and organizing all the people on a large estate was a full-time job. Elizabeth Berkeley, countess of Warwick (d. 1422), had fifty people in her employ whom she fed, clothed, and administered, and in one year spent the astonishing sum of £511 6s. 8d. on provisions to feed them (the equivalent of $797,000 in 2022 dollars) (Leyser 1995, 166). Women who were not so wealthy had similar duties toward their households. The *Ménagier de Paris* contains a long section on managing servants, cautioning the young wife to keep close watch on her servants to ensure their good behavior and even to do background checks if there were doubts about their honesty. The text encouraged her to guard the chastity of her female servants and instructed her to be "master, overseer, ruler and chief administrator" of her household (Bayard 2001, 93).

Elite women also handled the education of the children of the household. Households might have many children, those of servants along with the noble family, about whom the lady of the household might have to make decisions. As discussed in chapter two, upper-class children were often raised by nurses, and noble women interacted with their children only on more formal occasions. Queen Margaret of Scotland (1045–1093 CE) received praise from her biographer about her care for her children. He wrote that Margaret encouraged the steward of her household to strike her children when they were disobedient. As a result, her biographer wrote, "they happily and peacefully got on with each other, and the young ones always respected their older siblings" (Skinner and van Houts 2011, 192). In our modern society we no longer advocate hitting children, but medieval parents applied the proverb "Spare the rod and spoil the child" (Proverbs 13:24) literally.

Early religious education was also within a noblewoman's purview; Margaret of Scotland was particularly enthusiastic about increasing her children's knowledge of scripture. Many illustrations from books of hours show images of Saint Anne teaching her daughter, the Virgin Mary, to read. Although male children above age eight were no longer in the nursery, elite mothers might continue to be concerned about their religious beliefs. One of the most touching examples of this concern comes from the ninth century, when Dhuoda, a Frankish noblewoman, dictated a book for her son William to exhort him to take care of his soul. William, aged about seventeen at the time (about 841–843 CE), had not seen his mother for years, because his father had taken him away from her and had ordered her to stay in a city away from him. William had then been traded to Charles the Bald (823–877 CE) as a hostage, and Dhuoda wrote that she hoped her book would stand in for her motherly advice. She addressed William and his little brother, born in 841, who had also been taken from her, to advise them to put their trust in God. "May he make you successful in all your undertakings, and after the end of this life may he bring you rejoicing to heaven among his saints" (Amt 2010, 112). Dhuoda ended her book by asking her sons and anyone who read her book to offer prayers for her soul. (Read more about Dhuoda in chapter seven.)

LEISURE TIME

Medieval aristocratic women who spent most of their time managing their households seldom had the opportunity to spend much time at their leisure. However, the sources show us that aristocrats passed their time in games and pastimes when they had an opportunity to do so. The romance *The Castellan of Coucy*, written ca. 1285 by a writer named Jakèmes, described the after-dinner pastimes of a group of aristocrats: hunting, chess, and backgammon. Playing and gambling with dice spanned all ranks of society, and betting was common for board games as well. Chess and backgammon, in various forms, were very popular among the aristocrats of the middle ages (Gies and Gies 1990, 64). Playing cards, which originated in China, came to Europe in the fourteenth century. There were also games specific to medieval society that are rare today, such as Fox and Geese, a board game in which one piece, representing a fox, tries to jump (and therefore eat) a number of pieces representing geese, while the geese try to capture the fox by surrounding it.

Hunting was an aristocrat's hobby par excellence, and many noble households kept packs of hunting dogs. Although medieval women could and did ride after hounds, the most popular method of hunting for women was falconry. Numerous medieval manuscripts depict women mounted on horseback and carrying small birds of prey, often merlins or peregrine falcons. Since unmarried women and men could ride and hunt together, some medieval romances depicted falconry as an occasion when flirtation and courtly drama could take place. Hunting birds were expensive and difficult to train, so hunting in this way also emphasized wealth and status (Gies and Gies 1990, 69).

Literature

Aristocratic women were often patrons of artists and writers. Beginning in the twelfth century in France, poets and singers—men called troubadours, and women *trobairitz*—began to write poetry containing stories about and advice for lovers. The term for this love, which frequently occurred out of wedlock among people of high rank, was *amour courtois* or "courtly love." Two of the most

A man and woman enjoy a game of chess. (Purchase from the J. H. Wade Fund. The Cleveland Museum of Art.)

notable of the patrons of such literature were Marie, Countess of Champagne (1145–1198), daughter of Eleanor of Aquitaine and King Louis VII of France, and Eleanor of Aquitaine herself (1122–1204). While we do not know details of the lives of many of these writers, their passionate poetry entertained noble courts with songs about love and loss between lovers who were not married or who were married to other people. Andreas Capellanus, a writer in the twelfth century, set down (probably in satire) a series of rules for this kind of love. "Love gets its name (amor) from the word for hook (amus), which means 'to capture' or 'to be captured,' for he who is in love is captured in the chains of desire and wishes to capture someone else with his hook" (Larrington 1995, 61). Once captured, the lover would experience all the symptoms of the "illness" of love: sighing, paleness, and a belief that separation would kill him or her. The poems extolled both the joys of being in love and the pain of losing love. Although some of the poems by *trobairitz* writers were highly stylized, many were frankly sexual in nature and make clear that relationships outside of marriage were a part of the romantic culture of the time, at least in literature. We will look more at some of these female authors in chapter seven.

Popular stories called romances, beginning in the twelfth century, entertained noble audiences with stories about noble knights and the beautiful ladies who fell in love with them because of their prowess at fighting. The authors of romances, especially Marie de France (twelfth century) and Chrétien de Troyes (d. ca. 1180), set many of their stories at the fictional court of King Arthur, whose royal court provided many examples of couples who could be fitted into stories of courtly love and loss. In such stories, the central plot often revolved around a love affair and a grand adventure, with many trials for the hero and descriptions of the fine clothes and luxuries of King Arthur's court. Romances also described the standard of beauty. A beautiful woman was always fair and blond; her eyes were bright and either gray or blue; her lips were red; and she had a slender figure with small breasts but large hips (Phillips 2003, 45). Female saints and martyrs of the Middle Ages, including the Virgin Mary, were even portrayed in art using this ideal. When we think of the Middle Ages today, many of the fanciful images we imagine—knights, dragons, and beautiful ladies—are products of this kind of literature.

The character of the adulterous queen is a frequent presence in romance literature, as in the story of Lancelot and Guinevere or of Tristan and Isolde. Romance writers using several languages adapted these two stories in the twelfth century. Despite the risk that such adultery posed—adultery by the queen could result in a baby not sired by the king—medieval romances emphasized the love triangle created by the relationship rather than its dangers, and the adulterous queens in the stories rarely had children. The queens were, at the same time, deeply flawed people caught in sin and noble victims of a perfect, all-consuming passion. It is not likely that such literature represented reality but, rather, portrayed a fictionalized version of love and splendor that caught the imaginations of its noble audience.

Fashion and Beauty

The beautiful ladies of romances always had long, uncovered hair, but loose hair was the model only for young unmarried girls.

In the early Middle Ages upper-class married women braided or coiled their hair and wore it covered with a linen veil. In the twelfth century, a married woman concealed her hair with a wimple, which covered both the head and neck. In the thirteenth and fourteenth centuries, however, wimples gave way to fashionable hats such as the tall, conical **hennin**, which originated in the early fifteenth century (Piponnier and Mane 1997, 80). We may think of the **hennin** as the quintessential medieval headgear, but it shared space with headgear of many different shapes, including two-pronged shapes and shapes that featured a wing on each side. These headdresses might have thin floating veils made from silk.

With the headgear of the thirteenth and fourteenth centuries came a fashion for hairlessness and high, white foreheads like the women of romances. Fashionable ladies plucked the hair back from their foreheads to display a high forehead and covered their faces with a mixture of lead powder to increase the skin's whiteness. One twelfth-century recipe to whiten the face called for herbs, lead, camphor, borax, and gum arabic combined with rose water. The lady was instructed to take a small piece of this substance and mix it with water before applying it to her face. Her face could also be reddened with a mixture of herbs and rose water (Green 2001, 138–139). Eyebrows could be plucked back to almost nothing to accent the white hairlessness of the face.

Fashion in upper-class clothing changed slowly in the Middle Ages by our standards. In the early Middle Ages, men and women alike wore long gowns that covered linen shirts. Over time, skirts for men went up in length, until, in the fifteenth century, they barely covered the buttocks, and the legs were covered by hose made from wool yarn. Women's dress, meanwhile, changed mainly in the style of neckline and sleeve. Starting in the eleventh century, a long, full overtunic covered the undergown, and, in the twelfth century, women's sleeves became so long that they had to be knotted to keep them from dragging on the floor. The popular garment of this period was the **bliaut**, a tight-fitting dress with belled sleeves. Bodices, generally, were tight and skirts full to emphasize the hips (Piponnier and Mane 1997, 78–79). The sleeves, which were often laced onto the overdress, could be replaced or modified to support the current fashion, while necklines could be altered. In the fourteenth century, other overgarments were replaced by the **houppelande**, a sort of open coat, beautifully decorated and with wide sleeves and a high collar. Women's reached the ground and sometimes had trains, while men's were open in the front and considerably shorter, from

This miniature shows the fashion for elaborate headdresses, pale skin, and high foreheads popular with women in the fourteenth century. (Gift from J. H. Wade. The Cleveland Museum of Art.)

mid-calf to mid-thigh (Piponnier and Mane 1997, 68).

Good outer gowns were expensive and were passed down in wills. An Anglo-Saxon will from the tenth century divided the dead woman's **kirtles** (overdresses) among her kinswomen with great specificity: "And her blue kirtle, which is untrimmed at the bottom, and her best headdresses are to be given to Beornwynn. And her three purple kirtles are to be given to Lufetat and Aelfgifu and Godwif" (Skinner and van Houts 2011, 282). Purple, made from the murex snail native to Lebanon, was a very expensive dye, so it is not surprising that the deceased wanted to pass her fanciest dresses on to other women.

In the later Middle Ages, when a wider range of luxury goods became available as a result of expanding trade, wealthy people had access to silk and might have their clothes sewn with pearls or gold or studded with gemstones. In the thirteenth century, gold leaf was sewn onto ceremonial garments; by the fourteenth century, gold embroidery, made with thread twisted with gold wire, became popular. Other popular materials available to rich buyers included damask, a patterned silk that came from Damascus, and thin silks good for headdresses and veils. It became more common for upper-class people to have large wardrobes and to change those wardrobes more often. Advances in dye technology made more bright and dark colors available: dark red and purple were

Elaborate brooches like this one were often part of the inheritance that young women received from their mothers. (Purchase, Joseph Pulitzer Bequest, 1987. The Metropolitan Museum of Art.)

the most popular, but a green called perse and a dark azure blue were available as well. Noble houses and royal families kept full-time seamstresses, tailors, and furriers, along with armorers and embroiderers, to provide luxury clothes quickly and exclusively (Piponnier and Mane 1997, 28–29, 70–71).

Such luxuries in late medieval fashion had many critics. Moralists preached against the height of headdresses and the length of trains. Some cities and courts passed laws called **sumptuary laws** to rein in both what they considered to be excessive luxury and to ensure that lower-class people were easy to distinguish from upper-class people. The Venice statutes of 1299 forbade anyone to wear borders of pearls on their clothes, except brides on their wedding dresses, while the English statutes of 1363 set limits for how much given classes of people might spend on their clothes and what furs—ranging from ermine and miniver to cat or rabbit—each group was legally permitted to wear (Amt 2010, 63–65).

The changing fashions of royal courts could be punishingly expensive for wealthy people who wanted to display their social standing through their clothing. Some governments, like the English government in 1337, tried to protect their trade in fabric by prohibiting the wearing of foreign-made materials. Philip the Fair (1268–1314), the king of France, tried to limit the amount of money his nobles spent on clothing per year, probably to prevent them from squandering money that he could otherwise tax. Such restrictions were frequently loaded with criticism toward upper-class women, who were regarded as vain and loving luxury.

CONCLUSION

The contrast between lower-class and upper-class women in medieval society is still striking despite the time separating us from them. Aristocratic women of the period enjoyed many luxuries, but their lives were far from idle—the demands on their time and their fertility were constant. In the next chapter, we will explore the realm of women in the Roman Catholic church in the Middle Ages.

5

RELIGION AND THE CHURCH

From the origins of Christianity in the first century CE, women were intimately involved with the Christian religion and were full participants in the Roman Catholic Church. This chapter will first address how women expressed their religious views in medieval Christian society. The second part of the chapter will address those medieval women who made religious devotion their vocation and lived as nuns or members of religious communities. Religious devotion for women took many forms. Women lived in communities or by themselves; they might be virgins, married women, single women, or widows; and, despite the rigors of religious life, their vocations sometimes allowed them unusual forms of power and influence. They were often upper-class women, but poorer women could also seek to live religious lives. Religion could provide opportunities for self-expression and self-determination for women of many backgrounds.

DAILY RELIGIOUS PRACTICE

In the Middle Ages, belief in the Christian God and, by extension, the ritual and theology of the Roman Catholic Church, was dominant. In the early Middle Ages, as the Roman Catholic Church expanded across Europe, its leaders sought to make religious practice uniform and diverse customary beliefs orthodox. This effort stretched into the late twelfth and thirteenth centuries, when the church was at the peak of its power and influence. Views of God and religion shaped everyday life for medieval people.

In the fourth century CE, the doctrine on the nature of God had been decided by a series of meetings held between bishops of the major Roman cities, the most important of which was the Council of Nicaea (325 CE). By 400 CE, the church understood God to be three persons in one: God the Father, Christ the Son, and the Holy Spirit. Mankind, because of the errors of Adam and Eve, was doomed to be damned to a fiery hell but could hope for salvation through the merits and forgiveness offered by Jesus. Medieval women, therefore, lived in a society that believed that salvation should be the goal of every Christian. This salvation hinged on faith, religious practices such as prayer, and divine grace. As we saw in chapter two, women were considered to have a spiritual deficit because of the story of Adam and Eve, so preachers consistently emphasized to them that they were naturally inferior to men and were worse sinners than men.

Concern with salvation affected not only women's behavior on Sundays but also dictated the calendar of the year, which revolved around a series of major holidays, especially Christmas (December 25), Easter (in the spring on a varying schedule), and Pentecost (five weeks after Easter). As we saw in previous chapters, religious beliefs about salvation also informed the ceremonies that attended birth, marriage, and death. Seven of these ceremonies, called the **sacraments** (a word that means "to consecrate"), were understood as active signs of God's grace. Most of them required the presence and participation of a priest. *Baptism* took place shortly after a child's birth and *confirmation*, around age twelve or thirteen. *Marriage* was not considered a sacrament until the early thirteenth century, as discussed in chapter two. *Penance* was the ceremony by which an individual was forgiven of their sins, usually after confession to a priest. *Holy orders* consecrated a man (women were not allowed to be priests) to the priesthood. At the end of life, *extreme unction* followed the last confession and prepared the believer for death.

Among the sacraments, the *Eucharist*, or Holy Communion, particularly influenced medieval women's religious lives. The Eucharist consisted of a ceremony in which bread and wine were blessed in order to make them turn into the body and blood of Christ, a doctrine called **transubstantiation**. This made the Eucharist a way of directly having contact with Christ. Among medieval Christians, some people took part in the Eucharist only once a year, but some people with strong religious beliefs, like the **mystics** described below, took the Eucharist every week or sometimes even every day. The Eucharist was embedded in a larger ceremony called the *mass*, a series of religious practices done in a prescribed order several times a day. Beginning in the twelfth century, families sometimes financially supported masses or priests with money in the hopes that their sins or their relatives' sins would be forgiven (Lynch 1992, 280). Religion was intertwined with most issues in the daily life of medieval people.

Hours and Days

The medieval day was divided into sections referred to as the **canonical hours**, referring to the specific prayers that were said at particular times of the day and night. Monks and nuns, as we will discuss below, observed a worship schedule according to the **canonical hours**. Upper-class women outside of the cloister, some of whom had books of hours, could keep the **canonical hours** themselves by praying specific prayers at specific times of day. Cecily, Duchess of York (1415–1495 CE), provides an example of a noblewoman who organized her day around religious services: she rose at seven in the morning, prayed with her chaplain, heard two masses before lunch, prayed extensively in the afternoon, and heard the last service of the day before retiring at eight o'clock. Cecily also read the work of women **mystics** such as Mechtilde of Hackeborn and Catherine of Siena, introduced below (Leyser 1995, 232–233).

Women with less leisure to worship quite so extensively were also encouraged to observe religious practices whenever they could. In the early fourteenth-century poem "How the Good Wife Taught Her Daughter," the speaker advised her child to "Go to church whene'er thou may," and to be quiet and respectful while she prayed the rosary (Furnivall and Rickert 1908, 31). As in many societies, affluence and education allowed for a broader range of religious practices; only women who could afford to do so had the liberty to devote large parts of their lives to observation of religious duties.

Saints, Relics, and Pilgrimage

Medieval Christians believed that certain people, known as **saints**, had lived lives or had suffered deaths devoted to God and had the power to intercede with God on their behalf. As the people of the Middle Ages understood God to be remote and all-powerful, many chose to depend on saints to intercede for them before him. Contact with the saints could be achieved through prayer or by touching or venerating the **relic** of a saint, often a bone or personal item that had belonged to him or her. The most important saint of the Middle Ages was certainly the Virgin Mary, mother of Jesus, whose veneration as a saint became especially popular in the thirteenth century and continued throughout the late Middle Ages. Medieval women often devoted their prayers to Mary. According to the list of Mary's miracles compiled in the early fifteenth century, Mary heard all prayers made to her and performed dramatic miracles, even for those who had sinned. In one story, a nun called Beatrice, who had been very devoted to Mary, left the convent and became a prostitute. When she returned to her convent one day, she asked the gatekeeper if he knew a nun named Beatrice. He replied that he had never met her, because Beatrice was a nun who had never left the convent and who had lived a blameless life. To her astonishment, Beatrice found that the Virgin Mary had assumed her looks and had kept her place in the convent during the years when she had been a prostitute. She returned to the convent and confessed her sins (Shinners 1997, 135–136). Stories like this one, widely circulated in sermons and by word of mouth, increased devotion to Mary all around Europe.

Slightly below Mary in importance was a level of saint whose veneration was widespread, such as the twelve apostles or important historical martyrs like St. Catherine of Alexandria (ca. fourth century). Some of these saints were credited with healing specific health problems. Medieval people sometimes chose to make journeys called *pilgrimages* to visit the relics of an important saint, believing that their illnesses would be cured or that their sins would be forgiven. Pilgrimage became especially important beginning in the eleventh century, when peaceful travel became easier and more people chose to take the road to visit famous sites. Jerusalem and Rome were, by far, the most important pilgrimage sites, but there were many sites closer to home for medieval women. Two of the most visited were the cathedral of Cologne, which claimed to have relics of the Three Magi, and Santiago de Compostela, in Spain, which claimed the relics of the apostle James. After the murder of the archbishop of Canterbury Thomas Becket in 1170 in England, his relics also became the foundation of an important pilgrimage site, as is recorded in Geoffrey Chaucer's *Canterbury Tales* (late fourteenth century). Visiting some of these major sites earned the pilgrim a *plenary indulgence*, which meant forgiveness of all one's sins. Some smaller pilgrimage sites offered lesser spiritual benefits.

Aside from more well-known saints, many communities had their own local holy people—some approved by the central church and some not—whom they solicited for help. Before the church developed its official method of declaring sainthood in the twelfth century, communities venerated their local holy people as they chose; in the later Middle Ages, local communities pushed for the canonization of their holiest citizens through official channels. In 1318, the people of Cortona, Italy, sent representatives to the papal court to speak for the canonization of Margaret of Cortona (1247–1297), a local Franciscan **tertiary** who lived a life of intense piety and service. Unfortunately, the people of Cortona did not succeed in attracting the attention of anyone powerful in the papal government, so Margaret was not canonized. Instead of continuing to push for her official recognition, the city honored St. Margaret with a feast day and later built a church that was consecrated in her honor. In this way, local communities sometimes got around the requirements of the papacy by going forward on their own (Vauchez 1993, 158–160).

Documents from pilgrimage sites confirm that women often went on pilgrimage, despite worries from authorities that traveling out in public would be an opportunity for wanton sexual behavior (Craig 2009, 261). When women went on pilgrimage, they often emphasized their roles as caregivers of the ill and suffering, taking to the road to pray for others. As we saw in chapter two, women often connected relics to successful pregnancies or births, so many miracles recorded at saints' shrines were miracles having to do with fertility or with lactation (producing milk). Saints' relics were also understood to work on mental illness, interpreted as demonic possession, along with physical illness. Bishop Adalhelm of Sées (ninth century) recorded in his *Miracles of St. Opportuna* one example of such a miracle. A woman named Olbiregis suffered for a long time under a condition that caused her limbs to flail about uncontrollably. Her husband brought her to Opportuna's grave where, after some setbacks, she eventually regained control of her body and senses. She and her husband recognized this as a miraculous cure, and the story says Olbiregis spent the rest of her life serving God in thanks (Rubin 2009, 223–224).

One of the well-known woman pilgrims of the Middle Ages was Margery Kempe (1373–1438), whose autobiography told of the life experiences of a laywoman in England at the turn of the fifteenth century. Kempe's experiences provide us with one image of the everyday life of a middle-class medieval woman. Kempe began to have mystical experiences later in life and traveled to multiple pilgrimage sites, including Jerusalem, Rome, and Compostela. Her mystical experiences, which came with uncontrollable weeping and a great desire to correct other people's faults, did not always endear her to her traveling companions. We can appreciate, however, the ways in which spirituality became the backbone of her life, to the exclusion of all other commitments. (Read more about Margery Kempe in chapter seven.)

Origins of Female Monasticism

From the time of early Christianity, some women chose to dedicate their lives exclusively to serving God. This service, according to the early church, required self-denial, such as chastity, solitude, and devotion to prayer. By the fourth century CE, some Christian men and women chose to live solitary lives as hermits, often in the deserts of Syria and North Africa. Anthony of Alexandria (251–356 CE) was one of the early practitioners of desert asceticism, but his biographer states that before he became a hermit, Anthony settled his younger sister with a community "of faithful virgins of good repute to be brought up according to their example" (White 1998, 10). Specific information about these early communities is hard to find, but consecrated women of this period in church history seem to have lived in communities more often than men did. In the early fifth, century a bishop named Palladius surveyed the hermits in Egypt and reported that there were 18,900 men and 3,095 women living as hermits in the desert. He also reported finding twenty thousand women and ten thousand men living religious lives in Oxyrhynchus, an Egyptian city (Ranft 1996, 2). Almost constant devotion to prayer and sometimes intentional physical suffering, through self-whipping or long periods without food, made the life of a hermit difficult to sustain. Still, some women believed that their salvation depended on such ascetic practices. One famous example is that of St. Mary of Egypt (fourth to fifth century), who lived as a hermit in the desert. A former prostitute, she felt such guilt at her sinful nature that she stayed in the desert, naked except for her hair, for decades.

The harsh life required of hermits prompted some groups of men and women to gather in institutions called **monasteries**. In the fourth and fifth centuries, many important women's monasteries were founded in Europe. In France, Lérins, off the coast of southern France, was founded by Honoratus of Arles in 410; Marseilles was founded in 415 by John Cassian. Both of these communities had a women's and a men's house situated near each other. The French houses were founded before women's houses in Britain, the earliest of which date from the seventh century, and which were founded by Anglo-Saxon royal women (Schulenberg 1989, 265–266). German foundations followed in the eighth and ninth centuries, including Nonnberg, founded by Bishop Rupert of Worms, a nunnery that is still active today. Spain, Dalmatia, and Bohemia had Benedictine monasteries by the eleventh century, while Poland and Portugal had foundations that dated from the twelfth century. The Scandinavian countries of Norway, Sweden, and Denmark also had Benedictine foundations that dated from the early twelfth century (Ranft 1996, 45).

Recent scholarship has shown that early women's religious houses used many types of literature to form their own guidelines for living a religious lifestyle: letters, sermons, and saints' biographies could all provide guidance for women gathered together in a convent (Lifshitz 2014, 148–149). By the sixth century, some male writers had begun producing written rules for such communities. The first was Caesarius of Arles (ca. 470–542), who founded a convent for his sister Caesaria in honor of St. John in about 512 CE. Caesarius's *The Rule for Nuns of St. Caesarius of Arles* was informed by the theological writings of St. Augustine and other writers, but it was also a practical guide to the monastic life for women. Caesarius insisted that all the nuns of the convent of St. John be literate and specified that each nun should spend at least two hours a day reading. They were also to dress in undyed clothes and spend their work time producing wool fabric to supply the house (Caesarius 1960, 175–176, 179). Most importantly, Caesarius promoted what was called **enclosure**: the nuns were not allowed to leave the monastery at all without the abbess's permission. He wrote that "no one of you up to the time of her death, [should] be permitted to go forth from the monastery . . . or presume on her own to go out" (Caesarius 1960, 188). Ecclesiastical authorities argued that enclosure increased the safety both of the nuns and of the general public (meaning men), who might be tempted by unmarried women. The abbess controlled how strictly this rule was applied.

Apart from St. John's, the only other women's monastery that used the original rule of Caesarius was the monastery of Holy

Cross at Poitiers, founded around 560 by Radegund of Poitiers (ca. 520–587) alongside a men's monastery called St. Mary. Radegund is one of the best-known women of the early Middle Ages, because three different biographies of her are still extant. A daughter of the king of Thuringia, she was married to the Merovingian king Clothar I but eventually convinced him to help her found the monastery, where she became the guiding force for a vibrant community of nuns who were highly educated, wrote creatively, educated children, and cared for the poor and sick (Ranft 1996, 22–23).

Like Radegund, abbesses of women's monasteries in the sixth and seventh centuries enjoyed a period of unprecedented autonomy and influence. In Ireland, Brigid of Kildare (ca. 456–524/5), Moninne of Killeedy (d. ca. 518) and Ita of Killeedy (d. ca. 570) founded monasteries for women. Queen Bathilda of Ascania (ca. 620–ca. 679), wife of the Frankish king Clovis II, revived the monastery of Chelles; her contemporary, the Anglo-Saxon abbess Hilda (614–680), became the abbess of the powerful monastery of Whitby in the 650s. Many of these foundations were **double monasteries**, in which a men's monastery and a women's monastery were side by side, often sharing churches, and in which an abbess was the ruler of both houses (Ranft 1996, 16–27). The abbesses of these houses were powerful and prominent in their local communities, functioning as leaders, witnesses to legal contracts, and sometimes judges.

During the Carolingian period in the eighth and ninth centuries, monastic reformers sponsored by the crown sought to make monks and nuns observe more uniform instructions for the religious life. The most influential of the rule writers for this period was Benedict of Nursia (ca. 480–ca. 547), author of the *Rule of St. Benedict*. Benedict wrote in his rule that he wanted to found a "school" for serving God. Unlike some of the desert ascetics who ate and drank only sparingly and prayed constantly, Benedict's monks and nuns were devoted to prayer but also to shared communal work and would not practice the harsh asceticism of Anthony and the early hermits.

The moderation of Benedict's approach helped his rule become widely practiced. In 814, a church council under Charlemagne declared Benedict's rule the required rule for both monks and nuns, and the rule has continued to shape the monastic life into the twenty-first century. As more women became nuns, Benedict's rule provided the structure of much of their religious lives. This development carried with it, however, a disadvantage: early women's monasteries, under powerful, usually noble abbesses, had been largely independent of royal control. The imposition of the *Rule of*

St. Benedict robbed abbesses of the autonomy they had enjoyed in previous centuries by subjecting them to male church authorities (Ranft 1996, 32). Furthermore, the *Rule of St. Benedict* was designed primarily for men and had to be adjusted to make it usable for women's houses. In the twelfth century, Héloïse of Argenteuil, abbess of a monastery, complained in a letter to her former husband that the *Rule of St. Benedict* did not cover important questions for her nuns. These included methods for dealing with menstruation, since monks did not normally wear underwear. Héloïse also suggested that women were biologically able to drink more alcohol than men and should therefore be allocated more wine. (Read more about Héloïse in chapter seven.)

The *Rule of St. Benedict* set out four vows for nuns and monks who wanted to join a monastery: poverty, meaning having no personal possessions; chastity, refraining from all sexual activity; obedience to the abbot or abbess of the monastery and to the church hierarchy; and stability, meaning staying in the same monastic house for life. Some women were given to monasteries as children and raised there until they were old enough to take vows. Other women chose to become nuns on their own or were committed to the monastic life by their families, entering the monastery as teenagers or adults. Widows, particularly those who were well-off financially, sometimes retired to monasteries. Even women who were political prisoners might live out their lives in a monastery rather than a prison.

Professing, or taking vows as a nun, was, for the most part, confined to upper-class women who could afford to pay the required contribution for the monastic profession. Most women brought money or property to the monastery in the form of a **dowry**, which was often not as much as a genuine marriage portion might be but which would, in theory, support the new nun in her career. In France in the central Middle Ages, the average monastic dowry was less in comparison to dowries intended for marriage. A doctrinal controversy arose over the practice of accepting dowries in the late twelfth century. Some jurists regarded giving dowries as making payments, which made them a form of *simony*, selling church positions for money, an abuse that the church had been trying to eliminate. Parents, however, continued to wish to dower their daughters, and the practice remained in effect in nunneries all over Europe (Johnson 1991, 24–25).

A woman who professed as a nun became an important connection between her family and the monastery, and families often had close relationships with monasteries where their family members were nuns. Aunts and nieces or mothers and daughters might decide to profess at the same religious house. Sisters professing at the same house were even more frequent, either because younger sisters looked up to older sisters as examples or because their families already had relationships with the religious houses. Documents show that these relationships were often long-lasting. A knight called Walter of Rupefort gave land to make it possible for his three daughters, Joanna, Alice, and Philippa, to become nuns at the French abbey of Notre-Dame des Voisins in the thirteenth century, making a bargain to provide for his daughters' future (Johnson 1991, 20). Similar documents exist for many other women's monasteries throughout the Middle Ages.

Some moralists of the period criticized families who had several children and chose to commit some of them to the religious life, saying their motives were more to feed their excess children than to make offerings to God. Documents that record the profession of nuns, however, emphasized the gift of a child as benefiting the souls of her parents and further kinship group as an **oblate**—literally, an "offering." Becoming a nun required a trial period of one year, and then a period of learning called the *novitiate* for three years. **Novices** were clothed with a nun's habit but did not receive the nun's signature veil (an over-the-head covering, often black) until they made their final vows to stay in the monastery for the rest of their lives.

Daily Routine in a Benedictine Monastery

The central focus of the religious life under the *Rule of St. Benedict* was prayer. Religious women in monasteries performed a rigorous series of services in which texts from the book of Psalms were sung in a prescribed order according to a calendar. The sisters performed these **canonical hours** every day. They rose at around two o'clock in the morning to take part in the night service, called matins. Services then followed on a roughly regular schedule: lauds (at dawn), prime (about six o'clock), terce (about nine o'clock), sext (about noon), nones (about three o'clock), vespers (about six o'clock), and compline (just before bedtime at around nine o'clock). In winter, when the days were shorter, the intervals between services were shrunk so that the canonical hours would still be distinct from each other (Lawrence 1984, 29).

Between services, the *Rule* specified that the sisters would do manual labor and attend to the administration of the monastery, including producing food and clothing. By the High Middle Ages, the demands of the prayer schedule led to a class-based division between the nuns: in wealthy nunneries, the upper-class women who entered the monastery became choir nuns, whose job was to sing the church services, and lower-class women became lay sisters, who were charged with doing most of the manual labor. In wealthy houses, the choir nuns were given manual tasks such as needlework or manuscript copying. In poorer communities, however, the choir nuns did their own housework.

The person who oversaw the administration of the monastery was the **abbess**, whom the nuns called "mother." She supervised the other officers of the monastery: the *cellarer*, who was responsible for the food supply; the *sacristan*, who prepared the vessels and other items for religious services; and the *infirmarer*, who maintained an infirmary for nuns who fell ill or required care. In large houses, the abbess had a second in command who was called the *prioress*. These officers oversaw a group of buildings that generally included a church, a dormitory with a refectory (a dining hall), latrines, stables, a kitchen and bakery, and a chapter house where the nuns could congregate for periodic administrative meetings. The church and dormitory were often connected by a *cloister*, an open area surrounded by a covered walkway. In larger monasteries, the abbess might have her own residence, and in many, a guest house provided lodging for visitors (Williams and Echols 1994, 120).

The main meal of the day was luncheon, right after the canonical hour of Sext, which St. Benedict directed should consist of two or three cooked dishes in addition to bread (one pound or 0.45 kg per day, per person) and about half a bottle of wine per person (approximately half a liter). During the meal, one of the sisters read aloud from a religious book chosen by the abbess, but otherwise, the sisters ate in silence.

Clothing was to be simple and inexpensive and suited to the climate where the monastery was located. Nuns under the *Rule of St. Benedict* had little personal space, especially by modern standards, and very little privacy. St. Benedict directed that all the nuns in a given religious house should sleep in one room, if possible, though this directive was relaxed as the centuries passed to allow individual cells (small rooms) for sleeping. A light was kept burning in this dormitory all night to prevent sexual activity or disruption.

The *Rule* was very strict with regard to personal deportment and behavior. It required unquestioning obedience to the abbess without grumbling. A sister who grumbled might be privately chastised to show better respect, but if that sister continued to complain, the abbess might excommunicate her. In this context, excommunication consisted of banishment from the table during meals, eating only after the other sisters were served, or even solitary confinement. After a period of time, the abbess ordered a ceremony in which the excommunicated sister could attain forgiveness.

The abbess of a Benedictine monastery was required to question a potential novice at regular intervals over the course of a year to make sure the postulant truly wanted to adopt the religious life. If at any point the novice wished to, she could renounce the religious life and leave the monastery. If she stayed, she eventually took her solemn vows to stay in the monastery for the rest of her life (Fry et al. 1981, 220–223, 266–269).

It is difficult to know how often women who entered monasteries actively chose the life for themselves, since women's choices were constrained by class and family obligations. Sources on both sides show that some women had strong desires to fulfill their religious beliefs by taking the veil, and some women clearly chafed against the discipline of a religious life they had not chosen. One example is Christina of Markyate (ca. 1096–1155), an Anglo-Saxon woman who wanted to serve God so passionately that she ran away from home and from her fiancé to avoid the loss of her virginity. Christina eventually became an **anchoress** who was confined to a small room next to the church and lived the rest of her life in prayer, attracting a group of followers around her that developed into a monastic settlement (Ranft 1996, 43). Later medieval saints' lives have many examples of upper-class women who resisted their families' attempts to marry them off and pursued the religious life instead. Margaret of Hungary (1242–1270), having entered a Dominican convent, aroused the opposition of her father, King Bela IV of Hungary, by refusing to marry. When he attempted to take Margaret from her convent, she refused and said she would cut her face with a knife rather than be married, saying, "To me it is better to be without lips in paradise than to go to hell with my nose and lips" (Vauchez 1993, 179, 304). Horrified, her father gave up.

There are also examples of women who disliked the religious life or who found the vow of chastity to be a burden. When Archbishop Eudes Rigaud visited the French monastery of La-Salle-aux-Puelles in 1249 to conduct an inspection, he found that several of the nuns had relationships with men, and one of the sisters had even given birth to a child (Amt 2010, 203). In *chansons de nonne*, "nuns' songs," poems in which the narrator is a nun, the speakers complained about their circumstances and wished to leave the convent. One author wrote, "God give much unhappiness to the one who . . . put me in the cloister" (Williams and Echols 1994, 122–123). A story from the *Decameron* by Giovanni Boccaccio (1313–1375) depicted the nuns of a small convent as promiscuous, wearing out the man who worked in their garden with sex. One of the nuns in the story remarked that these sins were unimportant, for "We are constantly making [God] promises that we don't keep!" (Boccaccio 1995, 195).

FINANCES AND ENDOWMENTS

In the early Middle Ages, some nunneries became very large and wealthy, supported by donations from aristocratic families and by the property that women brought when they professed as nuns. Such wealthy monasteries were places where royal women could and did become nuns, living in comfort. Matilda of Ringelheim (ca. 894–968), queen of Germany and empress of the Holy Roman Empire, founded the monastery of Quedlinburg in 936 in memory of her husband, Henry I. Quedlinburg was a foundation made up of **canonesses** living under the rule of St. Augustine, and many noble women chose to become sisters there. One of the biographies of Queen Matilda states that the queen and her husband decided to move a group of nuns living at Wendhausen to the nunnery at Quedlinburg. At Wendhausen, the women were from good families but were distressingly poor, so much so that their "kinfolk were unhappy to have them remain amidst so much poverty" (Scheck 2009, 30). We must assume, then, that the foundation at Quedlinburg allowed the sisters to live in a more comfortable style. In contrast, some nunneries were smaller, poorer, and dependent on their donors for support. When Eudes Rigaud, archbishop of Rouen, visited the small Cistercian nunnery of Saint-Saens in 1257, there were sixteen nuns who farmed and subsisted on "income in coin and in kind from tenants." The nunnery was heavily in debt and was forced to sell some of its endowed property to keep the nuns fed (Johnson 1991, 221–222).

NEW AND REFORMED RELIGIOUS ORDERS

As new religious orders proliferated in the eleventh, twelfth, and thirteenth centuries, women and their monasteries enthusiastically sought entrance into them. Medieval ideas about women, however, shaped the opportunities that they had inside the newer religious orders. Some male monastics felt that women could not endure the tougher demands of some of the newer orders. Others resented the *cura monialium*, or care of nuns, which took away from men's resources and opportunities by demanding that they supervise nuns and provide their priestly services. As a result, the roles of women inside the new movements were constrained by rules and regulations designed to keep religious women and their houses under control.

In the eleventh century, a monastic reform emanated from the monastery of Cluny, located in Burgundy, under abbot Hugh of Cluny (1024–1109). The Cluniac order claimed to strictly observe the rule of St. Benedict, and the Cluniac message attracted many wealthy donors. Hundreds of affiliated monasteries (called priories) for men, subordinate to Cluny, were founded by the time Hugh founded its first women's house, Marcigny, in 1056. Marcigny was intended to be a religious house for women whose husbands or other male relatives chose to enter Cluny. Along with careful application of the rule of St. Benedict, Marcigny's nuns observed strict **enclosure**. This pattern applied to many women's monasteries founded under the guardianship of Cluny.

The founding of the order of Citeaux, or Cistercian order, in the early twelfth century in the region of Burgundy was the result of discontent with current Benedictine practices. The Cistercian experience provide a common model of women's entrance into male-dominated monastic orders: resistance first; then incorporation; and finally, increasing supervision. As the order spread, women's houses petitioned to be allowed into the order, but the Cistercian leadership resisted. Women, they argued, were not sufficiently strong to bear the discipline of the Cistercian practice. The leadership attempted to stop nunneries from being associated with the order several times. Powerful nobles intervened. Alfonso VIII of Castile (1155–1214) pressured the Cistercians to accept the nunnery he had founded, Las Huelgas de Burgos, in 1187, and the pope himself requested the incorporation of a nunnery at Vezella, in Lombardy, in 1230 (Ward 2016, 179). The number of Cistercian nunneries grew tremendously. The heads of the order prohibited letting more women's monasteries join the Cistercian fold in 1228, but this did not solve what they saw as a problem: increasing female interest in the order, such that there were more Cistercian women's monasteries than men's monasteries in Germany and the Low Countries, and growing numbers in other areas as well. In addition, supervising houses that contained aristocratic women used to governing their own affairs proved to be a challenge for the administrators of the order. Two abbots made a visit to the Cistercian nunnery at Colonges in 1250 to give the nuns instructions on how to elect a new abbess, but the prioress, not recognizing their authority over her, denied them access and would not follow their instructions (Lawrence 1984, 184–185). Some Cistercian women maintained the strict lifestyle of the order but rejected the supervision of their houses and maintained control over their own administrations.

In the early twelfth century, popular preachers like Robert of Arbrissel (ca. 1045–1116), Gilbert of Sempringham (1083–1190), and Norbert of Xanten (ca. 1075–1134) were also responsible for groups of women who demanded to live a religious life under their interpretations of monasticism. Robert founded the monastery of Fontevraud in western France in 1101 to provide his female followers with a place to live. Fontevraud was a **double monastery**—a place in which a community of nuns and a community of monks lived on the same site but were kept entirely separate from each other. Within the community of nuns, widows, virgins and married women made up one section, while another section housed repentant prostitutes. The house also included a section for those who were ill. An abbess controlled the entire monastery, including the men's community. Robert chose prominent noblewomen from the area to supervise the house: the first abbess was Petronilla of Chemillé, from a local noble family, whose leadership expanded the reputation of the house and its priories. The order of Fontevraud grew throughout the twelfth century and thrived throughout the Middle Ages. By 1200, the abbess of Fontevraud supervised almost seventy religious houses in central France, and the queen of England, Eleanor of Aquitaine (1122–1204), chose to retire and spend her last years at Fontevraud (Ranft 1996, 46–47; Venarde 1997, 63).

In England, Gilbert of Sempringham, founder of the Gilbertine order, also found that women were attracted to his preaching and wanted to pursue a monastic life under his direction. Gilbert placed the first seven nuns in an enclosure next to the church at Sempringham and recruited lay sisters and some lay brothers to minister to the nuns' needs. As the community grew, Gilbert requested to have it accepted into the Cistercian order, but he was unsuccessful. Ultimately, he established the order for nuns under the rule of St. Benedict and the order for male canons under the rule of St. Augustine in an arrangement similar to that of Fontevraud. The order grew rapidly, and the nunneries became quite large. The largest, Watton, housed 150 women and 70 men. Women generally outnumbered men in Gilbertine houses; altogether, the houses totaled nine hundred women and five hundred men (Venarde 1997, 80).

Norbert, founder of the Premonstratensian order, also kept his male canons and nuns in double monasteries, adapting some of their observances from the strict rule of the Cistercian order. The order spread across Flanders and Brabant in the 1130s. Women in the order were strictly enclosed, mostly tending the sick or cleaning and mending clothes, while the men of the order traveled to preach in the region (Venarde 1997, 69–70). The structure of the double houses, however, made the leaders of the order concerned about the opportunities for temptation inherent in having men and women too close to one another. The Premonstratensians were sufficiently worried about this problem that they attempted to reorganize their double houses after Norbert's death in 1134 (Ward 2016, 179). Houses of nuns were relocated to areas away from the male canons, ostensibly to resist temptation. As a result, some of the Premonstratensian houses for nuns were relatively short-lived, as the nunneries sometimes failed to thrive in their new locations (Venarde 1997, 70).

The orders of preaching friars also presented women with opportunities to serve, though not in the same ways as the male friars. Dominic (1170–1221), founder of the Dominican order or Order of Preachers, founded a monastery in 1206 for women who had been accused of the Albigensian heresy (discussed below) but had repented and were now serving penance. This early foundation included twelve nuns. Unlike the men recruited to the Dominican order, however, the sisters were not allowed to preach or teach publicly: they were to support the efforts of their male counterparts through prayer (Lawrence 1984, 215). Dominic understood the activities of the Dominican nuns as reflecting the part of Mary in the Bible (Luke 10: 38–42) and his order of male preaching friars as taking the role of Martha. Thus, both halves of the order were essential to making the work successful (Ranft 1996, 70).

Similarly, nuns of the Franciscan order, called the Poor Ladies or the Poor Clares after Francis of Assisi's friend and follower Clare of Assisi (1194–1253), were made to separate themselves from the world in monasteries under a rule very similar to the rule of St. Benedict. Francis set out in the rule for his order that the members should own no property and support themselves by the charity of others. Clare herself deeply felt the necessity for the nuns to own absolutely no possessions, which she considered an essential part of the *vita apostolica*, or apostolic life. Around 1215, believing that her nuns would be forced into owning property by the administrators of the order, Clare appealed to the pope, Innocent III, who wrote a papal **bull** supporting the Poor Clares' right to refrain from owning property. The bull, called the "Privilege of Poverty," declared that no one present or in the future could attempt to make the nuns give up apostolic poverty. After Innocent's death in 1215, however, later popes advocated the strict **enclosure** of all Franciscan nuns and required the houses to own property to support them. Clare was bitterly disappointed and spent the rest of her life attempting to restore what she saw as a genuine imitation of the apostles (Ranft 1996, 67).

The Bishop of Assisi gives St. Clare, founder of the Poor Clares, a palm leaf. (The Cloisters Collection, 1984. The Metropolitan Museum of Art.)

Their piety and asceticism made the women's orders of the Dominicans and the Poor Clares attractive to many women and made them very successful: by the 1300s there were 150 Dominican convents in Europe, and of the Poor Clares, there were twenty-five in Germany, twenty-three in Italy, and various other foundations from England to the crusader states (Ward 2016, 175–177). In terms of religious life, however, they had more in common with enclosed orders like the Benedictines than with the men's orders. It was considered to be dangerous not only to the women themselves but to society if nuns were allowed to wander freely to preach.

By the thirteenth century, many of the monastic orders incorporated third orders, called **tertiaries**, in order to allow for greater piety for laymen and women who wished to be part of a religious order but could not commit to the monastic life. Tertiaries followed the monastic lifestyle while living in their own homes, often fasting, praying, and caring for the poor. Beginning in the early 1220s, some men and women chose to live specifically as Franciscans, eventually being adopted into the Franciscan order as its third order. Other monastic groups, such as the Dominicans, also developed third orders during the thirteenth century.

LAY PIETY AND BEGUINAGE

Although their names are not in the sources, all these orders owed some of their success to the determination of women who fought to be part of religious life and, sometimes, distinguished themselves so highly that they became venerated as saints of the church. Not all these women, however, joined traditional religious orders. In the late twelfth century a movement broadly called the *Umiliati* appeared in northern Italy, made up of laypeople who wanted to live a religious life outside of the normal religious orders. The *Umiliati* were the beginning of a larger movement of laypeople who believed in living in poverty like the apostles. In 1221, Pope Innocent III approved the Order of the Penitents, called the *Ordo Poenitentiae*. Members of this order lived at home, wearing distinctive undyed robes. They fasted more strictly than regular Christians and recited the canonical hours daily. Married women who were part of this order had to have their husbands' permission to join, but otherwise women could participate fully in the lifestyle shaped by the movement (Vauchez 1993, 121–122).

In northern Europe, also beginning in the late twelfth century, the growth of cities and towns produced a surplus of women who were unmarried and who wished to pursue a religious life but who could not or did not want to become nuns or tertiaries in established religious orders. Some women chose to live lives of poverty and prayer in their own homes, and in northern cities, in areas such as Flanders and Brabant, groups of women collected together in urban houses that took the place of monasteries. Their purpose was to live the *vita apostolica*, or life in imitation of the apostles. They were called by many different names, including *mulieres sanctae*, meaning "holy women," and **Beguines**, a word of uncertain origin. Although they practiced poverty and chastity, Beguines did not take vows and could leave to marry if they wished. Some communities of Beguines worked lace, made textiles, or otherwise supported themselves by working in concert (Lawrence 1984, 187–188). Some women who began living as Beguines eventually became **tertiaries** of religious orders.

The Beguine movement gave rise to many important religious women, both inside and outside of orthodoxy. Marie of Oignies (1177–1213), who was from an upper-class family in Belgium, lived a life of harsh asceticism in the city of Liège. Her follower and confessor, Jacques de Vitry (ca. 1160–1240), praised her extraordinary ascetic practices and her devotion to prayer in the biography he wrote shortly after her death. Marie's example inspired many women, and her biography was central to the growth and support for the Beguine movement in Flanders (de Vitry 1989, 5–6). One of the most famous Beguines was Marguerite Porete (d. 1310), whose visions were recorded in her book the *Mirror of Simple Souls* (ca. 1300). The book circulated widely despite having been deemed heretical by ecclesiastical authorities. Porete refused to disavow her visionary experiences and was burned at the stake in Paris in 1310 (Ward 2016, 206). (Read more about Marguerite Porete in chapter seven.)

The burning of Porete, concern about the sexual habits and religious orthodoxy of the Beguines, and a heresy called the Free Spirit provoked Pope Boniface VIII into calling a church council at Vienne in 1311–1312. He decreed that Beguines were not to be allowed the privileges of an order of nuns because they did not take vows like nuns or follow a rule. Ecclesiastical officials began to force Beguines into more established (and usually **enclosed**) orders in the fourteenth century. By the fifteenth century, the movement had largely disappeared into the other monastic orders of the period.

MYSTICISM

A **mystic** is a person who seeks spiritual union with God through religious practices. Christian mysticism has deep roots in the scriptures, but mystical writing in the early Middle Ages belonged to men. Beginning in the twelfth century, however, women like Marie of Oignies and Marguerite Porete expanded on the notion of experiencing God personally through spiritual union. Over the course of the thirteenth and fourteenth centuries, women mystics proliferated around Europe. They came from very different backgrounds. Some were from wealthy families, like Mechtilde of Hackeborn

(1240–1298), who was born to a noble Thuringian house and entered the monastery of Helfta at the age of seven. Others were from middle-class families, like Margery Kempe (1373–1438), discussed above, who began having visions after she was married and had borne fourteen children. In general, female mysticism in the Middle Ages was emotional and ecstatic, often provoking intense feelings of love and joy. Women were stereotyped as being overemotional, but women mystics of the period succeeded in using this stereotype to their advantage, expressing their love and sometimes their sexuality through their visionary experiences. In this way, they made what was perceived as feminine weakness into a strength based on religious fervor.

One of the earliest of the medieval female mystics was Hildegard of Bingen (1098–1179), a Benedictine nun and natural philosopher who began experiencing visions as a small child. Hildegard wrote three major visionary works: *Scivias* (an abbreviation of *Sci vias domini, Know the Ways of the Lord*), *Liber vitae meritorum* (*Book of the Rewards of Life*), and *Liber divinorum operum* (*Book of Divine Works*). After Pope Eugenius III (ca. 1080–1153) approved her first book, *Scivias*, she became a famous preacher, traveling around Germany and as far as France (Fox 2002, 3–4). (Read more about Hildegard in chapter seven.) Hildegard was not afraid to challenge important people whose behaviors she thought to be immoral, and she even wrote letters to kings. She used the moral weight that she gained from her visions to have influence over others.

Many mystics experienced ecstasies in which they had personal experiences with Christ as an infant or as an adult. Angela of Foligno (1250–1309) had visions in which she saw and touched the baby Jesus. Lutgardis of Aywières (1182–1246) had a vision in which Jesus reached into her chest, plucked out her heart, and then replaced it with his own (Ward 2016, 216; Williams and Echols 1994, 123). These kinds of experiences were characteristic of the intense female spirituality which flourished during the period.

In the thirteenth century, the monastery of Helfta, founded in 1229, became a center of female mysticism and spirituality under the abbess Gertrude of Hackeborn (1232–1291). Although the nuns of Helfta followed Cistercian practices, they were influenced by the spirituality of the Dominican order, as well as the Beguine movement. In 1270, the brilliant and controversial mystic Mechtilde of Magdeburg, a former Beguine, joined Helfta, bringing with her a large mystical work titled *The Flowing Light of the Divinity*. Mechtilde was one of the first mystics to write in a language other than Latin;

her works were in Low German, making them more accessible to laypeople. She found a vibrant learned community and apt students for her particular form of spirituality at Helfta. Among them were Mechtilde of Hackeborn (1250–ca. 1298) and Gertrude of Helfta, often called Gertrude the Great (1256–ca. 1302). Both these women were writers and saints who became well-known for their works during the later Middle Ages (Ranft 1996, 74–75). (Read more about the women of Helfta in chapter seven.)

Mystics like Gertrude and Mechtilde occupied a difficult space within medieval religious life. Visionary experiences could give women a great deal of local and international fame. Women who spoke to God or the saints directly, however, could be accused of ignoring the role of the priesthood in mediating their relationships with God. The concept of sainthood was also becoming more complex. In the early Middle Ages, most saints were acclaimed by their local communities, and no papal authority was required; however, in the twelfth century, the church hierarchy took increasing control over the definitions and requirements for sainthood. As a result, women who were prominent in public because of their holiness had to be very careful to get an ecclesiastical stamp of approval. No one doubted that their mystical experiences were real, but visions were supposed to originate from either God or from the devil. Many writers tackled the difficult question of how to discern where visions came from. Raymond de Sabanac, a fourteenth-century writer, opined that a woman who had visions needed to be closely questioned to ascertain if she were "spiritual, discreet, mature, virtuous, Catholic and approved" (Rubin 2009, 290).

Catherine of Siena (1347–1380), an Italian mystic and Dominican **tertiary**, experienced ecstatic visions in which she talked to Christ, Mary, and several saints. She even envisioned a "mystical marriage," in which was married Jesus. Such experiences gave Catherine a great reputation for holiness, and in her many letters—380 of which are still extant—she exhorted her correspondents to obey the pope and to cooperate with the church in Rome. Catherine's fame and many travels, however, provoked criticism from those who thought she should stay home or in the cloister like a nun. Catherine replied that she traveled and preached with no other purpose in mind but the glory of God (Luongo 2006, 23–25). (Read more about Catherine in chapter seven).

Some mystics were credited with supernatural experiences that went beyond ecstasy. St. Margaret of Hungary (1242–1270) was reputed to have levitated while praying. She also received the

St. Catherine of Siena, an influential mystic, gives Christ her heart in one of her visions. (Jim Emmons)

stigmata, meaning that her hands, feet, and side were wounded as Jesus's had been during the crucifixion (Rubin 2009, 275). The Belgian mystic Christina Mirabilis (her name can be translated as "Christina the Astonishing"), according to her biographer Thomas of Cantimpré (1201–1272), levitated, balanced on the tops of fences, climbed into ovens, and submerged herself in frigid water. She believed she could allow others to exit purgatory and stop their suffering by willingly suffering in her own body (Petroff 1986). Motivations like this one characterized female mysticism throughout the Middle Ages, though few women engaged in such starkly unusual behaviors as Christina's.

JOAN OF ARC: SAINT OR HERETIC?

Joan of Arc (ca. 1412–1431) belongs in a discussion of women and the church because her controversial, tragically short career illuminated the broad conversation considering women and their lived experiences in society in the fifteenth century. Her life has inspired a multitude of published works in many different languages, a broad filmography, and even conspiracy theories. Joan was born in a village called Domrémy, in the Vosges region of France, during the Hundred Years' War. She belonged to a well-off peasant family. Her early life and everyday habits can, in some ways, be reconstructed from the testimony she gave at her trial and from the witnesses at her retrial some years after her death. Joan lived a normal life for a fifteenth-century girl: she had three brothers and one sister, shared a room with her sister, sewed, spun, and looked after her family's animals. She even told her inquisitors that "in sewing and spinning she feared no woman in Rouen" (Taylor 2009, 8). Her friends found her serious and devout.

As an adolescent, she began hearing voices that she eventually identified as Saint Margaret of Antioch, Saint Catherine of Alexandria, and the archangel Michael. These voices encouraged her to leave home and offer her military service to the dauphin of France, Charles de Valois (later Charles VII, 1403–1461), who was embroiled in a difficult war with England and its ally, Burgundy. Her first attempts to convince the local commander, Robert de Baudricourt, of her visions were unsuccessful, but in 1429, she persuaded him to allow her an escort to join the dauphin at Chinon. The dauphin required Joan to submit to questioning by ecclesiastical officials to determine whether her mystical experiences came from God or the devil. Joan convinced them that she could aid the dauphin both in raising a difficult siege at the city of Orléans and in freeing the city of Rheims, where he would be crowned king of France. She was a leader of the forces that achieved both these goals. Wearing armor and men's clothing, Joan became the inspiration of the forces in France.

Over the course of the next year, from the spring of 1429 to the spring of 1430, Joan and her allies, deputized by the new king of France, continued to take towns and strongholds for the French army. She carried a sword that she had predicted would be found behind a church altar, although it seems to have been purely honorary. It seemed that her forces could not lose. In May 1430, Joan was attempting to protect the city of Compiègne when she was cut off from her followers and captured by the Burgundian army. She was interrogated over the course of several weeks by the bishop of Beauvais and several other ecclesiastical officials, again to determine whether she was a saint or a heretic. Not surprisingly, the pro-English judges found her guilty of heresy and handed her over to the secular government to be executed. She was burned at the stake in Rouen on May 30, 1431. Several decades later, the papacy required a retrial, this time under French control, at which Joan's conviction for heresy was withdrawn and her reputation rehabilitated. She was made a saint in 1920.

Joan's story fascinates modern people because of the amazing circumstances: an ordinary peasant girl from northern France was catapulted into prominence because of her mystical voices. Unlike other mystics of the time, however, her prominence was political rather than religious. The records that survive of her interrogation in 1430 provide a window onto what the judges thought was most suspicious about her mystical experiences. It was simple for them to claim that her voices were of demonic rather than heavenly origin. They particularly emphasized that she wore men's clothing, against which a number of Bible verses could be quoted, and argued that she was indecent as a result. One English noble referred to her as "that disorderly and deformed travesty of a woman who dresses like a man" (Hotchkiss 1996, 57).

In her second trial, however, when the judges were more favorably disposed toward Joan, her voices and her wearing of men's clothes were recast as evidence of her heavenly inspiration. The theologian Thomas Aquinas (1225–1274) wrote that a woman might assume men's dress in times of necessity, particularly for the sake of modesty or protecting her virginity. Writers of the period argued that Joan, while certainly protecting her virginity, had also taken on an aspect of masculine identity in order to do God's will (Hotchkiss 1996, 57–60). By abandoning her everyday life and its chores, Joan provoked extremely strong reactions, both positive and negative, depending upon the political affiliation of those who wrote about her.

CONCLUSION

When we study women's everyday lives in the Middle Ages, we must take their religious lives strongly into account. Rituals and visions could provide ways through which medieval women connected directly with God, bypassing male control. The people of the Middle Ages believed in the afterlife, the need for the remission of sins, and most believed in the role of the church for forgiveness. Women of the period understood their duties and responsibilities to rest on a foundation of religious morality. Immoral behavior, therefore, was not just wrong but also dangerous to an orderly society. In the next chapter, we will discuss the women who violated the moral underpinnings that medieval society set.

6

WOMEN ON THE OUTSKIRTS

This chapter introduces those women who did not operate inside the approved circles of wives, nuns, and mothers because of their sexual habits, religious beliefs, or social activities. Since medieval society stereotyped women as less intelligent and more wayward than men, women in general may have benefited from laxer punishments and lesser requirements when they transgressed; similarly, however, activities that were permitted to men but not to women allowed women to be prosecuted for gender-specific crimes. Judicial courts developed a great deal across the Middle Ages as royal power grew and a higher population required clearer and more specific legal punishments. Church government also shaped punishments and ideas about right and wrong.

CRIMES AND INCARCERATION

People who broke the law in the Middle Ages seldom left their own impressions of their experiences. Our best sources are court records, which became more common beginning in the thirteenth century. Numerical data culled from these records may not be indicative of larger trends, given their spotty coverage and inconsistencies, but, in general, the number of women punished for crimes seems to have been significantly lower than the number of men. Women certainly committed petty crimes such as minor theft and violence, particularly violence against husbands and children. There were also crimes peculiar to women: yelling insults at someone or being a "common scold" could earn a woman public humiliation, probably to the satisfaction of her neighbors. The borough ordinance of Hereford, England, in the late fifteenth century stated that women damaged the peace of the city by "quarrelling, beating, defamation, disturbing the peace of the night, [and] discord frequently stirred between neighbors" (Goldberg 1995, 234). Such laws took advantage of the stereotype that women talked too much.

Women who committed minor crimes that were not sexual (we will discuss sex work below) often were publicly whipped or exhibited in a **pillory** or the **stocks**, the time calculated according to the gravity of the offense. People passing could insult or throw things at the convicted person or even cause them physical harm. In England, a pillory for women was called a **thewe**. Some communities also used a **cucking stool** or a **ducking stool** for minor transgressions like scolding. A **cucking stool** was a sort of chair that held the accused person in place so that passersby could see them, while a **ducking stool** was a chair that was lowered rapidly into water a number of times. Many of these punishments persisted through the early modern period into the eighteenth and nineteenth centuries. According to English records, the last time that a **thewe** was used was in 1817.

Theft was the most common property crime attributed to women. Small thefts in particular were often associated with sex work—a prostitute might filch some extra money or a small item from a customer. Women were also responsible for major thefts, which could carry a sentence of mutilation, as in branding on the cheek, or execution. A woman named Desiderata de Toryntone was convicted in 1337 of having stolen £40 worth of silver plate and salt cellars from a servant of Lady Alice de Lisle while he was staying in Salisbury. By the time she was arrested, Desiderata had already sold some of the plate but was caught with the rest and was sentenced to hanging (Labarge 1986, 207).

Medieval secular courts tended to punish people convicted of crimes physically or with fines or exile, while **canon law** courts punished them with religious penance, sometimes inside a church institution like a monastery. Imprisonment as a punishment in itself developed along with the Catholic Church, which emphasized isolation as one of the approved forms of penance. Such punishment was called *detrusio*, meaning an exclusion or thrusting away, presumably from society. In the Italian city-states beginning in the thirteenth century, urban authorities began building dedicated spaces for the incarceration of criminals. These required dedicated staffs of administrators, guards, cooks, and physicians to care for the people imprisoned there. Over the course of the late Middle Ages, prisons added women's wards to their all-male institutions.

SEXUAL TRANSGRESSIONS

Criticisms based on sexuality were a prominent feature of most anti-woman writing in the Middle Ages. Women were alternately blamed in courtly literature for being cold and unwilling to have sex and criticized by religious writers as sexually promiscuous. Like most human beings, those who judged women in the Middle Ages were able to believe both these criticisms at once, without perceiving them to be at odds.

Adulterous Wives

Perhaps because adultery could interfere with the inheritance of property, legal authorities treated it as a particularly serious crime. Altogether, female adulterers received more attention and condemnation than male adulterers in the early medieval period, but in different places, the laws could vary widely. Roman law had generally understood adultery to be a crime against the men in the family. Any sexual activity outside of marriage for a free woman was forbidden. The Julian marriage laws of 18 BCE allowed a husband who surprised his wife with her lover to kill her lover without retribution, and a father who similarly caught his daughter with a lover was empowered to kill them both. Wives were not permitted similar rights with regard to their husbands and could not sue for divorce. There were some women who were exempt from charges of adultery: concubines, enslaved women, and prostitutes could not have legally valid marriages and, therefore, could not be prosecuted for betraying them. By extension, neither could the men who had sex with them, unless a man were trespassing on another man's sexual territory (Brundage 1987, 31). Upper-class Roman women who had sex with lower-class men, however, could be sentenced to death. This double standard was persistent throughout the Middle Ages: men's infidelity with their social inferiors was seldom punished, while women's infidelity, particularly with a man of lower social station, was punished severely.

In Germanic law codes, as well, adultery was defined as a female crime. The first year of a Germanic marriage was a sort of trial period in which a husband could freely divorce his wife unless a pregnancy resulted. After the first year, a man might choose to divorce his wife for sorcery, adultery, or (strangely) tomb violation, but in the Burgundian code, a woman who wanted a divorce could be buried alive in mud. Unmarried fornication was regarded as less serious than adultery, because an adulterous wife could bring illegitimate children into her husband's family. In many Germanic codes, the husband could kill both his wife and her lover if he found them in the act. Visigothic laws even extended this right to the woman's father and brothers (Brundage 1987, 130–32).

In the Christian Roman empire, writers on morality attempted to make adultery a serious crime both for men and for women. According to the doctrine of the **marriage debt** (see chapter two), wives and husbands owned the rights to each other's bodies. The writers of **canon law** (church law) forbade husbands with unfaithful wives from killing them, because that would constitute murder. Unfaithful spouses, male and female, were instead subject to excommunication and sometimes more physical punishments such as whipping. In Sicilian law, a man who learned that his wife was unfaithful was permitted to cut off her nose (Butler 2020).

Husband and wife might also be permitted to separate from one another, although neither could marry again. This kind of separation was called a *divortium a mensa et thoro*, a "divorce from bed and board," meaning that the parties no longer cohabited and otherwise had no marital duties. Some canonical writers specifically forbade adulterous husbands from marrying their lovers if the betrayed spouse died. Others made the distinction between private adultery, revealed only in confession and punished by penance, and public adultery, which was a prosecutable crime. Local folk law and custom, however, still allowed betrayed husbands to kill their wives in practice; no court would prosecute a man for doing so (Brundage 1987, 208, 388). Johannes Teutonicus, a legal writer from the thirteenth century, noted that it had at one time been customary in his region to punish adulterous wives with head shaving, whipping, public humiliation, and sometimes even with death. He rejected these punishments, arguing that it was preferable, as in his own time, to make the accused adulteress enter a monastery, where she could do penance for her sin and be separated from her husband (and her lover) at the same time. The option of entrance into a monastery, however, would likely have been restricted to upper-class women. Decisions about how to punish an adulteress were shaped by class and position (McDougall 2014, 499–500).

Medieval Swedish secular laws from the thirteenth century provide interesting samples of instances in which adulterous women were punished more harshly than men. In general, Swedish secular laws understood adultery to be a crime against the honor of the woman's husband. A betrayed husband could throw his wife out of the house and take her dower and personal property. She might be humiliated by having her cloak and skirt slit up the back so that her backside showed. There were also some shaming rituals that punished both man and woman. In one, a married man who had slept with an unmarried woman and could not afford the fine was sentenced to have a rope tied around his penis and to be led around the town by his lover, who was forced to wear two heavy stones and a chain around her neck (Ekholst 2014, 177–178).

The church generally oversaw prosecutions of unfaithful spouses in high medieval Europe. The idea that marriages, once made, were unbreakable pushed church authorities to seek reconciliation between spouses rather than separate them. Many religious writers argued that men and women who sinned equally should be equally punished. In fourteenth-century northern French church courts, such punishment took the form of fines, and more men were prosecuted than women. The church courts seemed to have believed that adulterous women who were under their husbands' guardianship were their husbands' responsibility to punish. Since both canon law and customary law recognized a husband's right to beat his wife, the assumption may have been that beating was to be expected. The attitude toward adultery emphasized the husband's moral dominance; when he strayed, he was made to pay, but he was also required to enforce the law in the household or be thought a weakling.

Local laws around Europe mentioned a number of other punishments for adulterous wives, including the traditional punishments of having their hair shorn, being whipped, and being paraded through town with their clothes torn. However, there are many cases in which accused adulterers were allowed to pay a fine rather than be publicly whipped. These fines ranged in amount depending on the ability of the sinner to pay—from as low as a few pennies (when a farm laborer might earn 35–50 pennies per year), to much more. Investigations into who was prosecuted and under what circumstances showed quite different patterns. In northern Europe, the records show a predominance of married men being arrested and fined for adultery. But further south, in Switzerland, women were more often prosecuted in adultery trials (McDougall 2014, 506–507).

Since adultery was frequently unprovable through the use of witnesses or other definitive evidence, some women in the High Middle Ages submitted to a judicial process called an **ordeal**. In an ordeal, the accused person, or his or her representative, agreed to undergo a physical challenge to allow God to reveal which of the parties was telling the truth. An ordeal might be unilateral (having one person involved) or bilateral (usually a duel). In a unilateral ordeal by hot water, the proband (the person undergoing the ordeal), after hearing mass and swearing an oath, plunged his or her hand into a pot of boiling water to take out a stone. In an ordeal by hot iron, the proband carried a red-hot piece of iron in his or her bare hand for a certain distance. In both of these situations, the proband then had the injured hand wrapped and left that way for three days. After three days, a panel made up of the local priest and other important people would view the hand and determine whether the wound showed God's favor (by healing) or not (by becoming infected). A unilateral trial by ordeal might also require the proband to eat some dry bread without choking or walk across red-hot coals without being burned. Ordeals seem to have taken place throughout the early and High Middle Ages, but in 1215, Pope Innocent III (ca. 1160–1216) ordered priests to stop participating in trial by ordeal, and the practice of unilateral ordeals gradually died out. Duels lasted longer; we will discuss this below.

Adultery was a particularly serious accusation against a queen and could be challenged by the ordeal. Several queens are recorded to have been accused of adultery and proven their innocence by walking over nine red-hot plow blades. Kunigunde (ca. 975–1040), queen of Henry II of Germany, is the most famous, but there is a similar story about Emma of Normandy (ca. 984–1052), wife of King Aethelred of England. Both stories are probably later embellishments by writers who believed in the sainthood of both women. There were real instances, however, in which paternity was proven by means of the ordeal. In 1218, a woman named Inga of Varteid undertook the ordeal of hot iron in order to prove that her son was fathered by King Hakon III of Norway. The ordeal proved the boy's paternity, and he became King Hakon IV (1204–1263) (Bartlett 1986, 20).

There are also some famous examples of adulterous wives who were tried by ordeal in medieval literature. For example, Queen

Isolde, wife of King Mark of Cornwall and lover of the great Arthurian knight Tristan, cleverly manipulated the ordeal to prove herself innocent of adultery in the romance of *Tristan*, written by Gottfried of Strassburg in the twelfth century. Isolde asked her lover, who was disguised as a leper, to carry her on his back across a wet patch of ground. When asked to swear her innocence, she swore that no man had been between her legs but her husband and the leper who had carried her. Isolde's manipulation of the ordeal process—since she was actually guilty—led Gottfried to remark in the romance that "Christ in his great mercy is pliant as a wind-blown sleeve." This remark suggests that even in Gottfried's time, some people felt the ordeal was an unreliable proof of guilt or innocence (Bartlett 1986, 17–20).

For upper-class people, trial by combat was also an option; women who chose trial by combat appointed a champion to represent their interest in a duel. This might provoke us to imagine situations in which armored knights battled for their ladies. This did sometimes happen, as in the rape case related by the chronicler Jean Froissart (see chapter one). Champions might also be chosen from among common people. In a 1063 case from the western French nunnery of Le Ronceray in Angers, a dispute over a piece of property was tried in an ordeal by battle in which the two champions were blacksmiths (Marchegay 1854, 3:125). Ordeal by combat was used as a proof later in history than the unilateral ordeal. Although many governments eventually made dueling illegal, the habit of dueling over matters of pride and honor lasted into the nineteenth century.

Toward the end of the Middle Ages, royal courts began to have more control over adultery cases as the structure of medieval justice became more secular. One justification for this change was the accusation that church courts were arresting innocent people for adultery and extorting money from them. Gradually, over the late fifteenth and sixteenth centuries, the prosecution of adultery changed focus from the husband to the wife. The jurists of the period restated the ancient legal doctrine that a wife's chastity was more important than a husband's purity because an unfaithful wife would interrupt the orderly inheritance of property from one generation to the other. By the mid-sixteenth century, Protestant and Catholic jurists accepted as given that women were temptresses whose unfaithfulness endangered both their husbands' money and the moral state of all of society. The "double standard" was firmly established in European legal precedent (McDougall 2014, 514–516).

Homosexuality

Sex between men merited serious punishment in medieval Europe. Historians have observed that beginning in the twelfth century, church authors increased their condemnation of men who committed sodomy, by which they meant anal or oral sex. St. Colomban (543–615 CE), an influential author of one of the early medieval Penitentials, prescribed ten years of penance for a single homosexual act. Female homosexuality, meanwhile, merited much less attention. The *Canons of Theodore*, written in the late seventh or early eighth century, prescribed a penance of three years for a woman who "commits fornication with a woman." The penance for female masturbation was also three years (Payer 1984, 41, 47). The lower punishment for women was possibly because the era's dominant idea of homosexuality was phallocentric—church authors did not recognize sex that did not include the penetration of some bodily orifice as worthy of the same kind of condemnation. There were certainly writers who worried that women might use objects as replacements for the penis in sexual activities together. The ninth-century bishop Hincmar of Reims (806–882) was clear in his condemnation of women who "are reported to use certain instruments of diabolical operation to excite desire" (Murray 1996, 198).

Same-sex relationships between women are hard to discern in medieval sources: church sources were resolute in condemning same-sex eroticism, and firsthand sources for same-sex relationships are rare. Sometimes the sources clearly avoid discussing them. A fifteenth-century poet named Michel Beheim wrote a series of poems on the seven deadly sins in which sins of "unchastity" are all described in detail, except for a sin that is so terrible that he cannot even bring himself to discuss it; this terrible sin was left to the reader's imagination, but it is not hard to imagine that he meant homosexuality (Puff 2013, 380–381). Such rhetoric, unfortunately, provides us unsatisfying information for what medieval people did or didn't do between them. Frequently, what little we know comes from judicial records in which sexual behavior was either a factor or a corollary. For example, in the early fifteenth century, a woman named Laurence petitioned the royal court of France to release her from prison. She claimed to have been seduced by a woman named Jehanne and to have entered into a passionate sexual relationship. When Laurence tried to end the relationship, Jehanne attacked her physically, bringing the affair into public view. Laurence succeeded in getting herself released from prison by claiming to have been Jehanne's unwilling victim; we know nothing of what happened to Jehanne (Bennett 2000, 18–19). This kind of judicial record is extremely rare. Literary historians, however, have found hints of same-sex eroticism in many medieval sources, even when sexual contact was not included. A Provençal poet named Bieris de Romans wrote a poem addressed to a "fair lady" named Maria in the thirteenth century; the text is much like comparable poems by men expressing their admiration for women, but the author is female (Dronke 1984, 98). Letters between nuns sometimes also contained intensely emotional, erotic language but in a celibate religious context.

Sex Work

Almost every culture in human history has had some instances in which people exchanged sex for money, property, or influence. In the Middle Ages, with its generally negative view of extramarital sex, religious leaders condemned prostitution as a form of fornication, and it was sometimes subject to harsh penalties. However, in certain circumstances, medieval society was willing to accept prostitution as a necessary evil. This ambiguity poses difficult questions for modern scholars. Not every person who exchanged sex for money or gifts would fit our modern definition of "prostitute" or "sex worker." Many women (and men) were victimized in situations that we would classify as rape, for which the term "prostitute" would not be accurate in a modern sense but which, in a medieval context, was condemned as illegal or sinful.

The word *whore* (Latin, *meretrix*) can provide us with a starting point. The word appears in ancient and medieval documents, but it is not a description of a profession but, rather, a reflection on the sexual behavior of a particular woman or women: a whore was someone who publicly displayed her sexuality, whether for money or not. Women who offered their sexual services for money were called *femmes publiques* (public women) in French, *meretrices publicae* (public whores) in Latin, and "common women" in English. Women could become "common women" willingly, but it was also quite easy to fall into "whoredom" against one's will. *Whore* could also be used for any women who transgressed social norms; since priests could not marry, their female companions were often called whores as well (Karras 1996, 27, 138).

Because medieval sex workers left no personal written sources for historians to explore, we are obliged to understand their lives by looking at court records and other legal documents that provide some clues. Some were itinerant, moving from place to place for clients, and some lived in hostels or in brothels. Some managed themselves, and some were under a **bawd** or pimp. Many made their living by working another job, like embroidery or wool working, and supplemented that income through prostitution. However, some laws, as in London in the mid-fourteenth century, prohibited sex workers from earning money by spinning or carding wool—probably to protect the livelihoods of women who worked wool (Karras 1996, 39). In rural areas, sex workers sometimes followed the progress of grape or grain harvests, where harvesters might be willing to hire them, or stayed in coastal towns to cater to men who traveled on the water (Rossiaud 1988, 3). In urban areas, where sex workers were numerous, demand was always high, and the need for new women was high as well.

We do not have much data telling us about the motivations of women who entered sex work. We might assume, probably correctly, that financial desperation played a role in some women's decisions. We know a little more about women who became sex workers through trauma or coercion. It would be a mistake to say that rape was rampant in the Middle Ages. However, young women were often assumed to owe sex to men who were of higher social status than they were. Chambermaids and lower female servants, in particular, were often considered the rightful prey of men in a wealthy household. If the sexual relationship became public or if the woman became pregnant, she often lost her place as a servant and had little recourse to anything besides prostitution to support herself. A study of late medieval Dijon based on the testimony of seventy-seven women who were sex workers showed that only eleven of those women claimed to have entered prostitution voluntarily. The others came to prostitution through the procuration of a family member, poverty, family conflict, by force, or after a rape (Rossiaud 1988, 33).

Young women who came to large cities looking for work were sometimes kidnapped and sold to brothel keepers or recruiters who worked for the large brothels of the city. A young woman named Ellen Butler, when looking for a job as a servant in fifteenth-century London, was taken and placed in a brothel by its owner, Thomas Bowde. Bowde demanded that Butler pay him a large sum of money when she refused to work as a prostitute. This left her to make a terrible decision between going to debtor's prison and entering sex work (Karras 1996, 57). Servants were sometimes sold into prostitution by their employers; some women were even sold by their families. Despite laws against this kind of sale, they continued all over Europe in cities where prostitution was big business.

When such cases ended up in law courts, it was rarely the actual clients who were convicted of crimes. Rather, the procurer, or **bawd**, whether male or female, was perceived as having "spoiled" a girl and could incur a penalty. This might be a monetary fine, or sometimes (if female), a physical sentence. Women in London could be sentenced to spending time in the **thewe**, a pillory that was reserved for the humiliation of women who committed minor crimes (Karras 1996, 57–58). Since procuring for sex work was regarded as a more serious crime than actually selling sex for money, laws sometimes allowed sex workers immunity from certain kinds of prosecution. A law of King Roger II of Sicily, dated about 1140, states that "known prostitutes" were to be considered immune to the laws that governed fornication and adultery. Prostitutes may have been "below the law, privileged in reverse," because they exchanged the stigma of sex work for some forms of legal immunity (Pullan 2016, 29).

A large percentage of bawds were women, which may strike us as surprising, but the trade was lucrative and provided women with money that they could use to supplement other jobs. Running a bathhouse, for example, was an opportunity to provide sex for customers; many bathhouses had a reputation for selling sex as much as bathing. Some bawds provided places for lovers to meet in secret. Sex workers could also procure sexual clients for each other, brokering deals with men who were interested in a particular woman and claiming part of her earnings. None of these events necessarily took place in a brothel. For an individual woman, selling sex for money might form only a part of the activities she undertook in order to survive—for the poorest, manual labor, petty theft, or rag picking; for women better off, spinning or sewing to make ends meet.

Sex workers were increasingly subject to restrictions from local laws and governments from the thirteenth to fifteenth centuries. City authorities increased the connection between local prostitution and city government by passing laws that were designed to keep them in particular parts of the city or to maintain control over them through their bawds. In justification for doing so, they claimed that having access to sex workers would keep the young men of the town from raping or seducing respectable wives and daughters. Gangs of young men, for example, troubled late medieval Dijon by singling out unprotected women and raping them. The town fathers provided for sex workers to offer sexual services to keep the young men satisfied; local prostitution was thought to be a way to prevent attacks on virtuous women. Young unmarried men who committed such crimes were regarded with sympathy, since their sexual needs were thought to have overwhelmed them (Rossiaud 1988, 20–21).

Surprisingly, church officials generally agreed that sex work was a necessary evil. Augustine of Hippo, the major fourth-century religious author, had used the metaphor that prostitution was like the sewer in a magnificent castle; evil things had to have some place to go in order to keep the castle from filling with filth—by which Augustine meant that young men were likely to turn to rape or to homosexuality without another outlet for their sexual needs. This way of understanding sex work continued into the High Middle Ages (Pullan 2016, 30).

In many places in the twelfth and thirteenth centuries, courts and municipalities wrote laws that restricted sex workers' clothing, living quarters, and activities. In Avignon, France in the 1240s, the municipal laws forbade them to live inside the city walls or to wear veils like respectable women. The statutes also forbade gambling after curfew in houses of prostitution. This indicates that there were houses of prostitution in Avignon and that sex workers were tolerated, even if they were regulated by the town. In Montpellier in the 1280s, after complaints from citizens about sex workers living in their neighborhoods, the bailiff of the king chose a street in a suburb of the city where they were required to live (Otis 1985, 18). Sex workers in London in 1351 were required to wear a hood of *ray*, a striped fabric, and were not allowed to wear fur linings in their garments (Karras 1996, 21). These laws represented steps toward the gradual municipal control of prostitution.

Municipal authorities had another reason for regulating prostitution: keeping the peace. Violence committed against sex workers was common. Some women had their heads shaved or their clothes torn; townspeople would break the doors and windows of their houses (Schuster 1994, 78). Many late medieval cities and towns built public or municipal brothels, a measure that was intended to protect, control, and manage sex work. These were usually funded by taxation and put under charge of a **bawd**, sometimes mockingly called an *abbess* if the manager was a woman. The abbess was responsible for recruiting women to the house and ensuring that they complied with any rules the city had for their conduct. Inmates of these official houses had to swear obedience to the town authorities, pay rent to the bawd once a week, pay the night watch protection money, and give money toward heating the house. Women who lived in these official houses of prostitution were sometimes a little older than women who were sex workers on their own. Most started their careers in their teens, sometimes as young as fifteen, while inmates of the official houses were often in their twenties. The existence of such "official" sex workers, of course, did not preclude other women from providing sex for money outside of state-sponsored brothels.

What happened to these women when they were no longer able to pursue sex work is a mystery. Some must have become bawds themselves. A few others entered real religious monasteries that were intentionally opened for reformed sex workers, particularly in the thirteenth and fourteenth centuries. Since medieval people understood Jesus's companion Mary Magdalene to have been a repentant prostitute, the stereotype of the reformed, holy woman carried much symbolic significance. Some refuges were called "Magdalene houses" for this reason. Preachers sometimes encouraged men of the faithful to marry repentant sex workers, and some upper-class people gave money to repentant prostitutes as dowries they could take into marriage. In Prague in the late fourteenth century, a popular preacher named Jan Milich of Kromeriz (d. 1374) preached to the city's common women with such success that he gathered a group of repentant women around him. Through donations, Milí could buy a series of properties around Prague to house his converts. The centerpiece of this community, which he named "Jerusalem," was a chapel built over the ruins of the city's largest public brothel. Milí 's success suggests that, in Prague at least, many women were eager to take advantage of the opportunity to leave sex work when their economic needs were met (Mengel 2004, 431). Such opportunities were rare.

It is not surprising that medieval people thought first of sexual sin when they thought of women. The overall rhetoric of gender, particularly attached to religion, guaranteed it. There were many other ways, however, in which medieval women might transgress society's norms. Religious orthodoxy also demanded beliefs and behaviors that some women rejected, or simply were accused of rejecting, throughout the late Middle Ages.

WOMEN AND RELIGIOUS HERESY

Mysticism and the ideal of apostolic poverty brought some groups into conflict with Catholic doctrine, and, beginning in the

Medieval people believed that Mary Magdalene, a companion of Jesus, was a repentant prostitute. In this ivory carving, Jesus appears to Mary Magdalene after resurrecting. (Gift of Mrs. Chester D. Tripp in memory of Chester D. Tripp. The Cleveland Museum of Art.)

twelfth century, women were active participants in heretical movements, or religious movements that the established church considered to be theologically wrong. The criteria that qualified thoughts as heretical were sometimes murky, and it is sometimes difficult to discern why one movement was called orthodox and one heretical. Individuals could be accused of heresy and be executed for it, but some believers also received lesser punishments from ecclesiastical authorities, such as penances on bread and water.

Historians have disputed whether heretical movements disproportionately attracted women away from orthodox practice because many movements featured expanded rights and positions for women. It is even possible that the church considered religious groups with female leadership as heresies from the start. However, other historians have pointed out that even when women joined heretical movements, they remained subordinate to the men in the sect; in most instances, women who joined heretical groups did not rise to higher office inside them. Because medieval society viewed women as gullible and given to error, they seldom held leadership positions. There were, however, a few notable exceptions.

An interesting example of a woman leader in a heretical sect is Guglielma (d. 1281), a daughter of the king of Bohemia, who gathered several dozen followers in Italy in the thirteenth century. Although she appears to have claimed to be an ordinary person during her lifetime, after her death, her followers, the Guglielmites, claimed that she had been the incarnation of the Holy Spirit, sent to convert Jews, Muslims, and pagans. Upon her resurrection, they believed, she would place a female pope, a "papesse," at the head of the Roman Catholic Church and begin a new phase of civilization dominated by a woman-led church. The female pope was already chosen: her follower, Mainfreda da Pirono, was set to take up the office. This open feminization of the godhead and of the church hierarchy made the Guglielmites the most radically pro-woman Christian sect of the period. As such, the sect was also in conflict with Catholic orthodoxy. Two decades after Guglielma's death, Sister Mainfreda and the other leaders of the sect were brought up before an inquisition. Three of them were executed, while Guglielma's body was exhumed and burned (Newman 2005, 4–5).

A larger movement called the Waldensians, or the Poor of Lyons, also faced persecution for unorthodox beliefs and practice. They were founded by a merchant named Valdes in the late 1170s. The Waldensian movement began in France, spread across the mountains to Italy and to Germany in the fourteenth and fifteenth centuries, and persisted until the Protestant Reformation. Among their doctrines was the belief that the Bible should be translated out of Latin and into vernacular languages so that ordinary people could understand it, an argument that was later echoed by the Lollards in England, by the Hussites in Bohemia, and eventually by Protestant movements.

Like the Franciscans, Waldensians had an understanding of apostolic poverty that included both begging and preaching. What differed was that some Waldensian women could also teach and preach. These "sisters" often lived in houses called *hospices* where traveling Waldensians could stop and receive a meal and where local women could come for religious teaching. Hospices were supported by donations from their local communities, and the sisters spun, wove, and cooked very like their counterparts who were married and in households. The simple lifestyle of Waldensian believers convinced many poor people that they were less greedy and more faithful than the wealthy church officials whom they only occasionally saw. Later, inquisitors asked locals whether they had given alms or donations of food or money to the Waldensians. For many people, the answer was "yes."

A study of the trial of four Waldensians, two men and two women, in Toulouse in 1319, has shown that the teachings that they believed in were gender-specific. Male Waldensians avoided venerating the Virgin Mary, discouraged visiting saints' shrines, and emphasized the masculinity of God. But the two Waldensian women still maintained their veneration of Mary and their faith in the saints. These gendered beliefs would have been hard for a medieval woman to give up, despite preaching to the contrary; Mary and the saints were important objects of prayer from women. It is often difficult to tell how much, or how little, the average person would have understood about the charges of heresy. It is likely that some of the people questioned had no idea they were heretics until they were summoned before an inquisition (Shahar 2001, 100–101).

The Cathars (the root word is the Greek word for "pure"), who were also called Albigensians, in southern France, were the most prominent heretical sect of late twelfth- and early thirteenth-century Europe and persisted in secret for centuries afterward. The two names, however, are modern innovations; their name for themselves was "Good Christians." Scholars have discussed whether Catharism was the theological heir of other heresies from earlier in the Middle Ages, or whether this particular sect was native to southern France, where it was most prominent. However, believers ranged significantly further afield as well: the Netherlands, Italy, and even, for a short time, in England (Peters 1980, 103). The basic theology of Catharism was *dualist*: followers believed that the world was a battleground between two gods, a good god and an evil god, who were equally powerful. The Cathars reasoned that since the world was so full of evil, it could have no connection with a benevolent and all-good God. They believed that humans had blessed souls whose natural place was heaven but that these souls were confined to their bodies by the Evil One. Death, therefore, was not something to be feared, and birth was not an occasion for celebration, because once the child cried, another angelic soul would be imprisoned in flesh (Brenon 1992, 94–95).

Cathars believed that male and female souls were theologically equivalent, no matter what body they were enclosed in, so both men and women were considered to be able to attain spiritual perfection. Both men and women could become Cathar priests, who were called perfecti, or perfects, by inquisitors. Perfects received a blessed meal called the consolamentum and, afterward, were required to be completely celibate. (Ordinary believers, who were called *credentes*, or believers, usually waited until they were about to die before receiving the consolamentum and did not normally practice celibacy.) Perfects practiced ascetic habits in meals and dress, rejecting any meat and refusing to kill animals. Cathar theology stated that the believer who died without the consolamentum was doomed to reincarnation, which could happen up to seven times, until the soul had fulfilled its penance and was ready to become angelic again (Peters 1980, 124). Asking suspected heretics to kill chickens or other animals was one technique with which the inquisition could uncover perfects hiding in the population.

Inquisitorial records that preserve the testimony of accused Cathars in southern France give us a picture of a rural everyday life affected by basic questions about Catholicism: whether the communion wafer was really Christ's flesh; whether pleasure in sex was sinful or not; and under what circumstances souls would be allowed into heaven. A fourteenth-century priest in Montaillou, France named Pierre Clergue used Cathar beliefs to deceive and rape his female parishioners while reassuring them that extramarital sex was not sinful. One young woman, Grazida Lizier, twenty-one years old when she was interrogated, had a long sexual relationship with Clergue after she lost her virginity to him in a local barn. When she married, the relationship continued with the full knowledge of her husband. When asked if she thought her relationship with Clergue was sinful, Grazida replied that Clergue had told her, "To lie with a woman was no sin as long as it gave her pleasure." She agreed with him, stating that "I still would not have thought it a sin, because of the shared joy of love." In contrast, Mengarde Buscalh, who also had a sexual relationship with Clergue, claimed he had threatened her into having sex (Dronke 1984, 204–205, 210).

Mengarde's testimony also included information about use of the consolamentum. She had a son about four months old who was ill and in danger of death. A Cathar perfect approached her about giving him the consolamentum so that, when he died, he would immediately become "an angel of God." Mengarde refused, however, when she learned that after the ritual, she would no longer be allowed to nurse her son because his purity could not be violated through consuming food. "I said I'd never stop giving him my breast as long as he was alive," she testified (Dronke 1984, 210).

While many heretical movements of the central Middle Ages were supported chiefly by lower-class believers, the Cathars were an exception: among the noble people attracted to Catharism was the countess Esclarmonde de Foix (ca. 1165–1215). Esclarmonde, widowed after having six children, became a perfect around 1200 and converted many people in her circle to Catharism. She attended a meeting in Pamiers in 1207 when a Catholic representative debated the Cathars on theology. She apparently spoke up so much that the Catholic legate told her, "Go to your **distaff**, madam, it is not proper for you to speak at such a gathering" (Labarge 1986, 211). Some of Esclarmonde's family were also active Cathars, notably her sister-in-law, Philippa de Montcada, and her nephew, Roger Bernart de Foix. Besides the better-known noblewomen like Esclarmonde, numerous young girls and elderly women sought to become consecrated "good women." Many of these women had passed their childhoods with good women, who might be their relatives, only to leave when they wished to marry (Pegg 2008, 86–87).

Esclarmonde died in 1215 of natural causes, but her relatives were soon caught up in the violent series of events that is known now as the Albigensian Crusade. This crusade was, in part, an attempt by Pope Gregory IX (1227–1241) to restore church power in southern France and to rein in the power of southern French nobles. In this conflict, the nobles of the region lost their power and holdings to the king of France, Louis IX (1214–1270). The papacy was then free to send in inquisitors to try to root out the heresy from the population. Repeated inquisitions, however, failed to entirely eradicate Cathar beliefs from southern France. Some scholars have posited that surviving Cathar beliefs were one of the reasons that southern France quickly became a Protestant stronghold during the Reformation.

MAGIC AND WITCHCRAFT

While popular culture today often identifies witchcraft with the Middle Ages, the most important period for witch trials and executions was the early modern period, between 1500 and 1700 CE. In modern times, some popular writers have promoted the belief that the witch trials were, in actuality, the persecution of an ancient nature religion that survived throughout the Roman period and the Middle Ages. No evidence exists for this point of view, however. Modern neo-pagans practice a number of rituals and beliefs that are based on ancient models, but there is no connection between these practices and medieval witchcraft as it is described in contemporary documents. Medieval beliefs about witchcraft existed firmly inside the medieval Christian worldview that Satan and his demons were constantly attempting to damn souls to everlasting torment. This was true of both accusers and defendants. While inquisitors were imagining the activities of witches, many people who were arrested believed in those activities as much as their accusers did, even if they were not guilty of attempting magic themselves.

Belief in magic—the belief that particular words, actions, or materials could cause visible effects on the natural world or on a person—was widespread during the whole of the Middle Ages. In Roman times, the use of magic was universal and not considered significant unless it was used against someone else, in which case it was labeled ***maleficium*** (literally "a bad deed," often translated as "sorcery"). The person affected by ***maleficium*** could sue for damages. In Christian Rome, writers against magic identified the nature spirits (in Greek, *daimones*) who provided magic power with demons, evil spirits who were uniformly the tools of Satan (Bailey 2001, 963). Church authorities later ignored some magic, particularly the normal everyday magic habits of peasants, which they dismissed as superstition. A work called the *Canon Episcopi* (ca. 900 CE) stated with deep condescension that "Some wicked women are perverted by the Devil and led astray by illusions and fantasies induced by demons, so that they believe they ride out at night on beasts with Diana, the pagan goddess, and a horde of women" (Russell and Alexander 2007, 53). The canon writer's intent may have been to dismiss superstitious fantasies but, over time, Diana was replaced with Satan, and widespread belief in such "shabbats" or Sabbaths grew (Bailey 2001, 961–962).

Old prejudices and stories that dated from the ancient world also reemerged and became identified with witchcraft, including accusations of cannibalism, orgies, and infant sacrifice. The early Christians and Gnostics of the first and second centuries had been the targets of such accusations, which probably originated in a misunderstanding of the Eucharist as an infant-killing ritual. The first medieval accusations of the kind were in 1022 in the city of Orléans, France, when a group of people accused of heresy were charged with participating in orgies and eating communion wafers made from the ashes of newborn babies. These accusations were easy to transfer onto accused witches. In the high Middle Ages as well, some learned upper-class men, some of them churchmen, were believed to be trying to affect the natural world through more complex magic that used astrology and alchemy. In 1326, Pope Innocent II issued a **bull**, *Super illius specula*, that condemned practitioners of all sorcery and commanded all papal inquisitors to seek out those who "enter an alliance with death and make a pact with hell" (Bailey 2001, 966).

By the early fourteenth century, folklore and theology had combined to create a shared belief in witchcraft that could then be used to punish people, especially women, who were, for one reason or another, transgressors of society's expectations. From the eleventh century onward, the punishment for women who committed heresy was burning at the stake, which functioned as a sort of official punishment for all actions that were particularly heinous. These terrible executions increased in number as the central church expanded the work and scope of inquisitions, and witchcraft became a crime that was punished by burning as well (Russell and Alexander 2007, 64–66, 70).

Torture was an acknowledged part of the medieval justice system and was sometimes used on accused witches and heretics. In general, women were tortured less often than men, in part because they were considered to be physically and mentally weaker. In questions of treason, magic, and heresy, however, the crimes were thought to be so serious that torture was warranted. In the late fourteenth century, King Juan I of Aragon (1387–1396) accused his stepmother, Queen Sibilla of Aragon (d. 1406), of both treason and sorcery, alleging that she was making him ill through black magic. We know of this case because a well-known legal author of the period, Baldus de Ubaldis (d. 1400), was asked to give his opinion, particularly since the accused was a queen. Baldus wrote that torture should be used only in cases in which the evidence was particularly strong and that any testimony given under torture was not valid unless confessions were made not only during torture but afterward, when the fear of torture was no longer a factor. He mentioned that Sibilla was, in fact, tortured, but we do not know the outcome of the trial. Since Sibilla outlived her stepson, who died in 1396, she may have been exonerated (Pennington 2012, 2–4).

Two key facets of late medieval witch accusations are particularly important: the concept of a pact with the Devil and the belief in demonic sex. In 1233, Pope Gregory IX accused Waldensian heretics of selling their souls to the devil and of worshipping the devil at their meetings (Russell and Alexander 2007, 71). By the early fourteenth century, kings such as Philip IV of France used accusations of devil worship to discredit churchmen who tried to block their political agendas, and since condemned prisoners forfeited all their possessions, money gave prosecutors a considerable motive. Late in the fourteenth century, the University of Paris declared that all magic involved demonic power, and witchcraft was labeled a serious, Europe-wide problem. As with heresy, courts often used torture to elicit confessions from the accused. Secular authorities such as royal courts took responsibility for physical punishments of heretics, since officials of the church were forbidden to shed blood (Russell and Alexander 2007, 76–77). When church courts handed over convicted witches or heretics to secular courts, they avoided having the taint of bloodshed attached to them.

The trial of Alice Kyteler in 1324 is often cited as the first witchcraft trial in which a woman was accused of intercourse with a demon and of practicing sorcery (***maleficium***). Alice Kyteler was a wealthy moneylender who lived in Kilkenny, Ireland. She was married four times and was accused of heresy and sorcery by her stepchildren. She reaped financial benefits from all her marriages and used that wealth to support the career of her biological son, William, but not his stepbrothers and sisters. According to her accusers, Alice Kyteler had a familiar demon who appeared as a black man, dog, or cat and with whom she had sexual intercourse. This demon supposedly gave her both money and magical power. The stepchildren brought their accusation to the English bishop of Ossory, Richard Ledrede, who opened up a case against Alice, accusing her of *maleficium* and of devil worship, including leaving the parts of dead animals at crossroads to create magic power and denying Christ and the church. Local Irish officials (probably correctly) interpreted Bishop Ledrede's action as an attempt to extend the power of the English church into Ireland, and fought back. The ensuing political morass led to Alice's flight from Kilkenny, probably to England or to Flanders, the execution of her maid, and the trial and penance of her son, William Outlaw (Williams 1994, 20–24).

In Alice Kyteler's case, we can see some of the trends that developed into a full-blown movement against witchcraft: accusations of devil worship and deliberate rejection of the church and descriptions of foul potions or mixtures that forced people to do things against their will. The growth of these beliefs led to the publication of the witch-hunter's manual called the *Malleus Maleficarum* (*Hammer of Witches*). Published in 1486, this book was the work of two Dominican inquisitors, Joseph Sprenger and Heinrich Kramer, who laced it with vicious assertions that women were at the most serious risk of becoming witches. Their reasons included claims that women were more "stupid, fickle, lighter-headed, weaker, and more carnal than men" (Russell and Alexander 2007, 79). Papal approval and the newly arrived printing press helped the *Malleus Maleficarum* to be one of the most important books of the period, issued in print fourteen times between 1486 and 1520 in various languages.

The *Malleus Maleficarum*, although it was very important for shaping beliefs about witches and women, did not invent the **misogyny** that underlay witchcraft accusations. Its authors were parroting older views attached to women, their sexuality, and their intelligence. They may also have been influenced by the changes to the population before, during, and after the **Black Death** (the outbreak of **bubonic plague** that took place from 1347 to 1351). Although most women in the Middle Ages lived under the protection of a husband or of a male relative, in the thirteenth century, women who were unable or unwilling to marry could choose the monastic life or join a community of **Beguines** (see chapter six). During and after the Black Death, convents became closed to everyone except the rich by requiring higher dowries, and the Beguine movement gradually died out. This left a subset of women who, because they never married or were widowed, had no place to go and no male protectors. Some historians have suggested that this demographic twist accented and intensified popular views of solitary women as sexually promiscuous and dangerous. Such women were easy to accuse with little fear of criticism, and the arguments of the *Malleus Maleficarum* served to confirm misogynistic stereotypes with ecclesiastical backing (Russell and Alexander 2007, 113–115). Official propaganda about the dangers of witchcraft helped develop the "witch craze" of the sixteenth and seventeenth centuries.

There is no way of knowing how many people (many women, but some men as well) were accused or executed as witches in the entire period of the witch-hunts; there are no aggregate numbers that are reliable, and witchcraft accusations took place all over Europe and in the European colonies of the New World. Modern scholars have arrived at an estimate of around one hundred and ten thousand accusations and around sixty thousand deaths, some by burning and some by hanging or other methods (Levack 1987,

21). It is important to remember that the period of the witch-hunts lasted about three hundred years. Additionally, our knowledge of what happened comes from authorities who were responding to or making the accusations against witches. Sometimes courts obtained information about the accused through judicial torture, either of the accused or of witnesses, so even legal sources must be used with caution. Sources also survive unevenly in history; for some places, there are plentiful records to be investigated for witchcraft trials and, for some places, no sources survive at all.

CONCLUSION

Thus far in this book, we have traced some of the major ideas and experiences that shaped medieval women's everyday lives. In the next chapter, we will look directly at some women whose writings we can still access. Although these women do not always give us the answers to our questions, they provide an exciting window into daily lives.

7

WOMEN IN THEIR OWN WORDS

This chapter will discuss a selection of women writers from the Middle Ages in their everyday lives. Finding the writing of women authors from the medieval period can be challenging, not least because fewer women were able to become literate than men. Some people in the Middle Ages could read but not write, as the two skills were taught separately from each other, and it is possible that was true for some women. Even in the later Middle Ages, when more women became able to both read and write, their writing was circumscribed by the control of books and education by men: fathers, uncles, church superiors, and husbands. Those women who did write were fortunate enough to have the physical space and economic privilege that they needed for writing.

While scholars are fortunate to have surviving writing from women in the Middle Ages, we certainly do not have all of it. Much of women's writing must have been destroyed, labeled as old-fashioned or unimportant over the many centuries, or simply suppressed. For example, letters from nuns in the early and central Middle Ages, such as Constance of Angers below, only survived because those nuns were correspondents of important male authors whose letters were considered worthy of being copied and saved. Writing by women may also have been rewritten by male authors;

medieval scholars relied on the concept of authority to judge the merits of texts, and male writers may have co-opted women's works to increase the texts' authority. However, women's writing should not be seen as inferior to men's simply because there is less of it surviving. Scholars have pointed out that at least some of the time, an "anonymous" text might have had a female author.

This chapter will expand the information given about individual women earlier in this book in brief biographies centered around what women's writing can tell us about daily life. The authors are listed in chronological order. There are fewer women writers for the early Middle Ages than for the late Middle Ages, a result of the expanding literacy taking place in the later period. In addition, they are mostly upper-class women; the voices of lower-class women are seldom heard in their own words. Many of these writers wrote of themselves as weak or ignorant—so much so that one might wonder if they had deep problems with self-confidence. Some of them may well have, but it is a cliché of writers in the Middle Ages, men as well as women, that they never compliment themselves. Scholars have, therefore, looked past these statements to see what the true messages of the authors really were.

BRUNHILDA (SIXTH CENTURY CE)

Brunhilda, a Visigothic princess, married Sigebert, King of Austrasia, northern Gaul, in 566 CE. She had a son, Childebert, and a daughter, Ingund. Ingund married a Visigothic prince, Hermenigild, and had a son. But Hermenigild fell out with his father, and his father had him killed. Ingund, now a widow, attempted to flee back to Austrasia with her little boy but was captured along the way by some soldiers of the Byzantine emperor Maurice. Ingund herself then died. Only the little boy, named Athanagild, reached Constantinople; the emperor hoped to hold him as a hostage that he could use to influence Childebert, the boy's uncle, to enter a war in Italy.

Heartbroken by the loss of Ingund, Brunhilda wrote a letter to the empress of the Byzantines to plead for her to send Athanagild to Gaul. "Let me," she wrote, "who have lost a daughter, at least not lose her sweet child, who remains for me . . . let me be consoled by you through my captive grandson's safe return" (Dronke 1984, 27). It is not known what happened to Athanagild or whether Brunhilda ever got her grandson back. The letter is one of a very few from women of Brunhilda's time period, showing that grandmotherly love was as present in the Middle Ages as it is today.

BAUDONIVIA (ca. 600 CE)

Baudonivia was a nun at the monastery of Holy Cross in Poitiers, France. She undertook a project of writing the *Vita* (life) of the convent's founder, the Frankish queen Radegund (ca. 520–587 CE). Her *Life of Radegund* is unusual because a prominent churchman and author, Venantius Fortunatus (ca. 530–ca. 609 CE), had already written a *vita* of the saint, and Baudonivia both knew him personally and knew his work. It may seem strange that a nun would write what was essentially a second biography of the saint when she had already been profiled by such an illustrious author. Baudonivia's work, however, presents a different view of Radegund than Venantius's work. While Venantius had emphasized Radegund's larger story as queen, wife, and then nun, Baudonivia preferred to emphasize Radegund's role as a bride of Christ and as a role model for the nuns of Holy Cross. It is a more personal biography and gives a different view of the famous queen.

DHUODA (NINTH CENTURY)

All we have of the Frankish noblewoman Dhuoda is her *Book for William*, dictated to a scribe in Latin somewhere around 841–843 CE. Scholars have posited that she was born about 803 because she married Bernard of Septimania in June 824 and was probably from the northern Frankish lands because her first language was Germanic. Bernard was a noble at the court of Louis the Pious (814–840 CE), emperor of the Franks, and deeply involved with the intrigue and backbiting of that court. He spent very little time with his wife. Dhuoda had one son, William, in 826, and another, whose name was to her unknown, in 841. In the meantime, she lived in the city of Uzès in southern France, where she may have been in exile or may have been in charge of Bernard's interests in the region. Their father took both children away from her, William at approximately fourteen years of age and the younger son (whose name she did not know) when he was still a newborn infant. William was then traded as a hostage as a guarantor of his father's loyalty to King Charles the Bald. This heartbreaking situation was what prompted Dhuoda to dictate the *Book for William* (Dronke 1984, 37).

The premise of the *Book for William* was that because she was far away from her sons, Dhuoda wanted to give them the religious education that she would ordinarily have given them had they been with her. The book shows both Dhuoda's deep religious faith and her complete loyalty to her husband and to the emperor. She urged both her sons to take care of their immortal souls and gave them many suggestions about how to do this. She also, however, admonished them to be loyal to their father; even if William was at a foreign court, she wrote, he should strive to make his father's interests his focus.

It is unknown whether Dhuoda knew her family's eventual fates. Bernard, her husband, was executed for treason. William became a rebel against Charles the Bald and was executed as well, four years later. Dhuoda's date of death is also unknown, as is the story of what happened to her second son. Only a few small places in the text give more information about Dhuoda's life. Scholars have learned that she had to borrow money to support Bernard's military debts, "not only from Christians but also from Jews" (Dronke 1984, 53). She asked William to make sure that in the event of her death, these debts and any others should be paid. She also wrote that she had many illnesses but did not describe them further.

What makes Dhuoda's writing unusual is the degree of feeling she imparts in her short work—personal feeling as much as religious feeling. It is easy to sympathize with a mother whose children have been taken from her and whose attitude toward her own future is so resigned. It is a work that reminds us that though there are many years between Dhuoda and the twenty-first century, we can see many human qualities in the writing of the past.

HROSVITHA OF GANDERSHEIM (ca. 935–ca. 973)

The clever and highly educated Hrosvitha was born to a noble family in Lower Saxony and spent most of her life as a canoness in the abbey of Gandersheim, an extremely wealthy monastic house. The noble canonesses were allowed to study not only the writers of the church but also classical Roman poets and writers. Under the tutelage of a superior named Rikkardis, Hrosvitha learned the foundational topics of classical education: the trivium, made up of grammar, logic, and rhetoric; and the quadrivium, made up of astronomy, arithmetic, music, and geometry. She wrote many works of poetry and the history of the monastery but is most well-known for her six plays. She was the first woman playwright in European history and is the only woman playwright in this collection from the early Middle Ages.

Hrosvitha designed her plays in the style of a Roman playwright called Terence (second century BCE). The plays of Terence were popular in the tenth century as examples of fine Latin-language style, and many people studied them as exemplary texts. Terence's plays were comedies, usually farces that featured sexual intrigues, slapstick comedy, and happy endings. Hrosvitha did not want to replicate Terence's subjects along with his style, writing disapprovingly, "Many Catholics can be found who prefer the vanity of pagan books to the utility of holy scripture" (Dronke 1984, 69). Therefore, three of her plays are stories of virgin martyrs, and three are about ascetic saints. The stories still have their elements of humor. For example, in the play *Dulcitius*, a Roman governor who wants to rape three Christian virgins is deceived by God into thinking the pots and pans in his kitchen are the women. He embraces and kisses the pots and pans, gets soot all over him, and frightens his family and soldiers when he emerges. After this funny moment, however, the play goes into the martyrdom of the three virgins, whose executions form the "happy ending" of the play, since they will go to heaven afterward. The "happy" part of this ending may be hard for us to understand, but to Hrosvitha's medieval audience, this convention of martyr stories was expected.

Hrosvitha's daily life in the convent at Gandersheim was probably quite different from the lives of other Benedictine nuns. Gandersheim had been founded specifically to be a refuge for noblewomen and was very like a small city on its own, with a significant library, its own courts, and even its own coinage. As a canoness, she did not take full monastic vows, although Gandersheim had nuns who did. Canonesses like Hrosvitha were required to take vows of chastity and obedience but not poverty. She could, and probably did, have servants, see guests, buy her own books, and leave the nunnery when she wished. Hrosvitha also certainly spent some time at the emperor's court, where her plays were either read out loud or performed. She broadens our understanding both of dramatic literature and the lives of noble religious women in the central Middle Ages.

WYNFLAED, WULFWARU, AND WULFGYTH (TENTH TO ELEVENTH CENTURIES)

Some details of certain tenth- and eleventh-century Anglo-Saxon women were communicated through the wills they left behind them. About seventy-two of these wills survive. Wealthy Anglo-Saxon women controlled their personal property at a much higher rate than upper-class women elsewhere. Although they probably did not write down their wills themselves, the documents the scribes recorded for them tell a great deal about everyday life. Wynflaed, who lived ca. 950, began her will by detailing an extensive list of properties and objects that she wanted to leave to the church, including an altar cloth and a gold cross. Most of her belongings, however, went to her children, particularly to her daughter Aethelflaed. Aethelflaed received not only land but many personal items, including tableware, tapestries, jewelry, bedclothes, chests, and "books and such small things." A substantial part of Wynflaed's will also went to the freeing of numerous enslaved women, sometimes including their husbands and sometimes not. She also bequeathed particular enslaved women to others, including a weaver and a seamstress.

Wulfwaru, who lived during the reign of King Aethelred (984–1016), bequeathed both personal property and land to her four children, two sons and two daughters. The two sons and her elder daughter inherited manors, including their produce and the people who worked them. Her younger daughter, Aelfwaru, received half of an estate shared with her older brother. Wulfwaru's personal treasures went to her daughters. She mentioned especially two cups worth four pounds, two brooches, and the large sum of thirty **mancuses** of gold. Similarly, the will of Wulfgth, dated to 1046, parceled out large estates to Wulfgyth's children and gave a few small bequests to different churches. Wulfgyth's will ended with a threat of divine punishment for anyone who attempted to avoid enforcing her wishes: "May he be delivered into the abyss of hell to Satan the devil and all his accursed companions" (Amt 2010, 114–117). Curse clauses like this one were not unusual in medieval legal documents when the parties were uneasy about what might happen after their deaths.

Legal documents like wills are one important resource for modern scholars who want to know what everyday women owned and whether they had control over property. Although it is hard to know how the women made their decisions about who was to inherit what, one can still perceive what they thought was important and who they wanted to recognize with a bequest.

WALLADA BINT AL-MUSTAKFI (d. ca. 1091 CE)

The daughter of the caliph, or ruler, of Muslim Spain, Wallada bint al-Mustakfi is the most well-known of the female Andalusian (Spanish) Muslim poets from the Middle Ages. Her mother was probably an Ethiopian Christian slave named Bint Sakrah al-Mawruriyah. Wallada was well-known for her poetry as well as for the meetings, or salons, of upper-class learned people that she sponsored. The Spanish Muslim historian Al-Fath ibn Khaqan (d. 1134) wrote of her that "Her presence encouraged the old to behave like the young" (Fernea and Bezirgan 1977, 69). Wallada declined to wear a veil and had verses of her own work embroidered on her sleeves. She fell in love with a poet named Ibn Zaydun (d. 1071), and the two exchanged romantic verses. She wrote, "Before, when you visited me during the wintry season, I spurned the brazier, so great was my fire of passion!" When the relationship soured, however, Ibn Zaydun complained, "[Wallada] is like water, difficult to hold in hand; its seething foam prevents getting it easily!" (Fernea and Bezirgan 1977, 70–71). Wallada's unconventional life is interesting in itself, but it also tells us about the conventions for women in Spain in the eleventh century. It is one of very few glimpses into the life of women in Spain during the Muslim period.

CONSTANCE OF ANGERS (LATE ELEVENTH TO EARLY TWELFTH CENTURIES)

Constance of Angers is the name of a young nun that we know from a letter written to Baudry of Bourgeuil (ca. 1046–1130), a well-known French Benedictine abbot who wrote to many correspondents in the late eleventh and early twelfth centuries. Constance was a novice at the monastery of Our Lady of Charity of Angers, also called Le Ronceray, in the late eleventh or early twelfth century. Her letter survived in a manuscript of Baudry's poems that is now in the Vatican Library. Although the manuscript makes reference to the names of other nuns who exchanged letters with Baudry, Constance's poem is the only one that was copied into the manuscript. Both Baudry's poem and Constance's reply are in Latin and are the same length (179 lines) and in the same complex meter and rhyme style, based on the *Héroïdes* of Ovid (first century BCE), a Roman Latin writer. The texts are flirtatious and, in some ways, erotic. Constance spoke of having Baudry's letter in her lap, which "heated up my heart" (Tuten 2004, 261). Strangely, though, the flirtatious style was a commonplace for monastic letters at the time, even between men. Baudry had many correspondents, both male and female, for whom he made verses about love and longing, and some nuns of Ronceray seem to have exchanged letters with Marbode, bishop of Rennes, around the same time.

Letters like Constance's are rare in comparison to letters written to men and by men. Women's correspondence was not often preserved, and what is more, the convention of the flirtatious monastic letter fell out of fashion in the twelfth century as times changed. Still, there are enough letters to provide a tantalizing window into the daily life of Benedictine nuns. Angers in the eleventh and twelfth centuries had a cathedral school, a place in which young men were trained to be priests. Le Ronceray's nuns were connected to the cathedral school via the men, called canons, who administered their religious services. One contemporary during Constance's day was a canon named Hilary, who wrote numerous poems, some of them to the abbess of Le Ronceray. Constance and her fellow novices also learned under the tutelage of a nun named Emma who functioned as their *grammatica*, or grammar teacher. Constance playfully referred to her as their "mean stepmother." They clearly studied the formal Latin language, not just by reading and imitating Christian authors but ancient writers as well.

Evidence exists around Europe for literate nuns who wrote their own Latin texts. A collection of texts from eleventh-century Regensburg contains thirty letters from nuns to their magister, or teacher. Although they were not as skilled as Constance with the difficult rhymes and meters of Latin poetry, their poems are still emotionally complex and effective, sometimes even cheeky, as one woman wrote, "You praised my beauty—as if that deserved it" (Dronke 1984, 91). Another example—identified by some scholars as being by Héloïse (below)—is a text called the *Epistolae duorum amantium* (*Letters of Two Lovers*). In these love letters between a man and a woman, dating from the twelfth century, the woman writes, "I shall never have joys except when you give them" (Dronke 1984, 96). Such texts teach us that, far from being voiceless, nuns in the Middle Ages spoke in their daily writing, often enough that hints remain as to how they felt and what they thought.

TROTA OF SALERNO (TWELFTH CENTURY)

Very little is known about the woman called Trota who lived in the twelfth century in Salerno, Italy, and wrote medical advice for women. Scholarship has recorded the names of a number of women practicing medicine there in that period who were called the *mulieres Salernitanae* (women of Salerno). Despite popular guesses as to Trota's origin, nothing is known for certain about her family, her training, or her birth and death dates. She is only known to have written two works, one of which is still extant, a text called *De curis mulierum* (*Treatments for Women*), and another work called the *Practica*, which is now lost. *De curis mulierum* forms part of a three-part medical collection that is called the *Trotula*. The other two sections were anonymously written but were probably written by men (Green 2020).

From what we know about medical practice in the twelfth century, Trota would likely have diagnosed her patients' illnesses using a urine sample. The body was believed to be made up of four **humors** or substances whose imbalance could cause disease. Medieval doctors examined the urine of patients in special glass flasks through which they could study the color, smell, and sometimes even taste of urine, which they used to get an understanding of how the **humors** were working in the patient's body. After diagnosis, the medieval doctor would advise changes in diet and exercise, herbal remedies, or baths to raise or lower the body temperature to rebalance the body **humors**. In extreme cases, the physician might prescribe procedures such as bloodletting.

The cures in *De curis mulierum* are generally mild. Almost all the remedies included in the text are intended to be given in a bath or applied to the skin. They give excellent clues about the various complaints from which everyday medieval people might have suffered. There are reproductive concerns, including childbirth, fertility, and remedies for complaints of the penis. There are recipes for cosmetics designed both to whiten and to redden the face, and wrinkle and freckle removers. The treatise also includes detailed instructions for getting rid of body lice and worms, which were common complaints of the period (Green 2001, 116–165). Trota's work allows us an unusual way to peek into women's everyday concerns, their health, and their hygiene.

QASMUNA BINT ISMA'IL IBN BAGDALAH (TWELFTH CENTURY)

Born in Spain, Qasmuna was one of a number of women who wrote poetry in Arabic. We learn of her from al-Sayuti (ca. 1445–1505), a collector of women's poetry. He related that she was Jewish and was educated by her father, Isma'il, who was also a poet. Her three surviving poems are beautiful expressions of a young woman's longing for companionship. In one, she addressed a deer grazing in a meadow, writing, "I resemble you in wildness and in blackness of the eye" (Nichols 1981, 157). In Qasmuna's poems, we can catch a very small glimpse of what an educated Jewish woman in Muslim Spain could do.

HÉLOÏSE OF ARGENTEUIL (ca. 1100–1164)

The story of Héloïse and her husband, Peter Abelard, is one of the best known and most studied romantic stories of the Middle Ages. Even as a young woman, Héloïse was famous in learned circles; she was educated in Greek, Latin, and Hebrew and was the ward of her uncle Fulbert, a canon at the cathedral of Notre-Dame. Abelard, a scholar at the University of Paris, wrote down their story, which he titled "History of My Calamities." He had heard of Héloïse's reputation and calmly asserted that he set out to become her lover. Soon he had been made her tutor, and they fell in love—or at least in lust. She became pregnant, and they had a son together. They were then married, but Héloïse's uncle was still angry at Abelard. He sent a group of thugs to castrate Abelard in vengeance for his public embarrassment. Abelard considered this tragedy to be divine intervention and decided to become a monk and convinced Héloïse to become a nun, though it was initially against her wishes.

The writings of Héloïse that now survive began after she had read Abelard's account of their misfortunes. By that time, she was the abbess

The tomb of Abelard and Héloïse, the famously star-crossed lovers, is in the Père Lachaise cemetery in Paris. (Izanbar/Dreamstime.com)

of a nunnery that Abelard had founded for her. They exchanged eight letters that are still extant. Letters two through five are known as the Personal Letters and deal with their past and their relationship. Letters six through eight are known as the Letters of Direction, in which Abelard gives Héloïse advice and theological reasoning in answer to her questions about the nunnery. Although scholars in the past doubted that the letters attributed to Héloïse were actually her own writing, most scholars now consider her letters genuine.

Scholars have also identified some poems that they believe may also be by Abelard and Héloïse in the period before their affair was discovered. Traditionally called *Epistolae duorum amantium* ("The Letters of Two Lovers"), the manuscript containing the poems was discovered in the fifteenth century at the monastery of Clairvaux by a monk who copied sections of them—unfortunately, not all of them—as models for literary exercises. His manuscript, which survives today, provides enough of the texts to furnish scholars with an enjoyable controversy. These letters are from lovers who almost compete in their flowery language about each other, the woman just as much as the man, and they make references to a relationship similar to the one Abelard described in his "History of My Calamities." As sources for medieval love poetry of a high level, these letters are very much worth reading (Mews 1999).

HILDEGARD OF BINGEN (1098–1179)

Hildegard of Bingen was one of the most important female authors of the Middle Ages. She was born around 1098 CE to noble parents. She became an **oblate,** enclosed with an anchoress, Jutta of Spondheim, at the age of eight at the church of Disibodenberg, in what is now western Germany. Jutta's cell was attached to a wealthy community of Benedictine monks, and, in the early part of Hildegard's life, she and Jutta were under the supervision of the abbot. By the time Hildegard had grown up and Jutta had passed away, a small group of nuns had gathered around them. After the nuns chose Hildegard as their leader, she petitioned the abbot of Disibodenberg to allow her nuns to build their own independent monastery at Rupertsberg, a distance away. He was initially reluctant to do so, whether for the safety of the nuns in their new house as it was being built or because he realized that Hildegard was a visionary who would one day bring great attention to his monastery. Hildegard finally convinced him to allow the move when she was struck by an illness that left her unable to rise from her bed. She explained that God was punishing her for not following his direction to build the new monastery. This convinced the abbot, and Hildegard and twenty nuns founded the monastery at Rupertsberg in 1150.

Hildegard's visions left her weak and ill, and she often described herself as a "poor little woman." She emerged from her illnesses with detailed, highly metaphorical visions and messages from God to the faithful. Several manuscripts that are richly illustrated provide visual images to connect with the visions. Hildegard was forty-two when she had a vision in which God commanded her to tell her visions to other people. At that point, she sought ecclesiastical permission from her superiors and received official sanction from Pope Eugenius III in 1148 to record and circulate her visions. Several scholars have wondered whether a type of migraine headache provoked Hildegard's complex visions (Newman 1985, 167). However, even if we may wonder about the sources, we should remember that people in the Middle Ages took such visions very seriously.

In addition to her three mystical works, *Scivias* (an abbreviation of *Sci vias domini, Know the Ways of the Lord*), *Liber vitae meritorum* (*Book of the Rewards of Life*), and the *Liber divinorum operum* (*Book of Divine Works*), Hildegard wrote many letters; many musical works; a musical play called the *Ordo Virtutum* (*The Order of Virtues*); and two books on medicine, the *Physica* and *Causae et Curae* (*Causes and Cures*). There are also two biographies of Hildegard written by her confessor and secretary. Although none of these works is designed to illuminate Hildegard's daily life, this large body of work provides many clues to her points of view and the events of her life.

In between writing and sometimes dictating to a scribe, Hildegard managed a monastery of nuns who needed her leadership. The sisters observed the *Rule of St. Benedict* for their daily worship (see chapter three). One of Hildegard's many letters was an explanation of the *Rule of St. Benedict* for some Belgian nuns who had written to ask her advice. The nuns lived quietly, and Hildegard provided them with music to sing and perform—some of the earliest music that we know of that was written specifically for women. Hildegard also worked in the monastery's infirmary, where she applied her own theories to medical knowledge of the period and wrote her two medical books. Her remedies are largely made up of herbs and other natural substances, explained by her as having virtues sent by God.

Hildegard also caused some controversy. Some people were scandalized by her major preaching trips around the region, even though she had permission from the pope. She was criticized when she dressed her nuns as brides for communion (Bynum 1992, 134).

She also allowed a nobleman who had been **excommunicated** to be buried at the monastery, a position that placed her in opposition to all the local authorities, including her ecclesiastical superiors. During this time the monastery was placed under interdict—meaning that the nuns could not sing the **divine office**, confess, or take on new sisters—and the authorities threatened to **excommunicate** them all. Hildegard wrote a letter declaring that her nuns were commanded to worship and sing by God and that the interdict violated God's wishes for them. Eventually, the interdict was lifted (Morrison 2016, 108).

Hildegard is an unusual example of how women who were considered to be holy could participate in activities, such as preaching, that were normally closed to women.

HERRAD OF HOHENBURG (ca. 1130–1195)

Herrad of Hohenburg was probably given as an **oblate** to the monastery of Hohenburg, outside Strassburg, as a young child, and received the best education available to women at the time in this powerful Augustinian abbey, which had close connections to the emperor Frederick II Barbarossa (ca. 1123–1190). She has been connected by some authors to the territory of Landsberg, but the attribution dates only to the sixteenth century. What is more certain is that she became abbess of Hohenburg sometime between 1167 and 1176. After a number of years organizing the abbey's possessions and relationships, Herrad began the monumental work *Hortus Deliciarum*, or *Garden of Delights*. The *Hortus Deliciarum* was intended to be a compilation of current theological thought for the educational benefit of the nuns of Hohenburg. Herrad and her collaborators wrote and compiled the manuscript beginning in about 1175. Some of the many texts the manuscript contains have not yet been identified. The manuscript was also richly illuminated: 254 painted miniatures survive which illustrate people, concepts, and theological subjects. Although the original manuscript tragically burned in the nineteenth century, authors of the period preserved enough of the manuscript to give us the opportunity to wonder at and enjoy this extraordinary work.

CLEMENCE OF BARKING (LATE TWELFTH CENTURY)

Clemence was a nun of Barking Abbey in England in the late twelfth century, probably within the reign of Henry II (1154–1189) or Richard I (1189–1199). Barking was a very prosperous and powerful Benedictine monastery east of London, founded in the seventh century but most powerful in the twelfth. Like Gandersheim, it had a large library, and the abbess was responsible for administering both considerable wealth and many people. Almost nothing is known of Clemence apart from her name, though her command of Anglo-Norman French suggests that she was Anglo-Norman by birth, and since the abbey was full of noble women, she was probably from a prominent family.

Clemence translated a Latin biography of the legendary North African saint Catherine of Alexandria (fourth century), who refused to marry and was martyred around the age of eighteen under the Roman emperor Maxentius. Catherine was widely venerated around Anglo-Norman England, and Clemence wrote that she had translated the story "so that it will be more pleasing to those who hear it" (Auslander 2012, 171). The Latin *Life of St. Catherine* was set in the fourth century, but Clemence told the story in a way that may have reflected the politics of her own day. For example, it is easy to draw parallels between the violent emperor in Catherine's text and King Henry II (1154–1189), who had control over Barking and other women's monasteries. Both men, the character and the real king, were betrayed by their queens: Maxentius when his wife converted to Christianity, and Henry when his wife, Eleanor, rose up against him in conjunction with his sons in an armed revolt. This uprising happened in 1173–1174, which is the early end of the period when Clemence may have been translating the *Life of St. Catherine*. At the end of 1174, Henry imprisoned Eleanor in a castle, where she stayed for fifteen years. If Clemence was actively criticizing the king in her translation, her message "would be subversive then and even dangerous" (Auslander 2012, 179).

Looking at saints' lives written and translated by women, we can learn much about their everyday attitudes and values. Such stories tend toward religious imagery, but there is still plenty to find that reflects genuine everyday life.

THE *TROBAIRITZ* (TWELFTH TO THIRTEENTH CENTURIES)

There are about twenty women's names associated with poems produced in southern France in the late twelfth and early thirteenth centuries. Along with their male counterparts, who are known as troubadours, the *trobairitz* wrote popular poetry for singing before wealthy lay audiences. They wrote in Occitan, the language of southern France at that time (there were also female writers in northern French, who were called *trouvères*). Many of the *trobairitz* were from noble families, though little background is available for most of them. The Comtessa de Dia (early thirteenth century) was probably the wife of the lord of Die, and her first name was possibly Beatriz; but for many of the writers we have a single name or a name associated with a place. We know that their poems were set to music, but we have only one tune written down, the Comtessa de Dia's song "A chantar m'er de so qu'ieu non volria," meaning "I must sing a song I'd rather not."

Raw emotion jumps out from these poems as the poets express their love and describe their lovers, both positively and negatively. The object of the writer's love is often a man who is not the poet's husband, which was not unusual in courtly love literature of the time. Some poems take the form of laments that the lover has been unfaithful or cruel. Castelloza (early thirteenth century) wrote to a man she loved that "I don't know why you are always on my mind, for I have searched from top to bottom your hard heart; and yet my own's unswerving" (Bogin 1976, 121). Sometimes, they express all the bliss of love. Azalais de Porcairagues (b. ca. 1140) wrote to her lover, "Handsome friend, I'd gladly stay forever in your service" (Bogin 1976, 97).

It is a much-discussed question among scholars whether the people who wrote back and forth to one another as lovers—some of whom were married to other people—were ever physically intimate. In some of the poems, the love is unrequited and what we might call platonic love. In others, physical love and sex are clearly a part of the conversation. In one of the Comtessa de Dia's poems, she wrote frankly, "I'd give almost anything to have you in my husband's place" (Bogin 1976, 89). However, extramarital sex was taboo in medieval Europe, and, among the nobility, it was particularly important that the parentage of any child was known to be genuine. These variables leave us with the question unanswered.

MARIE DE FRANCE (FL. TWELFTH CENTURY)

The poet known as Marie de France is mysterious. She revealed in one of her works that she was French, but that is all that is known about her apart from her works. It has been guessed that she wrote in England between 1170 and 1190 and that she was known at the court of King Henry II (reigned 1154–1189) of England and

Queen Eleanor of Aquitaine. She wrote a religious poem called "Saint Patrick's Purgatory," in which a knight visited the afterlife, and a series of translations of Aesop (sixth century BCE), the ancient storyteller, called the *Fables*. She is most famous for her *Lais;* a lai or lay is a romance set in rhymed couplets. Marie wrote in Anglo-Norman French, but these poems were so popular that they eventually appeared in Middle English, Old Norse, Middle High German, Latin, Hebrew, and Italian. Marie herself seems to have been literate in Latin, French, and Breton (the language of the French duchy of Brittany).

Marie's poems are most useful to us as reflections of what upper-class people liked to hear in stories. Many of her stories are adaptations from Breton fairy tales. They are about true love, filled with drama and action. In one lay called *Lanval*, a knight of King Arthur fell in love with a beautiful, magical maiden who made him promise not to tell anyone about their relationship. Lanval could not resist telling Queen Guinevere about his love, though, when the queen invited him to become her lover (Queen Guinevere comes out very poorly in this story). When he broke his promise to keep silent, his magical lady disappeared, breaking his heart. Worse yet, the queen accused him of attempted rape. Just as it looked like he would be executed for treason, his love returned and carried him away to Avalon, and they were never seen again.

Apart from the romance of the story, the beauty of the lady, and the jealousy of the queen, there are a few clues in *Lanval* that indicate that Marie was thinking about the good and bad behavior of nobles. At the beginning of the story, Lanval was poor and not well-known among King Arthur's knights. Once his magical lady enriched him, though, he behaved as a good wealthy man should. "Lanval gave costly gifts, Lanval freed prisoners, Lanval clothed the jongleurs (musicians), Lanval performed many honourable acts" (Burgess 1986, 75). It is possible to read this list as a hint to the nobles who were the audience for this lay, particularly the part about "clothing the jongleurs"—no doubt Marie and her contemporary writers would have appreciated some extra clothing! We can also see everyday life in the descriptions of clothing and finery, a sort of fashion show for the rich listener.

MARGUERITE PORETE (d. 1310)

Marguerite Porete, a Belgian mystic, was persecuted during her life for stating what she believed to be the divine truth given to her by her mystical visions. She kept the habit of a **Beguine** as she went from place to place, preaching a message that eventually caused her to be imprisoned. Her work, the *Mirror of Simple Souls,* urged complete annihilation of the self in God. It was written in lyrical, poetic language, which sometimes drifted into the erotic, and which envisioned the soul and God as lovers. Marguerite asserted that those who completely gave in to God, freeing themselves from all wishes and earthly concerns, would become "free souls," so that they would neither want nor need anyone, including (and perhaps especially) the church. She criticized the Catholic Church as the "little church," calling it subordinate to the greater church of free souls because of its emphasis on reason rather than ecstatic experience; true faith did not need reason because the soul would be unable to sin if united with God. Her message led to her imprisonment twice: once for a year and a half, after which she was released and continued to preach, and once, which ended when she was executed by burning at the stake. At the time, the inquisitors searched for every copy of the *Mirror of Simple Souls* to destroy. However, copies remained in circulation: there is one French copy still extant, and five different translations into Latin, Italian, and English (Dronke 1984, 217–228).

Marguerite's insistence that her mystical experiences did not need to be approved by the church hierarchy situated her as one of the boldest religious writers of her time. Some scholars have identified a protofeminism in her work. Like Joan of Arc, who was her contemporary, she did not hide behind self-deprecatory language and never referred to her sex as a weakness. Her execution did not dim her message for future generations (Morrison 2016, 140–141).

JULIAN OF NORWICH (ca. 1343–ca. 1416)

Julian of Norwich was one of the most important spiritual writers of the late Middle Ages and the first woman known to have written in English. Very little is known about her early life, and scholars have made a number of educated guesses about her background that vary from a background as a wife and mother to a background as a professed nun who became a recluse or anchoress in midlife. What is definitively known about Julian is only that she became very ill at thirty years old, experienced sixteen revelations or "showings" from God, and spent the second half of her life as an **anchoress**, enclosed in a small cell attached to the church of St. Julian in Norwich, U.K. (McAvoy 2008, 3–5).

Two works detail the revelations that Julian experienced, as well as her attitudes about her own life and her gender. The *Vision of God Shown to a Devout Woman* (a title bestowed by editors of Julian's texts, also called the *Short Text*) is a brief work, written soon after the first revelations took place in or around 1373 CE and included Julian's reactions to the visions. The later reworking, or *Long Text*, also called the *Revelation of Divine Love*, added two newer revelations that occurred in 1388 and 1393 (McAvoy 2008, 3). A meditation on the life and death of Christ, the *Revelation of Divine Love* argues that God gave love to the world: "Wouldst thou learn thy Lord's meaning in this thing? Learn it well: Love was His meaning" (Julian of Norwich n.d.).

Although an anchoress was never supposed to leave her cell, Julian's living space was not severely uncomfortable; she was permitted blankets and bedding and even a cat. Her daily life enclosed in her cell was solitary and full of prayer, but we know she had some contact with people who came to visit her there, including Margery Kempe (profiled below). According to the thirteenth-century *Ancrene Wisse*, a guide for anchoresses, visitors (mostly women; anchoresses were directed to avoid talking to men) could speak to her through a small window covered by a curtain to ask for prayers and advice. She also had a window between her cell and the church, through which she could see Mass and take Communion, and a window for the two servants whose job it was to cook her meals and attend to her bodily needs (Millett 2009, 161–162).

CHRISTINE DE PISAN (1364–1430)

Christine de Pisan is arguably the best known of all the women writers of the Middle Ages, particularly the late Middle Ages, and is unusual in having been a prolific and popular writer outside of the convent. Born in Venice, she moved to Paris with her father, a physician and astrologer, at the age of four. She was married at fifteen and had three children. When her father and her husband died, Christine was left with her children, a niece, and her mother to support and turned to writing to bring in income from noble patrons. At the beginning of her career in the 1390s, she wrote poetry, especially love songs, allegory, and personal advice for people in the royal family. Her works were disseminated both in manuscript and in print during the fifteenth and sixteenth centuries.

Some of Christine's works were far ahead of their time: she directly challenged sexist stereotypes, proving not only that a woman could write works of literature but also that a woman could be the judge of what was true and right in French medieval society. After more than a decade writing love poetry and other prose works, she defended women from the invective of a book called the *Roman de la Rose*, written in two sections by Guillaume de Lorris and Jean le Meung. Although the *Roman de la Rose* was written in the thirteenth century, the work gained a new popularity at the end of the fourteenth and beginning of the fifteenth centuries. While the first section was a courtly love allegory, the second (and much longer) section was a satire, depicting women as vicious, unfaithful seducers. In 1399, Christine wrote the poem "Epitre au Dieu d'Amours" ("Letter to the God of Love"), arguing that the satire was indecent and vulgar and that it condemned all women for the faults of only a few. Her criticism spawned a flurry of letters from learned writers, both supporting and not supporting the *Roman de la Rose* and inaugurated a literary movement known as the *querelle des femmes* ("the debate about women"). The *querelle des femmes* is the name given by scholars to the centuries-long debate about the morality and intelligence of women, in which many writers sought to prove that women were the intellectual and moral equals of men (Kelly 1982, 10–11; Krueger 2013, 593–595).

In 1404, Christine responded to another thirteenth-century work, the *Lamentations of Matheolus*, a satire in which clerical marriage was lampooned, but which also contained hostile language toward women and, in particular, to women's bodies. Christine countered this book with *The Book of the City of Ladies* (1405), an adaptation and expansion of Giovanni Boccaccio's *Concerning Famous Women*. The *Book of the City of Ladies* was far from a copy though. It began with a description of Christine herself, sitting appalled after reading the *Lamentations of Matheolus*, and wondering why God made women if they were so lacking in virtue. Three women, Lady Reason, Lady Rectitude, and Lady Justice, appeared to her wearing crowns and commanded her to defend women against the invective of the *Lamentations*. Christine then portrayed one hundred important women, mostly taken from Christian classical literature. These women's stories formed a metaphorical wall for the City of Ladies, in which virtuous, courageous women could live without fear of slander (Krueger 2013, 595–596). Altogether, Christine produced twelve major works and many minor ones between 1400 and 1415.

Christine's everyday life as a writer was affected by her status as a widow, a group for whom she expressed sympathy in her work. As a widow, she had control over her own finances and professional life, but she was also vulnerable because she had no male protector. She may have worked as a copyist for a time, a trade in which she would have been paid by the page. She also depended on her father's court connections to gain audiences for her many works. Her biography of the French king Charles V was commissioned by his brother, Duke Philip of Burgundy; it has been suggested that she might even have had access to the royal library. She had such a good relationship with the earl of Salisbury that he kept her son in his household. However, it has been suggested that in the last years of her life, Christine and her female relatives retreated to the Dominican convent at Poissy, where they were safe both from the outside world and from the conflict that was raging in France at the time (Labarge 1986, 235–37). At Poissy, although they were not nuns, they would have lived simply and safely as boarders.

Since the 1980s, scholars have debated whether Christine de Pisan was a feminist for her time. Her writing does not fit the modern definitions of feminism that include the goal that women and men should have equal access to public roles; rather, she defended women inside the roles that medieval society expected them to have—the family and the church. She did, however, pioneer spaces in which secular female writers could take control of their own stories. The popularity of her works in the fifteenth and sixteenth centuries suggests that her audience was broad, until her works fell out of favor and out of print in the seventeenth century. She has found a new readership in modern times.

CATHERINE BENINCASA OF SIENA (1347–1380)

The mystic saint Catherine of Siena occupies a prominent place in the history of fourteenth-century Italy. Born the last of twenty-four children to a middle-class Italian family, early in life, Catherine decided to stay a virgin and strenuously resisted her parents' attempts to find her a husband. She joined the Dominican order as a **tertiary** in 1363 and adopted extremely harsh ascetic practices, denying herself nourishment to the extent that that she was known to chew food and spit it out or even cause herself to vomit (Vauchez 2018, 1–37). Catherine's severe practices attracted disciples, including her confessor Raymond of Capua (1330–1399), who was also her biographer. Over her lifetime, she dictated more than 380 letters—the most from any one medieval woman known—and a large work called the *Dialogue*, a four-section treatise on theology.

Catherine was far from a meek religious woman living quietly in a cloister. Her ascetic practices gave her a reputation for holiness that allowed her to affect the politics of Italy, particularly in her home town of Siena. Siena in the fourteenth century was a complex, commerce-driven society that was home to the bankers of the papacy and large trading interests. The city had gone from sixty thousand people to twenty thousand during the Black Death (1347–1353) and had a rivalry with Florence for the control of Tuscany. Different factions controlled the city during Catherine's lifetime, and, at one time, two of her brothers served in its government. She traveled south of Siena in 1377 with her disciples (whom she called her *famiglia*, family) and stayed at the manor of a local noble family, the Salimbeni. Magistrates from Siena demanded that she return to the city because her presence at the Salimbeni manor implied that she supported the family politically. In a letter of response, Catherine scolded them: "The citizens of Siena do a very shameful thing in believing or imagining that we are here for making plots in the lands of the Salimbeni, or in any other place in the world" (Luongo 2006, 1–2). She argued that she was staying there for the purpose of saving souls and claimed that the magistrates had no jurisdiction over her because she was serving the higher agenda of God.

Despite her assertions, Catherine did affect Italian politics in the wider sense. During the early fourteenth century, the papacy had moved to the city of Avignon, close to the French border, and in Catherine's day, the pope was threatened by a large alliance of northern city-states (including Siena) called the Florentine League. During this period, which was known as the "War of Eight Saints," Catherine attempted to reconcile the two factions with a vision of a united Christendom in which problems in the church would be reformed and the city-states recruited to a new relationship with the papacy. She died in 1380, aged about thirty-three, only two years after the pope moved back to Rome (Luongo 2006, 21). Whether read for her theological discussions or to understand the politics of the late fourteenth century, Catherine's letters are important for anyone who wants to study Italy during the early Renaissance.

MARGERY KEMPE (1373–ca. 1439)

The *Book of Margery Kempe*, dictated to a priest by a townswoman in what is now King's Lynn, United Kingdom, in the fourteenth century, is a difficult text but is also full of insights for modern historians. Margery Kempe was born to a well-off family of merchants. Her father was mayor of Lynn five times and was also a member of Parliament. She was married when about twenty to a man from another middle-class family, John Kempe, who was a brewer. They were married until his death and had fourteen children together.

Margery Kempe began to have visions after the birth of her first child and continued to have mystical experiences for the rest of her life. Although it appears that she could neither read nor write, she had a knowledge of many of the religious works circulating in her day, including works about the mystics St. Birgitta of Sweden and St. Margaret of Hungary. She imitated the saints as best she could through prayer and loud, violent weeping. Her husband was baffled by her desire to cease having sexual intercourse (despite fourteen children!) and to devote herself to religious practices, but he finally granted her wish to be celibate in 1413.

Not long after, Margery resolved, partly inspired by divine visions, to visit Jerusalem, where she did so much weeping and wailing that she tried the patience of the other pilgrims. Returning from Jerusalem, she passed through Assisi and Rome. In Rome, she experienced a "mystical marriage" to Jesus, imagining a ritual in which she replaced her earthly husband with Christ. After returning home, she decided—again with divine encouragement—to visit the major pilgrimage site at Santiago de Compostela, Spain. Such experiences made Margery unusually well-traveled for the period she lived in, and it was even more unusual for her to travel alone, picking up companions along the way. It speaks to her determination and resourcefulness, despite her descriptions of herself as weak and sinful.

Upon her return to Lynn, Margery became caught in a controversy centered around an English priest and heretic, John Wyclif, whose followers were called "Lollards." Margery's odd behavior caused her to be accused of Lollardy several times, but, each time, she was able to call on the church to attest to her orthodoxy. She cared for her husband after a bad fall confined him to bed and eventually when he became senile and incontinent (Bale 2015, 161–162). After his death, she accompanied her widowed daughter-in-law to Prussia, returning to England only with great difficulty. She probably died around 1439.

Margery Kempe's *Book* contains many moments of everyday middle-class life, from Margery's attempts at starting businesses in brewing and milling (both failures), to her descriptions of her clothing before her conversion, which she later considered sinful (Bale 2015, 13). She recounts frank conversations with her husband, and there are glimpses of Margery's travels around her area of England, as well as her visits to Jerusalem and to Rome. Although there are not descriptions of everyday chores, her book records the voices of those who believed Margery was a living saint and those who thought she was a heretic. Because of this, Margery Kempe's *Book* is an unusual window onto medieval life.

BARTOLOMEA RICCOBONI (ca. 1369–1440)

Bartolomea Riccoboni was a member of the convent of the Corpus Domini (body of Christ) in Venice, Italy, in the late fourteenth and early fifteenth centuries. The convent had begun as a Benedictine house but, in 1394. was converted into a house of Dominican nuns that was wealthy and connected to the upper class of Venice. Bartolomea was twelve when she entered in 1394 and lived there until her death in 1440. Her writing is unusual for a medieval woman because she wrote chronicles. Chronicles are works that tell the history of a place or group, often in a yearly format, and she is one of the rare women who wrote such a work whose work survives. She also wrote a **necrology**, a list of the dead associated with the convent that served as a prayer guide for the nuns when they commemorated their supporters. Bartolomea's chronicle, the *Cronaca del Corpus Domini*, detailed not only the experiences of individual nuns in her convent but also the history of the papal schism that divided the church in the early fifteenth century. This schism was the result of infighting and political conflict in the Catholic Church that led to a feud over who was the pope: there were three candidates, each claiming to have more right to the position than the other two. Bartolomea supported a Venetian-born pope, Gregory XII (ca. 1326–1417), but the city of Venice declared its support for a different pope. Her recounting of the conflict, in which some sisters disagreed with their superiors, emphasized the sisters' respect for each other and the peaceful character of the convent. There were also moments of everyday life for the nuns. Bartolomea's biography of the convent's religious superior and supporter, Giovanni Dominici, is also interesting for its information about life in the convent. At one point, Dominici became worried that the nuns were punishing themselves too much through self-flagellation, a practice in which a person uses a whip or other device to provoke suffering during prayers. He asked them to surrender all the instruments they were using for this practice and was shocked by the number and severity of the instruments he received (Dunphy 2012, 185–190). Bartolomea's works have an authoritative tone that is often missing from the work of medieval women. She can also tell us how one small house of nuns managed to thrive during a period of intense political pressure.

HELENE KOTTANNER (ca. 1400–AFTER 1470)

The *Recollections (Denkwürdigkeiten)* of the fifteenth-century Austrian noblewoman Helene Kottanner are surprisingly little known by readers today. She described herself as "of humble birth," but she played a dangerous, secret role in the fortunes of the royal houses of Austria, Hungary, and Bohemia. She married twice, once to the mayor of her hometown of Ödenburg and later to a more prominent nobleman. His connections to the crown of Austria enabled her to become a lady-in-waiting to the duchess Elizabeth (1409–1442), wife of Duke Albert of Austria. When Duchess Elizabeth had a daughter (also named Elizabeth) in 1436, Helene Kottanner became part of the household of the new child. During this time, she became very close to the duchess and spent a great deal of time with her as she attempted to have a son for Albert. In 1438, Duke Albert was elected as the king of Germany and, in 1439, the king of Hungary. Queen Elizabeth was pregnant when Albert died of dysentery later in 1439. She was under pressure to remarry from the nobles of Hungary, who chose the sixteen-year-old king of Poland as her next husband, but Elizabeth was sure that the child she was carrying was a boy who could inherit Hungary under her guardianship. To ensure that her son could inherit, she asked Helene Kottanner to steal the holy crown of Hungary, which, according to legend, had been the crown given by the pope to the first Christian king of Hungary, Istvan, around the year 1000. The holy crown was so revered in medieval Hungary that possession of it enabled the holder to claim the approval of God.

The story of the theft of the holy crown reads like an adventure novel. The pregnant queen was on the move, worried that she would be forced to marry the king of Poland, when she asked Helene Kottanner to steal the holy crown. Kottanner and an unnamed servant made a difficult fifty-mile trek to the castle at Visegrád, where the crown jewels were stored. They broke the seals on the vault, stole the crown, and replaced all the locks and other safeguards that sealed it. Kottanner then sewed the holy crown into a pillow and loaded it into her sledge to return to the queen. On the way back, they had to cross the frozen Danube River; the ice cracked under the sledges, and one of them fell into the river. According to her own account, Kottanner arrived just in time to assist at the birth of Elizabeth's son, Ladislaus V. Ladislaus (called "Posthumous" because he was born after his father's death) was baptized and crowned in 1440, held in Kottaner's arms and wearing robes she had hand sewn. After Queen Elizabeth's death in 1442, the royal family honored Kottanner with an estate near Bratislava (Classen 2007, 315–317; Dunphy 2012, 190–192).

Helene Kottanner's *Recollections* allow us to take a look behind the scenes of the fraught political scene in fifteenth-century Eastern Europe and also into the closed world of aristocratic women at the mercy of their dynastic obligations. The adventures of Helene Kottanner introduce us to a resourceful woman who bravely changed the course of history.

THE PASTON WOMEN (FIFTEENTH CENTURY)

In 1735, a collection of about one thousand letters was found at Oxnead Hall in Norfolk. They are the letters of the Paston family, a prominent upper-class family in the area during the fifteenth and early sixteenth centuries. The letters express the activities and personalities of several women who married into the Paston family: Agnes Berry (ca. 1400–1479), Margaret Mauteby (ca. 1420–1484), and Margery Brews (ca. 1460–1495), as well as their husbands, sons, and other relatives. Although the women did not always write down the letters themselves, they dictated them, and their personalities shine through the letters.

Agnes, the wife of William Paston, comes through as a ruthless personality. She and William had five living children together, and some of her letters tell of her matchmaking for them. She arranged her oldest son John I's marriage to Margaret Mauteby in the late 1430s and expected his unquestioning obedience to her wishes. Later she quarreled with him over some property at Clere. Her daughter-in-law Margaret wrote to John, "She says she knows of no claims or legal right you have concerning it, unless you want a dispute with her, which will not earn you any respect" (Watt 2004, 75). Agnes was willing to cause a division within the family in order to maintain her personal rights.

Margaret, the person to or for whom most of the letters were written, had seven children with her husband, John Paston. The Wars of the Roses affected the fortunes of the whole family, and political quarrels with some of Norfolk's most powerful nobles caused them both personal and financial loss. At one point, Margaret worried that she would have to defend their home physically while John was in London. She wrote to him, asking him to buy crossbow quarrels and pikes. Others of her letters gave news of her attempts to marry off her own children and requests for more normal items, such as caps and dresses. In one letter from 1441, she humorously asked her husband for a new belt because her pregnancy had made it impossible for her to wear the others. "I am now grown so slim," she wrote, "that I cannot be girt into any girdle I have except one" (Virgoe 1989, 41). In a 1463 letter to her eldest son, John, she scolded him for angering his father and then went into detail about one of their horses, writing, "He shall never be any good for riding not much good for ploughing . . . I do not know what to do with him" (Watt 2004, 70). Everyday concerns and family matters are outlined in her letters.

Margaret's greatest challenge may well have been the love affair between her daughter, Margery Paston, and Richard Calle, the steward of their estate. Margery and Richard married secretly against her parents' wishes in 1469. When they discovered this, her parents were infuriated and separated them from one another until a church court determined that the marriage would stand. Margery endured being thrown out of the house by her mother, who directed the servants never to let her in again. The two women never made up. Margaret did, however, leave a small bequest for Margery's eldest son in her will (Watt 2004, 115).

CONCLUSION

This book introduces the wide world of European medieval women. Though strong social customs and formal laws restricted their choices, medieval women were not as oppressed and silenced as we in the twenty-first century often imagine. We know the most about the women who left us something behind, whether that is a text (used mostly by historians) or an artifact (used mostly by archaeologists). Source rarity certainly shapes what we have learned and will be able to learn about medieval women. A surprising number of sources do survive, however, and they provide us with opportunities to see inside the everyday lives of women whose hopes and experiences were not that different from our own.

PRIMARY DOCUMENT A

Héloïse to Abelard, Letter 4, ca. 1132

This letter is part of the "Personal Letters," a series of communications between Héloïse of Argenteuil and her husband, Peter Abelard. In this passage, written after Abelard's castration and her retreat to a convent,

Héloïse laments the all-consuming nature of her love for Abelard and her pain at their separation. She blames herself for all the negative things that have arisen from their relationship and expresses, in her guilt, anger at heaven for what she sees as its unjust punishment of them both.

Dear *Abelard*, pity my despair! Was ever anything so miserable! The higher you raised me above other women who envied me your love, the more sensible am I now of the loss of your heart. I was exalted to the top of happiness, only that I might have a more terrible fall. Nothing could formerly be compared to my pleasures, and nothing now can equal my misery. My glory once raised the envy of my rivals; my present wretchedness moves the compassion of all that see me. My fortune has been always in extremes, she has heaped on me her most delightful favors, that she might load me with the greatest of her afflictions. Ingenious in tormenting me, she has made the memory of the joys I have lost, an inexhaustible spring of my tears. Love, which possessed was her greatest gift, being taken away, occasions all my sorrow. In short, her malice has entirely succeeded, and I find my present afflictions proportionately bitter as the transports which charmed me were sweet.

But what aggravates my sufferings yet more, is, that we began to be miserable at a time when we seemed the least to deserve it. While we gave ourselves up to the enjoyment of a criminal love, nothing opposed our vicious pleasures. But scarce had we retrenched what was unlawful in our passion, and taken refuge in marriage against that remorse which might have pursued us, but the whole wrath of heaven fell on us in all its weight. But how barbarous was your punishment? The very remembrance makes me shake with horror. Could an outrageous husband make a villain suffer more that had dishonored his bed? Ah! What right had a cruel uncle over us? We were joined to each other even before the altar, which should have protected you from the rage of your enemies. Must a wife draw on you that punishment which ought not to fall on any but an adulterous lover?

Besides, we were separated; you were busy in your exercises, and instructed a learned auditory in mysteries which the greatest geniuses before you were not able to penetrate; and I, in obedience to you, retired to a cloister. I there spent whole days in thinking of you, and sometimes meditating on holy lessons, to which I endeavored to apply myself. In this very juncture you became the victim of the most unhappy love. You alone expiated the crime common to us both: You only were punished, though both of us were guilty.

You, who were least so, was the object of the whole vengeance of a barbarous man. But why should I rave at your assassins? I, wretched I, have ruined you, I have been the original of all your misfortunes! Good Heaven! Why was I born to be the occasion of so tragical an accident? How dangerous is it for a great man to suffer himself to be moved by our sex!

. . . If I have committed a crime in having loved you with constancy, I shall never be able to repent of that crime. Indeed, I gave myself up too much to the captivity of those soft errors into which my rising passion seduced me. I have endeavored to please you even at the expense of my virtue, and therefore deserve those pains I feel. My guilty transports could not but have a tragical end. As soon as I was persuaded of your love, alas! I scarce delayed a moment, resigning myself to all your protestations. To be beloved by *Abelard* was, in my esteem, too much glory, and I too impatiently desired it not to believe it immediately. I endeavored at nothing but convincing you of my utmost passion. I made no use of those defenses of disdain and honor; those enemies of pleasure which tyrannize over our sex, made in me but a weak and unprofitable resistance. I sacrificed all to my love, and I forced my duty to give place to the ambition of making happy the most gallant and learned person of the age. If any consideration had been able to stop me, it would have been without doubt the interest of my love. I feared, lest having nothing further for you to desire, your passion might become languid, and you might seek for new pleasures in some new conquest. But it was easy for you to cure me of a suspicion so opposite to my own inclination. I ought to have foreseen other more certain evils, and to have considered, that the idea of lost enjoyments would be the trouble of my whole life.

How happy should I be could I wash out with my tears the memory of those pleasures which yet I think of with delight? At least I will exert some generous endeavor, and, by smothering in my heart those desires to which the frailty of my nature may give birth, I will exercise torments upon myself, like those the rage of your enemies has made you suffer. I will endeavor by that means to satisfy you at least, if I cannot appease an angry God. For, to show you what a deplorable condition I am in, and how far my repentance is from being available, I dare even accuse Heaven every moment of cruelty for delivering you into those snares which were prepared for you.

. . . During the still night, when my heart ought to be in quiet in the midst of sleep, which suspends the greatest disturbances, I cannot avoid those illusions my heart entertains. I think I am still with my dear *Abelard*. I see him, I speak to him, and hear him answer. Charmed with each other, we quit our philosophic studies to entertain ourselves with our passion. Sometimes, too, I seem to be a witness of the bloody enterprise of your enemies; I oppose their fury; I fill our apartment with fearful cries, and in a moment I wake in tears. Even in holy places before the altar I carry with me the memory of our guilty loves. They are my whole business, and, far from lamenting for having been seduced, I sigh for having lost them.

I remember (for nothing is forgot by lovers) the time and place in which you first declared your love to me, and swore you would love me till death. Your words, your oaths, are all deeply graven in my heart. The disorder of my discourse discovers to everyone the trouble of my mind. My sighs betray me; and your name is continually in my mouth. When I am in this condition, why dost not thou, O Lord, pity my weakness, and strengthen me by thy grace?

You are happy, *Abelard*; this grace has prevented you; and your misfortune has been the occasion of your finding rest. The punishment of your body has cured the deadly wounds of your soul. The tempest has driven you into the haven. God who seemed to lay his hand heavily upon you, fought only to help you: he is a father chastising, and not an enemy revenging; a wise physician, putting you to some pain in order to preserve your life. I am a thousand times more to be lamented than you; I have a thousand passions to combat with. I must resist those fires which Jove kindles in a young heart. Our sex is nothing but weakness, and I have the greater difficulty to defend myself, because the enemy that attacks me pleases. I dote on the danger which threatens me, how then can I avoid falling?

. . . Happy enough, if I can escape shipwreck, and at last gain the port. Heaven commands me to renounce that fatal passion which unites me to you; but oh! my heart will never be able to consent to it. Adieu.

Source: Héloïse. *Letters of Abelard and Héloïse*. Translated by John Hughes. London: W. Osborne, and T. Griffin, 1782.

PRIMARY DOCUMENT B

Catherine of Siena, Dialogue of the Seraphic Virgin, ca. 1370

A Treatise on Divine Providence

In this section from the work of Catherine of Siena, a fourteenth-century nun who became internationally prominent because of her mystical experiences, Catherine speaks of a mystical union between the soul and God. Love, which allows a human soul to be as one with God, forms the backbone of the discussion. Catherine asks God to answer her own prayers but also includes a request for God to solve the infighting in the fourteenth-century Catholic church.

How a Soul, Elevated by Desire of the Honor of God, and of the Salvation of her Neighbors, Exercising Herself in Humble Prayer, after she had seen the Union of the Soul, through Love, with God, asked of God Four Requests.

The soul, who is lifted by a very great and yearning desire for the honor of God and the salvation of souls, begins by exercising herself, for a certain space of time, in the ordinary virtues, remaining in the cell of self-knowledge, in order to know better the goodness of God towards her. This she does because knowledge must precede love, and only when she has attained love, can she strive to follow and to clothe herself with the truth. But, in no way, does the creature receive such a taste of the truth, or so brilliant a light therefrom, as by means of humble and continuous prayer, founded on knowledge of herself and of God; because prayer, exercising her in the above way, unites with God the soul that follows the footprints of Christ Crucified, and thus, by desire and affection, and union of love, makes her another Himself. Christ would seem to have meant this, when He said: "To him who will love Me and will observe My commandment, will I manifest Myself; and he shall be one thing with Me and I with him."

In several places we find similar words, by which we can see that it is, indeed, through the effect of love, that the soul becomes another Himself. That this may be seen more clearly, I will mention what I remember having heard from a handmaid of God, namely, that, when she was lifted up in prayer, with great elevation of mind, God was not wont to conceal, from the eye of her intellect, the love which He had for His servants, but rather to manifest it; and, that among other things, He used to say: "Open the eye of your intellect, and gaze into Me, and you shall see the beauty of My rational creature. And look at those creatures who, among the beauties which I have given to the soul, creating her in My image and similitude, are clothed with the nuptial garment (that is, the garment of love), adorned with many virtues, by which they are united with Me through love. And yet I tell you, if you should ask Me, who these are, I should reply" (said the sweet and amorous

Word of God) "they are another Myself, inasmuch as they have lost and denied their own will, and are clothed with Mine, are united to Mine, are conformed to Mine."

It is therefore true, indeed, that the soul unites herself with God by the affection of love. So, that soul, wishing to know and follow the truth more manfully, and lifting her desires first for herself—for she considered that a soul could not be of use, whether in doctrine, example, or prayer, to her neighbor, if she did not first profit herself, that is, if she did not acquire virtue in herself—addressed four requests to the Supreme and Eternal Father. The first was for herself; the second for the reformation of the Holy Church; the third a general prayer for the whole world, and in particular for the peace of Christians who rebel, with much lewdness and persecution, against the Holy Church; in the fourth and last, she besought the Divine Providence to provide for things in general, and in particular, for a certain case with which she was concerned.

How the Desire of this Soul grew when God Showed her the Neediness of the World

This desire was great and continuous, but grew much more, when the First Truth showed her the neediness of the world, and in what a tempest of offense against God it lay. And she had understood this the better from a letter, which she had received from the spiritual Father of her soul, in which he explained to her the penalties and intolerable sadness caused by offenses against God, and the loss of souls, and the persecutions of Holy Church.

All this lighted the fire of her holy desire with grief for the offenses, and with the joy of the lively hope, with which she waited for God to provide against such great evils. And, since the soul seems, in such communion, sweetly to bind herself fast within herself and with God, and knows better His truth, inasmuch as the soul is then in God, and God in the soul, as the fish is in the sea, and the sea in the fish, she desired the arrival of the morning (for the morrow was a feast of Mary) in order to hear Mass. And, when the morning came, and the hour of the Mass, she sought with anxious desire her accustomed place; and, with a great knowledge of herself, being ashamed of her own imperfection, appearing to herself to be the cause of all the evil that was happening throughout the world, conceiving a hatred and displeasure against herself, and a feeling of holy justice, with which knowledge, hatred, and justice, she purified the stains which seemed to her to cover her guilty soul, she said: "O Eternal Father, I accuse myself before You, in order that You may punish me for my sins in this finite life, and, inasmuch as my sins are the cause of the sufferings which my neighbor must endure, I implore You, in Your kindness, to punish them in my person."

How Finite Works are not Sufficient for Punishment or Recompense without the Perpetual Affection of Love

Then, the Eternal Truth seized and drew more strongly to Himself her desire, doing as He did in the Old Testament, for when the sacrifice was offered to God, a fire descended and drew to Him the sacrifice that was acceptable to Him; so did the sweet Truth to that soul, in sending down the fire of the clemency of the Holy Spirit, seizing the sacrifice of desire that she made of herself, saying: "Do you not know, dear daughter, that all the sufferings, which the soul endures, or can endure, in this life, are insufficient to punish one smallest fault, because the offense, being done to Me, who am the Infinite Good, calls for an infinite satisfaction? However, I wish that you should know, that not all the pains that are given to men in this life are given as punishments, but as corrections, in order to chastise a son when he offends; though it is true that both the guilt and the penalty can be expiated by the desire of the soul, that is, by true contrition, not through the finite pain endured, but through the infinite desire; because God, who is infinite, wishes for infinite love and infinite grief.

"Infinite grief I wish from My creature in two ways: in one way, through her sorrow for her own sins, which she has committed against Me her Creator; in the other way, through her sorrow for the sins which she sees her neighbors commit against Me. Of such as these, inasmuch as they have infinite desire, that is, are joined to Me by an affection of love, and therefore grieve when they offend Me, or see Me offended, their every pain, whether spiritual or corporeal, from wherever it may come, receives infinite merit, and satisfies for a guilt which deserved an infinite penalty, although their works are finite and done in finite time; but, inasmuch as they possess the virtue of desire, and sustain their suffering with desire, and contrition, and infinite displeasure against their guilt, their pain is held worthy. Paul explained this when he said: 'If I had the tongues of angels, and if I knew the things of the future and gave my body to be burned, and have not love, it would be worth nothing to me' (1 Corinthians 13:1). The glorious Apostle thus shows that finite works are not valid, either as punishment or recompense, without the condiment of the affection of love."

How Desire and Contrition of Heart Satisfies, both for the Guilt and the Penalty in Oneself and in Others; and how Sometimes it Satisfies for the Guilt only, and not the Penalty

"I have shown you, dearest daughter, that the guilt is not punished in this finite time by any pain which is sustained purely as such. And I say, that the guilt is punished by the pain which is endured through the desire, love, and contrition of the heart; not by virtue of the pain, but by virtue of the desire of the soul; inasmuch as desire and every virtue is of value, and has life in itself, through Christ crucified, My only begotten Son, in so far as the soul has drawn her love from Him, and virtuously follows His virtues, that is, His Footprints. In this way, and in no other, are virtues of value, and in this way, pains satisfy for the fault, by the sweet and intimate love acquired in the knowledge of My goodness, and in the bitterness and contrition of heart acquired by knowledge of one's self and one's own thoughts. And this knowledge generates a hatred and displeasure against sin, and against the soul's own sensuality, through which, she deems herself worthy of pains and unworthy of reward."

The sweet Truth continued: "See how, by contrition of the heart, together with love, with true patience, and with true humility, deeming themselves worthy of pain and unworthy of reward, such souls endure the patient humility in which consists the above-mentioned satisfaction. You ask me, then, for pains, so that I may receive satisfaction for the offenses, which are done against Me by My Creatures, and you further ask the will to know and love Me, who am the Supreme Truth. Wherefore I reply that this is the way, if you will arrive at a perfect knowledge and enjoyment of Me, the Eternal Truth, that you should never go outside the knowledge of yourself, and, by humbling yourself in the valley of humility, you will know Me and yourself, from which knowledge you will draw all that is necessary. No virtue, my daughter, can have life in itself except through charity, and humility, which is the foster-mother and nurse of charity. In self-knowledge, then, you will humble yourself, seeing that, in yourself, you do not even exist; for your very being, as you will learn, is derived from Me, since I have loved both you and others before you were in existence; and that, through the ineffable love which I had for you, wishing to recreate you to

Grace, I have washed you, and recreated you in the Blood of My only begotten Son, spilt with so great a fire of love.

"This Blood teaches the truth to him, who, by self-knowledge, dissipates the cloud of self-love, and in no other way can he learn. Then the soul will inflame herself in this knowledge of Me with an ineffable love, through which love she continues in constant pain; not, however, a pain which afflicts or dries up the soul, but one which rather fattens her; for since she has known My truth, and her own faults, and the ingratitude of men, she endures intolerable suffering, grieving because she loves Me; for, if she did not love Me, she would not be obliged to do so; whence it follows immediately, that it is right for you, and My other servants who have learnt My truth in this way, to sustain, even unto death, many tribulations and injuries and insults in word and deed, for the glory and praise of My Name; thus will you endure and suffer pains.

"Do you, therefore, and My other servants, carry yourselves with true patience, with grief for your sins, and with love of virtue for the glory and praise of My Name. If you act thus, I will satisfy for your sins, and for those of My other servants, inasmuch as the pains which you will endure will be sufficient, through the virtue of love, for satisfaction and reward, both in you and in others. In yourself you will receive the fruit of life, when the stains of your ignorance are effaced, and I shall not remember that you ever offended Me. In others I will satisfy through the love and affection which you have to Me, and I will give to them according to the disposition with which they will receive My gifts. In particular, to those who dispose themselves, humbly and with reverence, to receive the doctrine of My servants, will I remit both guilt and penalty, since they will thus come to true knowledge and contrition for their sins. So that, by means of prayer, and their desire of serving Me, they receive the fruit of grace, receiving it humbly in greater or less degree, according to the extent of their exercise of virtue and grace in general. I say then, that, through your desires, they will receive remission for their sins. See, however, the condition, namely, that their obstinacy should not be so great in their despair as to condemn them through contempt of the Blood, which, with such sweetness, has restored them. . . .

"Now, therefore, you have understood how suffering satisfies for guilt by perfect contrition, not through the finite pain; and such as have this contrition in perfection satisfy not only for the guilt, but also for the penalty which follows the guilt, as I have already said when speaking in general; and if they satisfy for the guilt alone, that is, if, having abandoned mortal sin, they receive grace, and have not sufficient contrition and love to satisfy for the penalty also, they go to the pains of Purgatory, passing through the second and last means of satisfaction.

"So you see that satisfaction is made, through the desire of the soul united to Me, who am the Infinite Good, in greater or less degree, according to the measure of love, obtained by the desire and prayer of the recipient. Wherefore, with that very same measure with which a man measures to Me, does he receive in himself the measure of My goodness. Labor, therefore, to increase the fire of your desire, and let not a moment pass without crying to Me with humble voice, or without continual prayers before Me for your neighbors. I say this to you and to the father of your soul, whom I have given you on earth. Bear yourselves with manful courage, and make yourselves dead to all your own sensuality."

How very Pleasing to God is the Willing Desire to Suffer for Him

"Very pleasing to Me, dearest daughter, is the willing desire to bear every pain and fatigue, even unto death, for the salvation of souls, for the more the soul endures, the more she shows that she loves Me; loving Me she comes to know more of My truth, and the more she knows, the more pain and intolerable grief she feels at the offenses committed against Me. You asked Me to sustain you, and to punish the faults of others in you, and you did not remark that you were really asking for love, light, and knowledge of the truth, since I have already told you that, by the increase of love, grows grief and pain, wherefore he that grows in love grows in grief.

"Therefore, I say to you all, that you should ask, and it will be given you, for I deny nothing to him who asks of Me in truth. Consider that the love of divine charity is so closely joined in the soul with perfect patience, that neither can leave the soul without the other. For this reason (if the soul elect to love Me) she should elect to endure pains for Me in whatever mode or circumstance I may send them to her. Patience cannot be proved in any other way than by suffering, and patience is united with love as has been said. Therefore bear yourselves with manly courage, for, unless you do so, you will not prove yourselves to be spouses of My Truth, and faithful children, nor of the company of those who relish the taste of My honor, and the salvation of souls."

How every Virtue and every Defect is Obtained by Means of our Neighbor

"I wish also that you should know that every virtue is obtained by means of your neighbor, and likewise, every defect; he, therefore, who stands in hatred of Me, does an injury to his neighbor, and to himself, who is his own chief neighbor, and this injury is both general and particular. It is general because you are obliged to love your neighbor as yourself, and loving him, you ought to help him spiritually, with prayer, counseling him with words, and assisting him both spiritually and temporally, according to the need in which he may be, at least with your goodwill if you have nothing else.

"A man therefore, who does not love, does not help him, and thereby does himself an injury; for he cuts off from himself grace, and injures his neighbor, by depriving him of the benefit of the prayers and of the sweet desires that he is bound to offer for him to Me. Thus, every act of help that he performs should proceed from the charity which he has through love of Me. And every evil also, is done by means of his neighbor, for, if he do not love Me, he cannot be in charity with his neighbor; and thus, all evils derive from the soul's deprivation of love of Me and her neighbor; whence, inasmuch as such a man does no good, it follows that he must do evil. To whom does he evil? First of all to himself, and then to his neighbor, not against Me, for no evil can touch Me, except in so far as I count done to Me that which he does to himself. To himself he does the injury of sin, which deprives him of grace, and worse than this he cannot do to his neighbor. Him [i.e., the neighbor] he injures in not paying him the debt, which he owes him, of love, with which he ought to help him by means of prayer and holy desire offered to Me for him.

"This is an assistance which is owed in general to every rational creature; but its usefulness is more particular when it is done to those who are close at hand, under your eyes, as to whom, I say, you are all obliged to help one another by word and doctrine, and the example of good works, and in every other respect in which your neighbor may be seen to be in need; counseling him exactly as you would yourselves, without any passion of self-love; and he (a man not loving God) does not do this, because he has no love towards his neighbor; and, by not doing it, he does him, as you see, a special injury. And he does him evil, not only by not doing him the good that he might do him, but by doing him a positive injury and a constant evil. In this way sin causes a physical and a mental injury. The mental injury is already done when the sinner has conceived pleasure in the idea of sin, and hatred of virtue, that is, pleasure from sensual self-love [i.e., selfishness of soul] which has deprived him of the affection of love which he ought to have towards Me, and his neighbor, as has been said. And, after he has conceived, he brings forth one sin after another against his neighbor, according to the diverse ways which may please his perverse sensual will. Sometimes it is seen that he brings forth cruelty, and that both in general and in particular.

"His general cruelty is to see himself and other creatures in danger of death and damnation through privation of grace, and so cruel is he that he reminds neither himself nor others of the love of virtue and hatred of vice. Being thus cruel he may wish to extend his cruelty still further, that is, not content with not giving an example of virtue, the villain also usurps the office of the demons, tempting, according to his power, his fellow-creatures to abandon virtue for vice; this is cruelty towards his neighbors, for he makes himself an instrument to destroy life and to give death. Cruelty towards the body has its origin in cupidity, which not only prevents a man from helping his neighbor, but causes him to seize the goods of others, robbing the poor creatures; sometimes this is done by the arbitrary use of power, and at other times by cheating and fraud, his neighbor being forced to redeem, to his own loss, his own goods, and often indeed his own person. 'Oh, miserable vice of cruelty, which will deprive the man who practices it of all mercy, unless he turn to kindness and benevolence towards his neighbor!'

"Sometimes the sinner brings forth insults on which often follows murder; sometimes also impurity against the person of his neighbor, by which he becomes a brute beast full of stench, and in this case he does not poison one only, but whoever approaches him, with love or in conversation, is poisoned.

"Against whom does pride bring forth evils? Against the neighbor, through love of one's own reputation, whence comes hatred of the neighbor, reputing one's self to be greater than he; and in this way is injury done to him. And if a man be in a position of authority, he produces also injustice and cruelty and becomes a retailer of the flesh of men. Oh, dearest daughter, grieve for the offense against Me, and weep over these corpses, so that, by prayer, the bands of their death may be loosened!

"See now, that, in all places and in all kinds of people, sin is always produced against the neighbor, and through his medium; in no other way could sin ever be committed either secret or open.

A secret sin is when you deprive your neighbor of that which you ought to give him; an open sin is where you perform positive acts of sin, as I have related to you. It is, therefore, indeed the truth that every sin done against Me, is done through the medium of the neighbor."

How Virtues are Accomplished by Means of our Neighbor, and How it is that Virtues Differ to such an Extent in Creatures

I have told you how all sins are accomplished by means of your neighbor, through the principles which I exposed to you, that is, because men are deprived of the affection of love, which gives light to every virtue. In the same way self-love, which destroys charity and affection towards the neighbor, is the principle and foundation of every evil. All scandals, hatred, cruelty, and every sort of trouble proceed from this perverse root of self-love, which has poisoned the entire world, and weakened the mystical body of the Holy Church, and the universal body of the believers in the Christian religion; and, therefore, I said to you, that it was in the neighbor, that is to say in the love of him, that all virtues were founded; and, truly indeed did I say to you, that charity gives life to all the virtues, because no virtue can be obtained without charity, which is the pure love of Me. . . .

"And it cannot be otherwise, because love of Me and of her neighbor are one and the same thing, and, so far as the soul loves Me, she loves her neighbor, because love towards him issues from Me. This is the means which I have given you, that you may exercise and prove your virtue therewith; because, inasmuch as you can do Me no profit, you should do it to your neighbor. This proves that you possess Me by grace in your soul, producing much fruit for your neighbor and making prayers to Me, seeking with sweet and amorous desire My honor and the salvation of souls. The soul, enamored of My truth, never ceases to serve the whole world in general, and more or less in a particular case according to the disposition of the recipient and the ardent desire of the donor, as I have shown above, when I declared to you that the endurance of suffering alone, without desire, was not sufficient to punish a fault.

"When she has discovered the advantage of this unitive love in Me, by means of which, she truly loves herself, extending her desire for the salvation of the whole world, thus coming to the aid of its neediness, she strives, inasmuch as she has done good to herself by the conception of virtue, from which she has drawn the life of grace, to fix her eye on the needs of her neighbor in particular. Wherefore, when she has discovered, through the affection of love, the state of all rational creatures in general, she helps those who are at hand, according to the various graces which I have entrusted to her to administer; one she helps with doctrine, that is, with words, giving sincere counsel without any respect of persons, another with the example of a good life, and this indeed all give to their neighbor, the edification of a holy and honorable life. These are the virtues, and many others, too many to enumerate, which are brought forth in the love of the neighbor. . . . These, and many other virtues, I place, indifferently, in the souls of many creatures; it happens, therefore, that the particular one so placed in the soul becomes the principal object of its virtue; the soul disposing herself, for her chief conversation, to this rather than to other virtues, and, by the effect of this virtue, the soul draws to herself all the other virtues, which, as has been said, are all bound together in the affection of love; and so with many gifts and graces of virtue, and not only in the case of spiritual things but also of temporal.

"I use the word temporal for the things necessary to the physical life of man; all these I have given indifferently, and I have not placed them all in one soul, in order that man should, perforce, have material for love of his fellow. I could easily have created men possessed of all that they should need both for body and soul, but I wish that one should have need of the other, and that they should be My ministers to administer the graces and the gifts that they have received from Me. Whether man will or no, he cannot help making an act of love. It is true, however, that that act, unless made through love of Me, profits him nothing so far as grace is concerned. See then, that I have made men My ministers, and placed them in diverse stations and various ranks, in order that they may make use of the virtue of love.

"Wherefore, I show you that in My house are many mansions, and that I wish for no other thing than love, for in the love of Me is fulfilled and completed the love of the neighbor, and the law observed. For he, only, can be of use in his state of life, who is bound to Me with this love."

How Virtues are Proved and Fortified by their Contraries

"Up to the present, I have taught you how a man may serve his neighbor, and manifest, by that service, the love which he has towards Me.

"Now I wish to tell you further, that a man proves his patience on his neighbor, when he receives injuries from him.

"Similarly, he proves his humility on a proud man, his faith on an infidel, his true hope on one who despairs, his justice on the unjust, his kindness on the cruel, his gentleness and benignity on the irascible. Good men produce and prove all their virtues on their neighbor, just as perverse men all their vices; thus, if you consider well, humility is proved on pride in this way. The humble man extinguishes pride, because a proud man can do no harm to a humble one; neither can the infidelity of a wicked man, who neither loves Me, nor hopes in Me, when brought forth against one who is faithful to Me, do him any harm; his infidelity does not diminish the faith or the hope of him who has conceived his faith and hope through love of Me, it rather fortifies it, and proves it in the love he feels for his neighbor. For, he sees that the infidel is unfaithful, because he is without hope in Me, and in My servant, because he does not love Me, placing his faith and hope rather in his own sensuality, which is all that he loves.

"My faithful servant does not leave him because he does not faithfully love Me, or because he does not constantly seek, with hope in Me, for his salvation, inasmuch as he sees clearly the causes of his infidelity and lack of hope. The virtue of faith is proved in these and other ways. Wherefore, to those, who need the proof of it, My servant proves his faith in himself and in his neighbor, and so, justice is not diminished by the wicked man's injustice, but is rather proved, that is to say, the justice of a just man. Similarly, the virtues of patience, benignity, and kindness manifest themselves in a time of wrath by the same sweet patience in My servants, and envy, vexation, and hatred demonstrate their love, and hunger and desire for the salvation of souls. I say, also, to you, that, not only is virtue proved in those who render good for evil, but, that many times a good man gives back fiery coals of love, which dispel the hatred and rancor of heart of the angry, and so from hatred often comes benevolence, and that this is by virtue of the love and perfect patience which is in him, who sustains the anger of the wicked, bearing and supporting his defects.

"If you will observe the virtues of fortitude and perseverance, these virtues are proved by the long endurance of the injuries and detractions of wicked men, who, whether by injuries or by flattery, constantly endeavor to turn a man aside from following the road and the doctrine of truth. Wherefore, in all these things, the virtue of fortitude conceived within the soul, perseveres with strength, and, in addition proves itself externally upon the neighbor, as I have said to you; and, if fortitude were not able to make that good proof of itself, being tested by many contrarieties, it would not be a serious virtue founded in truth."

Source: Catherine of Siena. Thorold, Algar, trans. and ed. *The Dialogue of the Seraphic Virgin Catherine of Siena, Dictated by her while in a State of Ecstasy, to her Secretaries, and Completed in the Year of Our Lord 1370, together with an Account of her Death by an Eye-Witness, Translated from the Original Italian, and Preceded by an Introduction on the Life and Times of the Saint, A New and Abridged Version.* Originally published in 1907 by Kegan Paul, Trench, Trubner & Co., Ltd., London.

PRIMARY DOCUMENT C

Julian of Norwich, *Revelations of Divine Love*, ca. 1410

The reclusive English anchoress Julian of Norwich experienced visions that she called "shewings" (showings). There were sixteen of them, each centered around a single concept or vision. Several were visions of different stages of Jesus's persecution and death; others are more theologically complex, emphasizing the duty of a Christian to submit to God's authority and to be assured of a blessed afterlife.

REVELATIONS OF LOVE

Here beginneth the First Chapter
This is a Revelation of Love, that Jesu Christ
our endless blisse made in xvi. shewings : of
which,

The first is of his precious crowning of thornes,
and therein was conteined and specified the blessed
Trinity, with the incarnation and the uniting between God and mans soul, with manie faire shew
ings and teachings of endeless wisdom and love :
in which all the shewings that follow be grounded
and joyned.

The second, is of the discolouring of his faire face,
in tokening of his dear worthie passion.

The third is, that our Lord God Almighty, all
wisdom and all love, right also verilie as he hath

made all thinges that are right, also verilie he doth and worketh all things that are done.

The fourth is, scourging of his tender bodie with plenteous shedding of his precious blood.

The fifth is, that the fiend is overcome by the precious passion of Christ.

The sixth is, the worshipfull thanking of our Lord God, in which he rewardeth all his blessed servants in heaven.

The seventh is, oftentimes feeling of weale and woe. Feeling of weale is gracious touching and lightning, with true sikernes of endeles joy : the feeling of woe is of temptation by heavines, and wearines of our fleshlie living with ghostelie under standing, that we be kept also verelie in love, in. woe as in weal, by the goodnes of God.

The eighth is, the last paines of Christ and his cruell dying.

The ninth is, of the liking which is in the blessed Trinity of the hard passion of Christ after his rufull and sorrowful dying : in which joy and liking he will that we be in solace and mirth with him, till that we come to the glorie in heaven.

The tenth is, our Lord Jesu Christ [shewing] by love his blessed heart even cloven in two.

The eleventh is, an high ghostlie shewing of his cleare worthie Mother.

The twelfth is, that our Lord God is all soveraign being.

The thirteenth is, that our Lord God will that we have great regard to all the deedes which he hath done, in the great nobletie of all things making, and of the excellency of mans making, the which is above all his works ; and of the precious amends that he hath made for mans sin, turning all our blame into endeles worship. Than meaneth he thus, Beholde and see, for by the same might, wisdome and goodness that I have done all this, by the same might, wisdome and goodness I shall make well all that is not well, and thou shall see it. And in this he will that we keep us in the faith and truth of Holie Church, not willing to wit his privities, not but as it longeth to us in this life.

The fourteenth is, that our Lord God is the ground of our beseekinge. Herein was seen two fair properties : that one is rightful praier : that other is verie trust, which he will both be one like [alike] large, and thus our praier liketh him, and he of his goodness fulfilleth it.

The fifteenth is, that we should soudeinlie be taken from all our paine, and from all our woe, and of his goodnes we shall come up above, where we shall have our Lord Jesu to our meed, and for to be fulfilled with joy and blisse in heaven.

The sixteenth is, that the blessed Trinitie, our maker, in Christ Jesu our Saviour, endleslie dwelleth in our soule, worshipfullie rewarding and command ing all things, us mightilie and wiselie saving and keeping for love, and we shall not be over-come of our enemy.

Source: Julian of Norwich. *Revelations of Divine Love*. George Tyrrell, ed. London: Kegan, Paul, Trench, Truber & Co., 1902, 1–4.

PRIMARY DOCUMENT D

Margaret Paston, The Marriage of Margery Paston, 1469

In this letter, the redoubtable Margaret Paston, matriarch of the Paston family, tells her son Richard that she has disowned his younger sister, Margery, for having a relationship with a family retainer, Richard Calle.

The couple married without permission, and Margaret and her husband, John, tried to have the marriage dissolved, considering Calle unworthy to marry their daughter. They did not succeed, and the church declared the marriage valid. Margery and Calle had three sons.

On Friday the bishop he sent for her [Margery] by Ashfield and other[s] that are right sorry of her demeaning. And the bishop said to her plainly, and put her in remembrance how she was born, what kin and friends that she had, and should have more if she were ruled and guided after them; and if she did not, what rebuke, and shame, and loss should be to her, if she were not guided by them, and cause of forsaking of her for any good, or help, or comfort that she should have of them; and said that he had heard say that she loved such one [Calle] that her friends were not pleased with that she should have, and therefore he had her be right well advised how she did, and said that he would understand the words that she had said to him, whether it made matrimony or not.

And she rehearsed what she had said [in promising marriage to Calle], and said if those words made it not sure, she said boldly that she would make it surer ere than she went thence, for she said she thought in her conscience she was bound, whatsoever the words were. These lewd words grieve me and her grandam as much as all the remnant. And then the bishop and the chancellor both said that there was neither I nor no friend of her would receive her. . . .

I was with my mother at her place when she [Margery] was examined, and when I heard say what her demeaning was, I charged my servants that she should not be received in my house. I had given her warning, she might have been aware afore, if she had been gracious; and I sent to one or two more that they should not receive her if she came. She was brought again to my place for to have been received, and Sir James [Gloys] told them that brought her that I had charged them all and she should not be received; and so [the bishop has sent her to] Roger Best's . . . I am sorry that [Best and his wife] are cumbered with her, but yet am I better paid that she is there for the while than she had been in other place, because of the sadness [i.e., seriousness] and good disposition of himself and his wife, for she shall not be suffered there to play the brethel [i.e., whore].

I pray you and require you that you take it not pensily [i.e., heavily] for I wot [i.e., know] well it goes right near your heart, and so does it to mine and to other[s]. But remember you, and so do I, that we have lost of her but a brethel, and set it the less to heart, for, an' she had been good, wheresoever she had been, it should not have been as it is, for, an' he [Calle] were dead at this hour, she would never be at mine heart as she was. . . . For wot it well, she shall full sore repent her lewdness hereafter, and I pray God she might so.

Source: Warrington, John, ed. *The Paston Letters.* London: J. M. Dent and Sons, 1924.

PRIMARY DOCUMENT E

Margery Kempe, Excerpt from *The Book of Margery Kempe*, 1521

The Book of Margery Kempe *is the dictated autobiography of an early fifteenth-century English woman who was both a passionate mystic and the mother of fourteen children. She was convinced of her own sinfulness and experienced uncontrollable periods of intense crying when she thought about her wretched behavior. In this excerpt, Margery Kempe expresses her desire to suffer for God as he suffered for her (in the Crucifixion).*

SHE desired many times that her head might be smitten off with an axe upon a block for the love of our Lord Jesu. Then said our Lord Jesu in her mind : " I thank thee, daughter, that thou wouldest die for My love; for as often as thou thinkest so, thou shalt have the same meed in heaven, as if thou suffredest the same death, and yet there shall no man slay thee.

"I assure thee in thy mind, if it were possible for Me to suffer pain again, as I have done before, Me were lever to suffer as much pain as ever I did for thy soul alone, rather than thou shouldest depart from Me everlastingly.

"Daughter, thou mayst no better please God, than to think continually in His love."

Then she asked our Lord Jesu Christ, how she should best love Him. And our Lord said : "Have mind of thy wickedness, and think on My goodness."

THE CELL OF SELF-KNOWLEDGE

"Daughter, if thou wear the habergeon or the hair [a hair shirt], fasting bread and water, and if thou saidest every day a thousand Pater Nosters, thou shalt not please Me so well as thou dost when thou art in silence, and suffrest Me to speak in thy soul.

"Daughter, for to bid many beads, it is good to them that cannot better do, and yet it is not perfect. But it is a good way toward perfection. For I tell thee, daughter, they that be great fasters, and great doers of penance, they would that it should be holden the best life. And they that give them unto many devotions, they would have that the best life. And those that give much almesse, they would that it were holden the best life. And I have often told thee, daughter, that thinking, weeping, and high contemplation is the best life in earth, and thou shalt have more merit in heaven for one year thinking in thy mind than for an hundred year of praying with thy mouth; and yet thou wilt not believe Me, for thou wilt bid many beads.

"Daughter, if thou knew how sweet thy love is to Me, thou wouldest never do other thing but love Me with all thine heart.

"Daughter, if thou wilt be high with Me in heaven, keep Me alway in thy mind as much as thou mayst, and forget not Me at thy meat; but think alway that I sit in thine heart and know every thought that is therein, both good and bad.

"Daughter, I have suffered many pains for thy love; therefore thou hast great cause to love Me right well, for I have bought thy love full dear."

"Dear Lord," she said, " I pray Thee, let me never have other joy in earth, but mourning and weeping for will. These are fed at the table of penance, and are good and perfect; but unless they have great humility, and compel themselves to consider the will of God and not that of men, they oft times mar their perfection by making themselves judges of those who are not going by the same way that they are going, Thy love; for me thinketh, Lord, though I were in hell, if I might weep there and mourn for Thy love as I do here, hell should not noye me, but it should be a manner of heaven. For Thy love putteth away all manner of dread of our ghostly enemy ; for I had lever be there, as long as Thou wouldest, and please Thee, than to be in this world and displease Thee; therefore, good Lord, as Thou wilt, so may it be."

She had great wonder that our Lord would become man, and suffer so grievous pains, for her that was so unkind a creature to Him. And then, with great weeping, she asked our Lord Jesu how she might best please Him; and He answered to her soul, saying : " Daughter, have mind of thy wickedness, and think on My goodness." Then she prayed many times and often these words: "Lord, for Thy great goodness, have mercy on my great wickedness, as certainly as I was never so wicked as Thou art good, nor never may be though I would; for Thou art so good, that Thou mayst no better be ; and, therefore, it is great wonder that ever any man should be departed from Thee without end."

When she saw the Crucifix, or if she saw a man had a wound, or a beast, or if a man beat a child before her, or smote a horse or another beast with a whip, if she might see it or hear it, she thought she saw our Lord beaten or wounded, like as she saw in the man or in the beast.

The more she increased in love and in devotion, the more she increased in sorrow and contrition, in lowliness and meekness, and in holy dread of our Lord Jesu, and in knowledge of her own frailty. So that if she saw any creature be punished or sharply chastised, she would think that she had been more worthy to be chastised than that creature was, for her unkindness against God.

Then would she weep for her own sin, and for compassion of that creature.

Our Lord said to her: " In nothing that thou dost or sayest, daughter, thou mayst no better please God than believe that He loveth thee. For, if it were possible that I might weep with thee, I would weep with thee for the compassion that I have of thee."

Our merciful Lord Jesu Christ drew this creature unto His love, and to the mind of His passion, that she might not endure to behold a leper, or another sick man, specially if he had any wounds appearing on him. So she wept as if she had seen our Lord Jesu with His wounds bleeding; and so she did, in the sight of the soul; for, through the beholding of the sick man, her mind was all ravished in to our Lord Jesu, that she had great mourning and sorrowing that she might not kiss the leper when she met them in the way, for the love of our Lord: which was all contrary to her disposition in the years of her youth and prosperity, for then she abhorred them most.

Our Lord said: "Daughter, thou hast desired in thy mind to have many priests in the town of Lynn, that might sing and read night and day for to serve Me, worship Me, and praise Me, and thank Me for the goodness that I have done to thee in earth; and therefore, daughter, I promise thee that thou shalt have meed and reward in heaven for the good wills and good desires, as if thou haddest done them in deed.

"Daughter, thou shalt have as great meed and as great reward with Me in heaven, for thy good service and thy good deeds that thou hast done in thy mind, as if thou haddest done the same with thy bodily wits withoutforth.

"And, daughter, I thank thee for the charity that thou hast to all lecherous men and women; for thou prayest for them and weepest for them many a tear, desiring that I should deliver them out of sin, and be as gracious to them as I was to Mary Magdalene, that they might have as much grace to love Me as Mary Magdalene had; and with this condition thou wouldest that everich of them should have twenty pounds a year to love and praise Me; and, daughter, this great charity which thou hast to them in thy prayer pleaseth Me right well. And, daughter, also I thank thee for the charity which thou hast in thy prayer, when thou prayest for all Jews and Saracens, and all heathen people that they should come to Christian faith, that My name might be magnified in them. Furthermore, daughter, I thank thee for the general charity that thou hast to all people that be now in this world, and to all those that are to come unto the world's end; that thou wouldest be hacked as small as flesh to the pot for their love, so that I would by thy death save them all from damnation, if it pleased Me. And, therefore, daughter, for all these good wills and desires, thou shalt have full meed and reward in heaven, believe it right well and doubt never a deal."

She said: "Good Lord, I would be laid naked upon an hurdle for Thy love, all men to wonder on me and to cast filth and dirt on me, and be drawen from town to town every day my life time, if Thou were pleased thereby, and no man's soul hindered. Thy will be fulfilled and not mine."

"Daughter," He said, " as oftentimes as thou sayest or thinkest: Worshipped he all the holy places in Jerusalem where Christ suffered bitter pain and passion in: thou shalt have the same pardon as if thou were there with thy bodily presence, both to thyself and to all those that thou wilt give to.

"The same pardon that was granted thee aforetime, it was confirmed on Saint Nicholas day, that is to say, playne remission ; and it is not only granted to thee, but also to all those that believe, and to all those that shall believe unto the world's end, that God loveth thee, and shall thank God for thee. If they will forsake their sin, and be in full will no more to turn again thereto, but be sorry and heavy for that they have done, and will do due penance therefore, they shall have the same pardon that is granted to thyself; and that is all the pardon that is in Jerusalem, as was granted thee when thou were at Rafnys."

That day that she suffered no tribulation for our Lord's sake, she was not merry nor glad, as that day when she suffered tribulation.

Our Lord Jesus said unto her: "Patience is more worth than miracles doing. Daughter, it is more pleasure to Me that thou suffer despites, scorns, shames, reproofs, wrongs, and diseases, than if thine head were stricken off three times a day every day in seven year."

"Lord," she said, " for Thy great pain have mercy on my little pain."

When she was in great trouble, our Lord said: "Daughter, I must needs comfort thee, for now thou hast the right way to heaven. By this way came I and all My disciples; for now thou shalt know the better what sorrow and shame I suffered for thy love, and thou shalt have the more compassion when thou thinkest on My passion."

"O my dear worthy Lord," said she, " these graces Thou shouldest shew to religious men and to priests."

Our Lord said to her again: "Nay, nay, daughter, for that I love best that they love not, and that is shames, reproofs, scorns, and despites of the people; and therefore they shall not have this grace; for, daughter, he that dreadeth the shames of this world may not perfectly love God."

Here endeth a short treatise of a devout ancress called Margery Kempe of Lynn.

Source: Excerpt from *The Book of Marjory Kempe* in Edmund Gardner, ed. *The Cell of Self-knowledge: Seven Early English Mystical Treatises printed by Henry Pepwell in 1521*. London: Chatto & Windus, 1910, 51–59.

GLOSSARY

abbess: The head of a women's monastery or double monastery. The word is also used to refer humorously to a bawd.

abortifacient: A preparation or substance that brings about an abortion.

anchoress: A religious woman who chooses to live in a small space, isolated from others, in order to pray constantly. A man is called an anchorite.

annulment: A declaration, made by a church court, that a marriage between two people never existed. Having a marriage annulled was one of the few recourses available to medieval people who wanted to leave a marriage.

arpent: A measure of land that is approximately 0.85 acre, or 0.34 hectare.

ascetic: A person who abstains from sex, food, and other pleasures for religious reasons.

banns: Public declarations that two people plan to marry, given on three successive Sundays in a parish church and designed to give warning to those who might object to the marriage.

bawd: A woman who oversees a group of prostitutes or a brothel. Sometimes also called an abbess.

Beguine: A woman who lives a religious lifestyle but does not take religious vows. Beguines became widespread in northern Europe in the 1300s.

Black Death: The popular name given to the outbreak of bubonic plague that occurred in Europe from 1347 to 1351.

bliaut: A dress that fits tightly in the bodice and is full in the skirt.

braies: A men's loose garment, similar to short pants, tied around the waist with a cord, worn under other clothing.

bubonic plague: A bacterial disease caused by the bacterium *Yersinia pestis,* the foundation of the fourteenth century Black Death.

bull: An official papal document, sealed with a lead seal called a *bullum.* Bulls often set out matters of policy or settle questions of theology.

canon/canoness: Man or woman who lives a simple life and takes a vow of chastity and obedience. Regular canons and canonesses follow a rule based on the writings of St. Augustine (d. 430). *Canon* is also a term for a man who is in charge of administering a cathedral church.

canon law: The laws and regulations pertaining to church matters, including religious crimes such as heresy and everyday matters such as marriage and adultery.

canonical hours: Saying of prayers at specific times of day. Traditionally the canonical hours are matins, lauds, prime, terce, sext, nones, vespers, and compline. They are also collectively called the Divine Office.

celibacy: Abstaining entirely from sexual intercourse. In medieval Europe, celibacy was formally required of all clergy, although it did not always happen in practice.

chattel: A piece of movable property; this item can refer to either an object or an enslaved person.

chrisom: A cloth used during baptism to wrap the child and cover the oil and balm used in the ritual. Some newborns who died were buried in their chrisoms.

concubine: In some medieval communities, a woman who is in a regular sexual relationship with a man outside of marriage; sometimes these relationships were sealed with legal contracts.

conjugal debt: See "marriage debt."

consanguinity: Sharing the same blood; blood relationship.

cribra orbitalia: Abnormal bone growth in the eye sockets of the skull that is a sign of childhood malnutrition.

cucking stool: A punishment dating to the early Middle Ages in which the convicted person was tied to a chair, sometimes a latrine chair, and exhibited in public. Not to be confused with a "ducking stool."

denier: A penny; worth 1/12 of a solidus.

dental enamel hypoplasia: Horizontal lines on the teeth that are a sign of childhood malnutrition.

distaff: A long rod wound with raw wool that is going to be spun. This tool was associated with women's work in the Middle Ages to such an extent that the female side of a family tree is called the "distaff side."

Divine Office: See "canonical hours."

double monastery: A monastery in which a men's house of monks and a women's house of nuns exist side by side, ruled by an abbess, and in which the monks provide spiritual services for the nuns.

dower: The money or gifts given to a new wife by her husband or his family.

dowry: The sum of money paid from the wife's family to the husband's family; brought with a woman into her marriage.

ducking stool: A punishment in which the convicted person was placed in a chair suspended over water and repeatedly plunged in. Not to be confused with a "cucking stool."

emmenagogue: A preparation or substance that brings on a woman's menstrual period.

enclosure: In women's monasteries, the rule that nuns were not allowed to leave the monastery without permission and that outsiders could not enter the monastery.

excommunication: A situation in which an individual or group of individuals is denied membership in the Roman Catholic Church, often for a major sin.

farthing: A coin worth one quarter of a copper penny.

fulling: A process of shrinking woolen fabric, using urine and water, that makes the cloth softer and thicker.

garderobe: Literally, a wardrobe, but figuratively, a latrine or privy.

guild: A trade or craft organization that controlled the sale of goods or the production of crafts in medieval cities. Guilds provided both quality control and a social safety net for their members and forbade non-guild members from practicing in the craft or trade.

gynaeceum: A women's workshop, usually for spinning and cloth production.

Harris lines: Horizontal lines on the long bones of a skeleton that are a sign of childhood malnutrition.

hennin: A tall, cone-shaped headdress that became fashionable in the fifteenth century.

houppelande: A long open coat worn by both men and women in the late Middle Ages, usually with wide sleeves and sometimes lined with fur.

humors: The four substances that learned medieval people believed made up the body. They are blood, black bile, yellow bile, and phlegm.

jus primae noctis: The "right of the first night" in which the overlord of a serf had the right to have sex with her before her husband did. This idea is popular in fiction about the Middle Ages, but it did not exist.

kirtle: A garment for both men and women, worn over a linen chemise and sometimes laced on.

leprosy: A serious progressive illness, caused by the bacterium *Mycobacterium leprae*, that can cause bodily disabilities and breakdown of facial features.

Little Ice Age: A period beginning in the late thirteenth century and lasting through the fourteenth century in which average temperatures in Europe dropped by 0.6 degrees Celsius.

***maleficium*:** Literally "doing evil," a word often used for magic or sorcery.

mancus: A gold English coin worth thirty pennies, or about one-eighth of a pound.

marriage debt: Doctrine that husbands and wives, who theologically owned one another's bodies, were not allowed to deny sex to their spouses. Also called the "conjugal debt."

misogyny: Hatred of women.

monastery: A Christian community in which men or women live together under a rule for the purpose of prayer.

Morgengabe: In Germanic societies, the "morning gift" given to a bride after her first night with her husband.

mystic: A person who seeks spiritual union with God through religious practices, often including asceticism.

necrology: A list of deceased people kept by a monastery or church that serves as a reminder for prayer.

novice: A person who is in training to become a nun or a monk.

oblate: Literally an "offering." A word used to refer to a child who is given to a monastery to be raised as a monk or nun.

obol: One-half of one penny.

ordeal: A medieval judicial process in which an accused person submitted to a physical challenge in order to prove himself or herself in the right during a trial. Ordeals could be unilateral (for example, a person might be asked to pick up a hot poker in his/her bare hand) or bilateral (in which two representatives of the parties fought a duel to determine a winner).

paleopathology: The study of ancient diseases.

penitential: A list of sins and their corresponding penances intended for the use of a priest hearing confession.

penny: A coin of small value, one-twelfth of a shilling or sou.

pessary: An herbal tampon used medically to affect a woman's reproductive health.

pillory: A kind of public punishment in which an offender was sentenced to put head and hands through a pair of wooden boards that held them in place for a specific period of time. See also "stocks."

polygyny: Having more than one wife.

porotic hyperostosis: Abnormal bone growth on the skull that is a sign of childhood malnutrition.

pound: Also called a librus or livre: a coin made up of twenty silver solidi or shillings.

regent: A person who acts as the ruler of a country while the monarch is too young to rule, is absent, or is otherwise unable to rule.

relic: Something left behind by a saint or other holy person that was believed to have spiritual power. In the Middle Ages, relics often included personal belongings, bones or hair.

Renaissance: A term meaning "rebirth," usually of interest in scholarship or Greco-Roman culture. Although the most common use of the word refers to the late Middle Ages, the ninth and twelfth centuries have also been called Renaissances.

rule of thumb: Many modern people believe that a man could legally beat his wife in the Middle Ages as long as the stick used was not larger than his thumb. This belief is wrong; the rule of thumb did not exist, although most medieval communities tolerated domestic violence.

sacrament: One of seven major religious rituals in the Roman Catholic church that are believed to be outward manifestations of grace. They are baptism, confirmation, marriage, the Eucharist (communion), holy orders, penance, and extreme unction (anointment of the sick).

saint: A person who is considered holy either because they have died for the Christian faith or because they lived a strict religious lifestyle. Medieval people believed that saints could intercede with Christ in order to obtain forgiveness of sins for their followers.

serf: An unfree agricultural worker. In the early and High Middle Ages, serfs were bound to the land that they farmed and could be sold or traded along with the land by their lords. There were several other varieties of unfree workers with varying rights.

shilling: A silver coin valued as twelve pennies. Also called a sou or a solidus.

solidus: Also called a sou or shilling; a silver coin valued at twelve deniers or pennies. Twenty solidi make up a pound.

spindle: A small instrument used to spin loose wool, silk, or flax into thread.

stocks: A type of public punishment in which an offender had his or her ankles bound between two boards for a specified period of time. See also "pillory."

sumptuary laws: Laws from the late Middle Ages that governed what classes of people could purchase luxuries and wear certain types of clothing.

tertiary: A person who is attached to a religious or monastic order but who does not take vows; often called a "third order."

thatch: Bundles of straw used as roofing material.

thewe: In medieval England, a pillory in which a woman accused of a minor crime was sentenced to spend time.

transubstantiation: The Christian doctrine that holds that the bread and wine of the Eucharist turns into the body and blood of Christ once consecrated in the mass.

wattle and daub: A method of building that consists of sticks woven together ("wattle") into a wall that is plastered with mud ("daub").

wergild: In Germanic societies, an amount of money assessed for harm done to one person by another person.

wet nurse: A woman who is currently producing milk who is employed to nurse a wealthy person's child.

BIBLIOGRAPHY

Alfie, Fabian. 2017. "The Sonnet about Women Who Marry in Old Age: Filth, Misogyny, and Depravity." In *Bodily and Spiritual Hygiene in Medieval and Early Modern Literature: Explorations of Textual Presentations of Filth and Water*, edited by Albrecht Classen, 389–406. Berlin: De Gruyter.

Amt, Emilie, ed. 2010. *Women's Lives in Medieval Europe: A Sourcebook*. 2nd ed. London: Routledge.

Anastasiou, Evilena. 2015. "Parasites in European Populations from Prehistory to the Industrial Revolution." In *Sanitation, Latrines and Intestinal Parasites in Past Populations*, edited by Piers D. Mitchell, 203–217. Aldershot: Ashgate.

Atkinson, Clarissa W. 1991. *The Oldest Vocation: Christian Motherhood in the Middle Ages*. Ithaca, NY: Cornell University Press.

Auslander, Diane. 2012. "Clemence and Catherine: The Life of St Catherine in Its Norman and Anglo-Norman Context." In *Barking Abbey and Medieval Literary Culture*, edited by Jennifer N. Brown and Donna Alfano Bussell, 164–182. Rochester: Boydell & Brewer. https://www.jstor.org/stable/10.7722/j.ctt1r2gxr.14.

d'Avray, David. 2008. *Medieval Marriage: Symbolism and Society*. Oxford: Oxford University Press.

Bailey, Michael D. 2001. "From Sorcery to Witchcraft: Clerical Conceptions of Magic in the Later Middle Ages." *Speculum* 76 (4): 960–990. https://doi.org/10.2307/2903617.

Bale, Anthony, trans. 2015. *The Book of Margery Kempe*. Oxford World's Classics. Oxford: Oxford University Press.

Banks, Amanda Carson. 1999. *Birth Chairs, Midwives, and Medicine*. Oxford, MS: University Press of Mississippi.

Bardet, Jean-Pierre, and Jacques Dupâquier, eds. 1997. *Histoire des Populations de l'Europe, I: Des Origines aux prémices de la révolution démographique*. Paris: Fayard.

Bardsley, Sandy. 2014. "Missing Women: Sex Ratios in England, 1000–1500." *Journal of British Studies* 53 (2): 273–309.

Barker, Hannah. 2021. "The Risk of Birth: Life Insurance for Enslaved Pregnant Women in Fifteenth-Century Genoa." *Journal of Global Slavery* 6 (2): 1–31.

Barnhouse, Rebecca, ed. 2006. *The Book of the Knight of the Tower: Manners for Young Medieval Women*. New York: Palgrave Macmillan.

Bartlett, Robert. 1986. *Trial by Fire and Water: The Medieval Judicial Ordeal*. Oxford: Oxford University Press.

Bayard, Tania, ed. 2001. *A Medieval Home Companion: Housekeeping in the Fourteenth Century*. New York: HarperCollins.

Bayless, Martha. 2012. *Sin and Filth in Medieval Culture: The Devil in the Latrine*. London: Routledge.

Beach, Alison I. 2000. "Claustration and Collaboration between the Sexes in the Twelfth-Century Scriptorium." In *Monks and Nuns, Saints and Outcasts: Religion in Medieval Society*, edited by Sharon Farmer and Barbara H. Rosenwein, 57–76. Ithaca, NY: Cornell University Press. https://www.jstor.org/stable/10.7591/j.ctv3mtbkq.8.

Bednarski, Steven. 2014. *A Poisoned Past: The Life and Times of Margarida de Portu, A Fourteenth-Century Accused Poisoner*. Toronto: University of Toronto Press.

Bednarski, Steven, and Andrée Courtemanche. 2011. "'Sadly and with a Bitter Heart:' What the Caesarean Section Meant in the Middle Ages." *Florilegium* 28: 33–69.

Bennett, Judith M. 1996. *Ale, Beer, and Brewsters in England: Women's Work in a Changing World, 1300–1600*. New York: Oxford University Press.

Bennett, Judith M. 2000. "'Lesbian-Like' and the Social History of Lesbianisms." *Journal of the History of Sexuality* 9 (1/2): 1–24.

Bennett, Judith M., and Ruth Mazo Karras, eds. 2013. *The Oxford Handbook of Women and Gender in Medieval Europe*. Oxford: Oxford University Press.

Berman, Constance H. 2018. "Catching Glimpses of 'Those Who Worked' in Rural Europe in the Middle Ages." *Medieval Prosopography* 33:1–14.

Blamires, Alcuin, ed. 1992. *Woman Defamed and Woman Defended: An Anthology of Medieval Texts*. Oxford: Clarendon Press.

Bloch, Marc. 1975. *Slavery and Serfdom in the Middle Ages*. Translated by William R. Beer. Berkeley: University of California Press.

Blumenfeld-Kosinski, Renate, ed. 1997. *The Selected Writings of Christine de Pisan*. New York: W. W. Norton.

Boccaccio, Giovanni. 1995. *The Decameron*. Translated by G. H. McWilliam. New York: Penguin Classics.

Bogin, Meg. 1976. *The Women Troubadours*. New York: W. W. Norton.

Boswell, John. 1990. *The Kindness of Strangers: The Abandonment of Children in Western Europe from Late Antiquity to the Renaissance*. New York: Vintage.

Brenon, Anne. 1992. *Les Femmes Cathares*. Paris: Perrin.

Brereton, Geoffrey, trans. 1978. *Froissart: Chronicles*. New York: Penguin Classics.

Brundage, James A. 1987. *Law, Sex, and Christian Society in Medieval Europe*. Chicago: University of Chicago Press.

Brundage, James A. 2000. "Domestic Violence in Classical Canon Law." In *Violence in Medieval Society*, edited by Richard A. Kaeuper, 183–195. Woodbridge: Boydell Press.

Burgess, Glyn, ed. 1986. *The Lais of Marie de France*. New York: Penguin.

Butler, Sara M. 2020. "Violence and Murder in Europe." In *The Cambridge World History of Violence: Volume 2: AD 500–AD 1500*, edited by Matthew S. Gordon, Richard W. Kaeuper, and Harriet Zurndorfer, 2:330–346. The Cambridge World History of Violence. Cambridge: Cambridge University Press. https://doi.org/10.1017/9781316661291.017.

Bynum, Caroline Walker. 1992. *Fragmentation and Redemption: Essays on Gender and the Human Body in Medieval Religion*. New York: Zone.

Cabré, Montserrat. 2008. "Women or Healers? Household Practices and the Categories of Health Care in Late Medieval Iberia." *Bulletin of the History of Medicine* 82 (1): 18–51.

Cadden, Joan. 1984. "It Takes All Kinds: Sexuality and Gender Differences in Hildegard of Bingen's 'Book of Compound Medicine.'" *Traditio* 40:149–174.

Caesarius of Arles. 1960. *The Rule for Nuns of St. Caesarius of Arles*. Translated by Maria Caritas McCarthy. Catholic University of America. Studies in Mediaeval History, New Ser. v. 16. Washington, DC: Catholic University of America Press.

Carlin, Martha, and Joel T. Rosenthal, ed. 2003. *Food and Eating in Medieval Europe*. London: Bloomsbury.

Classen, Albrecht. 2007. *The Power of a Woman's Voice in Medieval and Early Modern Literatures: New Approaches to German and European Women Writers and to Violence Against Women in Premodern Times*. Berlin: De Gruyter.

Craig, Leigh Anne. 2009. *Wandering Women and Holy Matrons: Women as Pilgrims in the Later Middle Ages*. Studies in Medieval and Reformation Traditions 138. Leiden: Brill.

Crawford, Sally. 1999. *Childhood in Anglo-Saxon England*. Gloucestershire: Sutton.

Crawford, Sally, Martin Ingram, Alysa Levene, Heather Montgomery, Kieron Sheehy, and Ellie Lee. 2010. "Infanticide, Abandonment and Abortion." In *Childhood and Violence in the Western Tradition*, edited by Laurence Brockliss and Heather Montgomery, 1:57–104. Barnsley: Oxbow. https://doi.org/10.2307/j.ctt1cd0p9q.8.

Davis, James. 2004. "Baking for the Common Good: A Reassessment of the Assize of Bread in Medieval England." *Economic History Review* 57 (3): 465–502.

Dean, Trevor. 2004. "Domestic Violence in Late-Medieval Bologna." *Renaissance Studies* 18 (4): 527–543.

Dean-Jones, Lesley. 1994. *Women's Bodies in Classical Greek Science*. Oxford: Clarendon Press.

Donahue, Charles. 2007. *Law, Marriage and Society in the Later Middle Ages: Arguments about Marriage in Five Courts*. Cambridge: Cambridge University Press.

Drew, Katherine Fischer, trans. 1972. *The Burgundian Code: Book of Constitutions or Law of Gundobad, Additional Enactments*. Philadelphia: University of Pennsylvania Press.

Dronke, Peter. 1984. *Women Writers of the Middle Ages: A Critical Study of Texts from Perpetua to Marguerite Porete*. Cambridge: Cambridge University Press.

Duby, Georges. 1978. *Medieval Marriage: Two Models from Twelfth-Century France*. Baltimore: Johns Hopkins University Press.

Dunphy, Graeme. 2012. "*Perspicax ingenium mihi collatum est*: Strategies of Authority in Chronicles Written by Women." In *Authority and Gender in Medieval and Renaissance Chronicles*, edited by Juliana Dresvina and Nicholas Sparks, 166–201. Newcastle upon Tyne: Cambridge Scholars.

Einhard, and Notker the Stammerer. 2008. *Two Lives of Charlemagne*. Translated by David Ganz. London: Penguin.

Ekholst, Christine. 2014. *A Punishment for Each Criminal: Gender and Crime in Swedish Medieval Law*. Leiden: Brill.

Evergates, Theodore, ed. 1999. *Aristocratic Women in Medieval France*. Philadelphia: University of Pennsylvania Press.

Farmer, Sharon. 2017. "Gender, Work, and the Parisian Silk Industry." In *The Silk Industries of Medieval Paris*, 106–136. Philadelphia: University of Pennsylvania Press.

Fernea, Elizabeth Warnock, and Basima Qattan Bezirgan, eds. 1977. *Middle Eastern Muslim Women Speak*. Austin: University of Texas Press.

Ferraro, Joanne M. 2012. "Childhood in Medieval and Early Modern Times." In *The Routledge History of Childhood in the Western World*, edited by Paula S. Fass. London: Routledge Handbooks Online. https://doi.org/10.4324/9780203075715.ch3.

Finch, Andrew J. 1990. "Parental Authority and the Problem of Clandestine Marriage in the Later Middle Ages." *Law and History Review* 8 (2): 189–204. https://doi.org/10.2307/743991.

Finlay, Nyree. 2000. "Outside of Life: Traditions of Infant Burial in Ireland from *Cillín* to Cist." *World Archaeology* 31 (3): 407–422.

Finucane, Ronald C. 1997. *The Rescue of the Innocents: Endangered Children in Medieval Miracles*. New York: St. Martin's.

Fleming, Robin. 2006. "Bones for Historians: Putting the Body Back in Biography." In *Writing Medieval Biography: Essays in Honour of Frank Barlow*, edited by David Bates, 29–48. Woodbridge: Boydell Press.

Flori, Jean. 2007. *Eleanor of Aquitaine: Queen and Rebel*. Edinburgh: Edinburgh University Press.

Fox, Matthew. 2002. *Illuminations of Hildegard von Bingen*. Rochester, VT: Bear.

French, Katherine. 2016. "The Material Culture of Childbirth in Late Medieval London and Its Suburbs." *Journal of Women's History* 28 (2): 126–148.

French, Katherine. 2008. "'My Wedding Gown to Make a Vestment': Housekeeping and Churchkeeping." In *The Good Women of the Parish: Gender and Religion After the Black Death*, 17–49. Philadelphia: University of Pennsylvania Press. https://www.jstor.org/stable/j.ctt3fhmtr.5.

Fry, Timothy, Imogene Baker, Timothy Horner, Augusta Raabe, Mark Sheridan, and Jean Neufville, eds. 1981. *RB 1980: The Rule of St. Benedict in Latin and English*. Collegeville, MN: The Liturgical Press.

Furnivall, Frederick James, and Edith Rickert. 1908. *The Babees' Book: Medieval Manners for the Young: Done into Modern English from Dr. Furnivall's Text*. London: Chatto and Windus. https://archive.org/details/thebabeesbook00furnuoft.

Garver, Valerie L. 2009. "Textile Work." In *Women and Aristocratic Culture in the Carolingian World*, 224–268. Ithaca, NY: Cornell University Press. https://www.jstor.org/stable/10.7591/j.ctt7zjz4.11.

Garver, Valerie L. 2012. "Childbearing and Infancy in the Carolingian World." *Journal of the History of Sexuality* 21 (2): 208–244.

Gies, Frances, and Joseph Gies. 1990. *Daily Life in Medieval Times*. New York: Barnes and Noble.

Gilchrist, Roberta. 2012. *Medieval Life: Archaeology and the Life Course*. Woodbridge: Boydell and Brewer.

Goldberg, P. J. P., ed. 1995. *Women in England c. 1275–1525: Documentary Sources*. Manchester: Manchester University Press.

Gravdal, Kathryn. 1991. *Ravishing Maidens: Writing Rape in Medieval French Literature and Law*. Philadelphia: University of Pennsylvania Press.

Greco, Gina L., and Christine M. Rose, trans. 2009. *The Good Wife's Guide (Le Ménagier de Paris): A Medieval Household Book*. Ithaca, NY: Cornell University Press.

Green, Monica H., ed. 2001. *The Trotula: A Medieval Compilation of Women's Medicine*. Philadelphia: University of Pennsylvania Press.

Green, Monica H. 2013. "Caring for Gendered Bodies." In *The Oxford Handbook of Women and Gender in Medieval Europe*, edited by Judith

M. Bennett and Ruth Mazo Karras, 345–361. Oxford: Oxford University Press.

Green, Monica H. 2020. "Who or What Is Trotula? 2020." https://www.academia.edu/41537366/WHO_WHAT_IS_TROTULA_2020.

Grossman, Avraham. 2004. *Pious and Rebellious: Jewish Women in Medieval Europe*. Translated by Jonathan Chipman. Waltham, MA: Brandeis University Press.

Hammond, P. W. 1993. *Food and Feast in Medieval England*. Phoenix Mill, Gloucestershire: Sutton.

Hanawalt, Barbara A. 1986. *The Ties That Bound: Peasant Families in Medieval England*. New York: Oxford University Press.

Hanawalt, Barbara A. 2000. "Violence in the Domestic Milieu of Late Medieval England." In *Violence in Medieval Society*, edited by Richard A. Kaeuper, 197–214. Woodbridge: Boydell Press.

Hanawalt, Barbara A. 2007. *The Wealth of Wives: Women, Law and Economy in Late Medieval London*. Oxford: Oxford University Press.

Hanson-Smith, Elizabeth. 1979. "A Woman's View of Courtly Love: The Findern Anthology, Cambridge University Library Ms. Ff.1.6." *Journal of Women's Studies in Literature* 1:179–194.

Harrison, Ann Tukey, ed. 1994. *The Danse Macabre of Women: Ms. Fr. 995 of the Bibliothèque Nationale*. Kent, OH: Kent State University Press.

Harris-Stoertz, Fiona. 2012. "Pregnancy and Childbirth in Twelfth- and Thirteenth-Century French and English Law." *Journal of the History of Sexuality* 21 (2): 263–281.

Hawthorne, John G., and C. S. Smith, eds. 2012. *On Divers Arts*. North Chelmsford, MA: Courier Corporation.

Hellman, Robert, trans., and Richard O'Gorman. 1965. *Fabliaux: Ribald Tales from the Old French*. Westport, CT: Greenwood Press.

Heng, Geraldine. 2018. *The Invention of Race in the European Middle Ages*. New York; Cambridge: Cambridge University Press.

Henry, Philippa A. 2005. "Who Produced the Textiles? Changing Gender Roles in Late Saxon Textile Production: The Archaeological and Documentary Evidence." In *Northern Archaeological Textiles: The North European Symposium for Archaeological Textiles VII*, edited by Frances Pritchard and John Peter Wild, 51–57. Barnsley: Oxbow. https://www.jstor.org/stable/j.ctvh1dpt9.13.

Herlihy, David. 1985. *Medieval Households*. Cambridge, MA: Harvard University Press.

Herlihy, David. 1990. *Opera Muliebria: Women and Work in Medieval Europe*. New York: McGraw-Hill.

Hotchkiss, Valerie R. 1996. *Clothes Make the Man: Female Cross Dressing in Medieval Europe*. Garland Reference Library of the Humanities, V. 1991. New York: Garland.

Jacquart, Danielle, and Claude Thomasset. 1988. *Sexuality and Medicine in the Middle Ages*. Translated by Matthew Adamson. Princeton, NJ: Princeton University Press.

Jestice, Phyllis G. 2018. *Imperial Ladies of the Ottonian Dynasty: Women and Rule in Tenth-Century Germany*. Queenship and Power. Cham: Palgrave Macmillan.

Johnson, Penelope D. 1991. *Equal in Monastic Profession: Religious Women in Medieval France*. Chicago: University of Chicago Press.

Johnston, Dafydd. 1993. *Galar y beirdd: marwnadau plant / Poets' Grief: Medieval Welsh Elegies for Children*. Caerdydd: Tafol.

Jones, Peter Murray, and Lea T. Olsan. 2015. "Performative Rituals for Conception and Childbirth in England, 900–1500." *Bulletin of the History of Medicine* 89: 406–432.

Julian of Norwich. "Julian of Norwich: Revelations of Divine Love - Christian Classics Ethereal Library." n.d. Accessed December 18, 2020. https://ccel.org/ccel/julian/revelations.xviii.xx.html.

Karras, Ruth Mazo. 1996. *Common Women: Prostitution and Sexuality in Medieval England*. Oxford: Oxford University Press.

Kelly, Henry Ansgar. 1994. "'Rule of Thumb' and the Folklaw of the Husband's Stick." *Journal of Legal Education* 44 (3): 341–365.

Kelly, Joan. 1982. "Early Feminist Theory and the 'Querelle des Femmes,' 1400–1789." *Signs* 8 (1): 4–28.

Klapisch-Zuber, Christiane. 1985. *Women, Family, and Ritual in Renaissance Italy*. Chicago: University of Chicago Press.

Kowaleski, Maryanne. 2014. "Medieval People in Town and Country: New Perspectives from Demography and Bioarchaeology." *Speculum* 89 (3): 573–600.

Krueger, Roberta L. 2013. "Towards Feminism." In *The Oxford Handbook of Women and Gender in Medieval Europe*, edited by Judith M. Bennett and Ruth Mazo Karras, 590–606. Oxford: Oxford University Press.

Labarge, Margaret Wade. 1986. *A Small Sound of the Trumpet: Women in Medieval Life*. Boston: Beacon Press.

Larrington, Carolyne. 1995. *Women and Writing in Medieval Europe: A Sourcebook*. London: Routledge.

Lawrence, C. H. 1984. *Medieval Monasticism: Forms of Religious Life in Western Europe in the Middle Ages*. London: Longman.

Leslie, Teresa. 1993. "Mortuary Rolls as a Source for Medieval Women's History." *Journal of the Georgia Association of Historians* 14: 116–124.

Levack, Brian P. 1987. *The Witch-Hunt in Early Modern Europe*. London: Longman.

Leyser, Henrietta. 1995. *Medieval Women: A Social History of Women in England 450–1500*. London: Phoenix Press.

Lifshitz, Felicia. 2014. "'An Eternal Weight of Glory' (2 Corinthians 4:17): Discipline and Devotion in Monastic Life." In *Religious Women in Early Carolingian Francia: A Study of Manuscript Transmission and Monastic Culture*, 148–182. New York: Fordham University Press. https://www.jstor.org/stable/j.ctt13x0c7h.14.

de Lorris, Guillaume, and Jean de Meun. 1962. *The Romance of the Rose*. Translated by Harry W. Robbins. New York: Dutton.

Luongo, F. Thomas. 2006. *The Saintly Politics of Catherine of Siena*. Ithaca, NY: Cornell University Press.

Lynch, Joseph. 1992. *The Medieval Church: A Brief History*. London: Longman.

Mackay, Christopher S. 2009. *The Hammer of Witches: A Complete Translation of the Malleus Maleficarum*. Cambridge: Cambridge University Press.

Magnusson, Roberta J. 2001. *Water Technology in the Middle Ages: Cities, Monasteries, and Waterworks after the Roman Empire*. Johns Hopkins Studies in the History of Technology. Baltimore, MD: The Johns Hopkins University Press.

Marchegay, Paul Alexandre. 1854. *Archives d'Anjou: Recueil de documents et mémoires inédits sur cette province*. Vol. 3. Angers: Ch. Labussière.

McAvoy, Liz Herbert. 2008. "Introduction: 'God Forbede . . . That I Am a Techere': Who, or What, Was Julian?" In *A Companion to Julian of Norwich*, 1–16. Rochester: Boydell & Brewer. https://www.jstor.org/stable/10.7722/j.ctt14brrrs.7.

McDougall, Sara. 2014. "The Transformation of Adultery in France at the End of the Middle Ages." *Law and History Review* 32 (3): 491–524.

McLaren, Angus. 2007. *Impotence: A Cultural History*. Chicago: University of Chicago Press.

McNamara, Jo Ann, John E. Halborg, and E. Gordon Whatley, eds. 1992. *Sainted Women of the Dark Ages*. Durham, NC: Duke University Press.

Mengel, David C. 2004. "From Venice to Jerusalem and beyond: Milich of Kromeriz and the Topography of Prostitution in Fourteenth-Century Prague." *Speculum* 79 (2): 407–442.

Métais, Charles, ed. 1889. *Marmoutier: Cartulaire Blésois*. Blois: E. Moreau et Cie.

Metzler, Irina. 2006. *Disability in Medieval Europe: Thinking about Physical Impairment during the High Middle Ages, ca. 1100–1400*. London: Routledge.

Metzler, Irina. 2015. "Disabled Children: Birth Defects, Causality and Guilt." In *Medicine, Religion and Gender in Medieval Culture*, edited by Naoë Kukita Yoshikawa, 161–180. Gender in the Middle Ages. Cambridge: D. S. Brewer.

Mews, Constant J. 1999. *The Lost Love Letters of Abelard and Heloise: Perceptions of Dialogue in Twelfth-Century France*. New York: St. Martin's Press.

Millett, Bella. 2009. *Ancrene Wisse / A Guide for Anchoresses: A Translation*. Exeter: University of Exeter Press.

Montanari, Massimo. 2012. *Medieval Tastes: Food, Cooking, and the Table*. Translated by Beth Archer Brombert. New York: Columbia University Press.

Morrison, Susan Signe. 2016. *A Medieval Woman's Companion: Women's Lives in the European Middle Ages*. Oxford: Oxbow.

Müldner, Gundula. 2016. "Marine Fish Consumption in Medieval Britain: The Isotope Perspective from Human Skeletal Remains." In *Cod and Herring: The Archaeology and History of Medieval Sea Fishing*, edited by James H. Barrett and David C. Orton, 239–249. Barnsley: Oxbow. https://www.jstor.org/stable/j.ctvh1dw0d.24.

Murray, Jacqueline. 1996. "Twice Marginal and Twice Invisible: Lesbians in the Middle Ages." In *Handbook of Medieval Sexuality*, edited by Vern L. Bullough and James A. Brundage, 191–222. New York: Garland.

Murray, Jacqueline, ed. 2001. *Love, Marriage and Family in the Middle Ages: A Reader (Readings in Medieval Civilization and Culture)*. Peterborough: Broadview Press.

Newman, Barbara. 1985. "Hildegard of Bingen: Visions and Validation." *Church History* 54 (2): 163–175. https://doi.org/10.2307/3167233.

Newman, Barbara. 2005. "The Heretic Saint: Guglielma of Bohemia, Milan, and Brunate." *Church History* 74 (1): 1–38.

Nicholas, Karen S. 1999. "Countesses as Rulers in Flanders." In *Aristocratic Women in Medieval France*, edited by Theodore Evergates, 111–137. Philadelphia: University of Pennsylvania Press.

Nichols, James Mansfield. 1981. "The Arabic Verses of Qasmuna bint Isma'il ibn Bagdalah." *International Journal of Middle East Studies* 13 (2): 155–158. https://doi.org/10.1017/S0020743800055264.

Nutz, Beatrix. 2013. "Bras in the 15th Century? A Preliminary Report." In *The North European Symposium for Archaeological Textiles XI*, edited by Johanna Banck-Burges and Carla Nübold, 221–225. Rahden: Verlag Marie Leidorf GmbH.

Nye, Eric W. 2022. *Pounds Sterling to Dollars: Historical Conversion of Currency*. https://www.uwyo.edu/numimage/currency.htm.

Orme, Nicholas. 2001. *Medieval Children*. New Haven: Yale University Press.

Osborn, Marijane. 2008. "Anglo-Saxon Ethnobotany: Women's Reproductive Medicine in Leechbook III." In *Health and Healing from the Medieval Garden*, edited by Peter Dendle and Alain Touwaide, 145–161. Woodbridge: Boydell Press.

Otis, Leah Lydia. 1985. *Prostitution in Medieval Society: The History of an Urban Institution in Languedoc*. Chicago: University of Chicago Press.

Payer, Pierre J. 1984. *Sex and the Penitentials: The Development of a Sexual Code, 550–1150*. Toronto: University of Toronto Press.

Pegg, Mark Gregory. 2008. *A Most Holy War: The Albigensian Crusade and the Battle for Christendom*. New York: Oxford University Press.

Pennington, Kenneth. 2012. "Women on the Rack: Torture and Gender in the Ius Commune." In *Recto Ordine Procedit Magister. Liber Amicorum E. C. Coppens*, edited by Jan Hallebeek, Louis Berkvens, Georges Martyn, and Paul Lucien Nève, 1–14. Iuris Scripta Historica 28. Brussels: Flemish Academy of Arts and Sciences.

Perez, Rosa A. 2017. "Troubled Waters: Bathing and Illicit Relations in Marie de France's 'Equitan' and in *Flamenca*." In *Bodily and Spiritual Hygiene in Medieval and Early Modern Literature: Explorations of Textual Presentations of Filth and Water*, edited by Albrecht Classen, 275–292. Berlin: De Gruyter.

Peters, Edward, ed. 1980. "The Cathars." In *Heresy and Authority in Medieval Europe*, 103–138. Philadelphia: University of Pennsylvania Press. https://www.jstor.org/stable/j.ctt3fh8qt.6.

Petroff, Elizabeth Alvilda, ed. 1986. "Christina Mirabilis: The Life of Christina of St. Trond by Thomas de Cantimpré." In *Medieval Women's Visionary Literature*, 184–189. New York: Oxford University Press.

Phillips, Kim M. 2003. *Medieval Maidens: Young Women and Gender in England, 1270–1540*. Manchester: Manchester University Press.

Phillips, Rod. 2016. "The Middle Ages: 1000–1500." In *French Wine: A History*, 34–62. Berkeley: University of California Press. https://www.jstor.org/stable/10.1525/j.ctv1xxz5z.7.

Piponnier, Françoise, and Perrine Mane. 1997. *Dress in the Middle Ages*. Translated by Caroline Beamish. New Haven: Yale University Press.

Puff, Helmut. 2013. "Same-Sex Possibilities." In *The Oxford Handbook of Women & Gender in Medieval Europe*, edited by Judith M. Bennett and Ruth Mazo Karras, 379–395. Oxford: Oxford University Press.

Pullan, Brian. 2016. "Prostitution, Sin and the Law." In *Tolerance, Regulation and Rescue*, 29–47. Manchester: Manchester University Press.

Ranft, Patricia. 1996. *Women and the Religious Life in Premodern Europe*. New York: St. Martin's Press.

Riddle, John M. 1992. *Contraception and Abortion from the Ancient World to the Renaissance*. Cambridge, MA: Harvard University Press.

Rider, Catherine. 2006. *Magic and Impotence in the Middle Ages*. Oxford: Oxford University Press.

Rio, Alice. 2017. *Slavery After Rome, 500–1100*. Oxford: Oxford University Press.https://doi.org/10.1093/acprof:oso/9780198704058.001.0001.

Rossiaud, Jacques. 1988. *Medieval Prostitution*. Translated by Lydia G. Cochrane. New York: Basil Blackwell.

Roth, Norman. 2005. *Daily Life of the Jews in the Middle Ages*. Westport, CT: Greenwood Press.

Rousseau, Constance M. 2014. "Neither Bewitched nor Beguiled: Philip Augustus's Alleged Impotence and Innocent III's Response." *Speculum* 89 (2): 410–436.

Rubin, Miri, ed. 2009. *Medieval Christianity in Practice*. Princeton Readings in Religion. Princeton, NJ: Princeton University Press.

Russell, Jeffrey B., and Brooks Alexander. 2007. *A History of Witchcraft: Sorcerers, Heretics and Pagans*. 2nd ed. London: Thames and Hudson.

Salmon, André, ed. 1864. *Livre Des Serfs de Marmoutier*. Tours: Imprimerie Ladevèze.

Saunders, Corinne. 2001. "Secular Law: Rape and Raptus." In *Rape and Ravishment in the Literature of Medieval England*, 33–75. Rochester: Boydell and Brewer. https://www.jstor.org/stable/10.7722/j.ctt81qfk.5.

Scarborough, Connie. 2012. "Women as Victims and Criminals in the Siete Partidas." In *Crime and Punishment in the Middle Ages and Early Modern Age: Mental-Historical Investigations of Basic Human Problems and Social Responses*, edited by Albrecht Classen and Connie Scarborough, 225–246. Fundamentals of Medieval and Early Modern Culture Ser. 11. Berlin: De Gruyter.

Scheck, Helene. 2009. "Queen Mathilda of Saxony and the Founding of Quedlinburg: Women, Memory, and Power." *Historical Reflections/Réflexions Historiques* 35 (3): 21–36.

Schofield, Roger. 1986. "Did the Mothers Really Die? Three Centuries of Maternal Mortality in 'The World We Have Lost.'" In *The World We Have Gained: Histories of Population and Social Structure*, edited by Lloyd Bonfield, Richard M. Smith, and Keith Wrightson, 231–260. Oxford: Basil Blackwell.

Schulenberg, Jane Tibbetts. 1989. "Women's Monastic Communities, 500–1100: Patterns of Expansion and Decline." *Signs* 14 (2): 261–292.

Schuster, Beate. 1994. "L'imaginaire de la prostitution et la sociéte urbaine en Allemagne (XIIIe-XVIe Siècles)." *Médiévales* 27:75–93.

Scott, Robert A. 2010. "Life in the Middle Ages." In *Miracle Cures: Saints, Pilgrimage, and the Healing Powers of Belief*, 3–28. Berkeley: University of California Press. https://www.jstor.org/stable/10.1525/j.ctt1ppj66.6.

Sears, Elizabeth. 2019. *The Ages of Man: Medieval Interpretations of the Life Cycle*. Princeton, NJ: Princeton University Press.

Shahar, Shulamith. 2001. *Women in a Medieval Heretical Sect: Agnes and Huguette the Waldensians*. Translated by Yael Lotan. New York: Boydell Press. https://www.jstor.org/stable/10.7722/j.ctt9qdk0k.

Shinners, John Raymond. 1997. *Medieval Popular Religion, 1000–1500: A Reader*. Readings in Medieval Civilizations and Cultures 2. Orchard Park, NY: Broadview Press.

Singman, Jeffrey L. 1999. *The Middle Ages: Everyday Life in Medieval Europe*. New York: Sterling.

Skinner, Patricia, and Elisabeth van Houts, eds. 2011. *Medieval Writings on Secular Women*. London: Penguin.

Soranus of Ephesus. 1956. *Gynecology*. Translated by Owsei Temkin. Publications of the Institute of the History of Medicine, Johns Hopkins University. 2d Ser.: Texts and Documents, v. 3. Baltimore: Johns Hopkins Press.

Sperling, Jutta Gisela, ed. 2013. *Medieval and Renaissance Lactations: Images, Rhetorics, Practices*. Women and Gender in the Early Modern World. Aldershot: Ashgate.

Steckel, Richard H., Clark Spencer Larsen, Charlotte A. Roberts, and Joerg Baten, eds. 2019. *The Backbone of Europe: Health, Diet, Work, and Violence over Two Millenia*. Cambridge: Cambridge University Press.

Stuard, Susan Mosher. 2013. "Brideprice, Dowry and Other Marital Assigns." In *The Oxford Handbook of Women and Gender in Medieval Europe*, edited by Judith M. Bennett and Ruth Mazo Karras, 148–162. Oxford: Oxford University Press.

Taylor, Larissa Juliet. 2009. *The Virgin Warrior: The Life and Death of Joan of Arc*. New Haven: Yale University Press. https://www.jstor.org/stable/j.ctt5vm27v.9.

Thomasset, Claude. 1992. "The Nature of Women." In *A History of Women in the West, II: Silences of the Middle Ages*, edited by Christiane Klapisch-Zuber, 44–69. Cambridge, MA: Harvard University Press.

Thorpe, Louis, ed. 1974. *Gregory of Tours, The History of the Franks*. New York: Penguin.

Tierney, Brian. 1999. *Western Europe in the Middle Ages, 300–1475*. 6th ed. Boston: McGraw-Hill.

Tuten, Belle S. 2004. "Who Was Lady Constance of Angers?" *Medieval Perspectives* 19: 255–268.

Uitz, Erica. 1988. *The Legend of Good Women: Medieval Women in Towns and Cities*. Mount Kisco, NY: Moyer Bell Limited.

Vauchez, André. 1993. *The Laity in the Middle Ages: Religious Beliefs and Devotional Practices*. Translated by Margery J. Schneider. Notre Dame: University of Notre Dame Press.

Vauchez, André. 2018. *Catherine of Siena: A Life of Passion and Purpose*. Translated by Michael F. Cusato. New York: Paulist Press.

Venarde, Bruce L. 1997. *Women's Monasticism and Social Change: Nunneries in France and England, 890–1215*. Ithaca, NY: Cornell University Press.

Virgoe, Roger, ed. 1989. *Private Life in the Fifteenth Century: The Illustrated Letters of the Paston Family*. New York: Weidenfeld & Nicolson.

de Vitry, Jacques. 1989. *The Life of Marie d'Oignies*. Translated by Margot King. Toronto: Peregrina.

Wallis, Faith, ed. 2010. *Medieval Medicine: A Reader*. Readings in Medieval Civilizations and Cultures 15. Toronto: University of Toronto Press.

Ward, Jennifer. 2016. *Women in Medieval Europe, 1200–1500*. 2nd ed. London: Routledge.

Watt, Diane, ed. 2004. *The Paston Women: Selected Letters*. Woodbridge: D. S. Brewer.

Weisl, Angela Jane. 1998. "'Quitting' Eve: Violence against Women in the Canterbury Tales." In *Violence Against Women in Medieval Texts*, edited by Anna Roberts, 115–136. Gainesville: University of Florida Press.

Wemple, Suzanne Fonay. 1981. *Women in Frankish Society: Marriage and the Cloister, 500 to 900*. Philadelphia: University of Pennsylvania Press.

White, Carolinne, trans. 1998. *Early Christian Lives*. New York: Penguin Classics.

Williams, Bernadette. 1994. "The Sorcery Trial of Alice Kyteler." *History Ireland* 2 (4): 20–24.

Williams, Marty, and Anne Echols. 1994. *Between Pit and Pedestal: Women in the Middle Ages*. Princeton, NJ: Markus Weiner Publishers.

Youngs, Deborah. 2006. *The Life Cycle in Western Europe, c. 1300–1500*. Manchester: Manchester University Press.

INDEX

Note: Most people in the Middle Ages did not have surnames. You will find many medieval people listed under their first names.

About the Author

BELLE S. TUTEN is Charles A. Dana Professor of History at Juniata College in Huntingdon, Pennsylvania. She has published on women's history, the history of female monasticism, and gender in medieval medicine. Her most recent work is "Care of the Breast in the Late Middle Ages: The *Tractatus de passionibus mammillarum*," in Sharon Strocchia and Sara Ritchey, eds., *Gendered Histories of Health, Healing and the Body, 1250–1550* (2020).

www.ingramcontent.com/pod-product-compliance
Lightning Source LLC
LaVergne TN
LVHW050510100826
845148LV00002B/297